The Law of Renewable Energy

The Law of Renewable Energy

Louise Smail
Mike Appleby
Charlotte Waters

Bloomsbury Professional
LONDON • DUBLIN • EDINBURGH • NEW YORK • NEW DELHI • SYDNEY

BLOOMSBURY PROFESSIONAL
Bloomsbury Publishing Plc
50 Bedford Square, London, WC1B 3DP, UK

British Library Cataloguing-in-Publication Data

A catalogue record for this book is available from the British Library.

ISBN:	PB	978 1 52651 512 4
	ePDF	978 1 52651 514 8
	ePub	978 1 52651 513 1

Typeset by Evolution Design and Digital Ltd (Kent)

Preface

"One must not believe, despite the silence of modern writings, that the idea of using solar heat for mechanical operations is recent. On the contrary, one must recognize that this idea is very ancient and its slow development across the centuries it has given birth to various curious devices."

Although the wording betrays that this is not a recent quote, readers may be surprised to learn that it was said over 140 years ago by Augustin Bernard Mouchot at the Universal Exposition in Paris, France in 1878. Mouchot was a nineteenth-century French inventor of the earliest solar-powered engine and demonstrated that concentrating solar heat could produce a steady stream of electricity. So renewable energy is nothing new.

The one change which has happened very quickly over the last few years, observed while working with many types of organisation, has been the move towards renewable energy. Much of this change is driven by the need for sustainability, which looks at how an organisation operates in the ecological, social and economic environment. Renewable energy not only decreases greenhouse gas emissions, but it also makes business sense not to be so dependent on diminishing fossil fuels, and it therefore increases an organisation's energy security.

Renewable energy isn't just wind and solar (although these days it's hard to travel very far in the UK without seeing solar farms and onshore and offshore wind farms). There are other forms of renewable energy which also have an exciting future.

Innovative ways of storing energy are important if you rely on energy from a source affected by the seasons and the weather. Battery development and energy storage, despite the challenges, are making renewable energy more viable.

This book looks at the types of renewable energy available, how they work, and where they are installed, alongside the advantages and disadvantages. It also covers some of the legal issues surrounding the installation and use of energy capture devices.

It is expected that half of the UK's electricity will come from renewable sources by 2025[1]. The UK, like many countries, has challenging binding targets to meet. This book considers not only the UK but other countries and their initiatives for renewable energy.

1 Analysis of government projections (Carbon Brief).

This book aims to provide an observer of the industry with plenty of resources for a curious reader to explore further. Sustainability of organisations is important for their survival and for our planet. At the heart of this is renewable energy.

Dr Louise Smail

October 2020

Contents

List of abbreviations

A1P1	Article 1 Protocol 1 to the ECHR
AD	anaerobic digestion
ADFD	Abu Dhabi Fund for Development
AONB	Area of Outstanding Natural Beauty
ARP	Adaptation Reporting Power
ASEAN	Association of Southeast Asian Nations
BEIS	Department for Business, Energy and Industrial Strategy
BRE	Building Research Establishment
BRI	Belt and Road Initiative
BTES	borehole thermal energy storage
CAES	compressed air energy storage
CCA 2008	Climate Change Act 2008
CCC	Committee on Climate Change
CCRA	Climate Change Risk Assessment
CCS	carbon capture and storage
CfD	contracts for difference
CGS	Clean Growth Strategy
CHP	combined heat and power
CPRE	countryside charity, formerly Campaign to Protect Rural England
CRT	Canals and Rivers Trust
CSP	concentrated solar power
DCO	development consent order
DECC	Department of Energy and Climate Change
DETI	Department of Enterprise, Trade and Investment (Northern Ireland)
DfE	Department for the Economy (Northern Ireland)
EA	Environment Agency
ECHR	European Convention on Human Rights
EER	energy efficiency requirement
EGS	enhanced geothermal system
EIA	Environmental Impact Assessment
ERDF	European Regional Development Fund
ETS	Emissions Trading Scheme
EU	European Union
EV	electric vehicle
FIT	Feed-in Tariff
FPV	floating photovoltaics
GEI	Global Energy Interconnection

GHG	greenhouse gas
GHP	geothermal heat pump
GIC	groundwater investigation consent
GSHP	ground-source heat pump
GW	gigawatt
GWh	gigawatt hour
HVO	hydrated vegetable oil
IEA	International Energy Agency
ILUC	indirect land use change (pronounced i-luck)
IPCC	Intergovernmental Panel on Climate Change
IRENA	International Renewable Energy Agency
kW	kilowatt
kWh	kilowatt hour
LAES	liquid air energy storage
LCCC	Low Carbon Contracts Company
LCOE	levelised cost of energy/electricity
LPA	local planning authority
mCHP	micro-combined heat and power
MCS	Microgeneration Certification Scheme
MSW	municipal solid waste
MW	megawatt
MWh	megawatt hour
NAP	National Adaptation Programme
NECP	National Energy and Climate Plan
NFFO	Non-Fossil Fuel Obligation
NIAUR	Northern Ireland Authority for Utility Regulation
NPPF	National Planning Policy Framework
NREL	National Renewable Energy Laboratory
NRMM	non-road mobile machinery
NSIP	Nationally Significant Infrastructure Project
Ofgem	Office of Gas and Electricity Markets
ONS	Office for National Statistics
OPV	organic photovoltaic
PEC	photoelectrochemical
PHES	pumped heat energy storage
PPC	Pollution Prevention and Control
PSH	pumped-storage hydro
PV	photovoltaic
REAL	Renewable Energy Assurance Limited
RED	Renewable Energy Directive
RED II	recast Renewable Energy Directive
RO	Renewables Obligation
ROC	Renewables Obligation Certificate
ROO-FIT	Renewables Obligation Order Feed-in Tariff
RTFC	Renewable Transport Fuel Certificate

RTFO	Renewable Transport Fuel Obligation
SEF	Strategic Energy Framework (Northern Ireland)
SEG	Smart Export Guarantee
SEM	Single Electricity Market
SEPA	Scottish Environment Protection Agency
SIDS	Small Island Developing States
SMES	superconducting magnetic energy storage
SNG	synthetic natural gas
SSSI	Site of Special Scientific Interest
TES	thermal energy storage
TW	terawatt
TWh	terawatt hour
UNFCCC	United Nations Framework Convention on Climate Change
VRE	variable renewable energy
WHO	World Health Organisation
WML	Waste Management Licence
WRAP	Waste and Resources Action Plan
WVO	waste vegetable oil

Table of statutes

[*All references are to paragraph numbers*]

Table of statutory instruments

[*All references are to paragraph numbers*]

Table of Cases

[*All references are to paragraph numbers*]

Chapter 1

Introduction and Climate Change Law

INTRODUCTION

1.1 This book looks at the renewable energy market and the increase in different types of renewable energy. It explains the types and trends and the effects of the law and feed-in tariff changes that alter the moves towards renewable energy. It also lists some of the legal cases that have shaped planning and government policy.

WHAT IS RENEWABLE ENERGY?

1.2 Renewable energy, often referred to as clean energy, comes from natural resources or processes that are constantly replenished (such as wind, sunlight and waves), even if this is dependent on weather and time. Renewable energy is not new; the ability to harness wind for windmills and sunshine that provided warmth during the day and helped kindle fires to last until the evening has been around for a long time. Until recently, the trend was to use other energy resources such as oil, gas and coal. These sources are not renewable in a short time frame and in fact, once used, will be gone for a long time. So, attention has now turned to the use of renewable resources. There are increasingly new ways to capture and retain renewable energy. Some of this has been on a small scale (for example, solar panels on domestic dwellings) and others have seen countries turn away from fossil fuels and generate electricity for the national grid using renewable energy.

The main types of renewable energy are:

- Solar – according to the National Renewable Energy Laboratory (NREL), 'more energy from the sun falls on the earth in one hour than is used by everyone in the world in one year'. Solar energy is used to heat homes and businesses, warm water and drive power devices.
- Wind – in the past, wind was used to drive windmills for the grinding of corn; nowadays large wind turbines drive generators which supply electricity to the National Grid.
- Hydroelectric – this relies on water, either fast-moving or descending from a high point; this water force can then be used to drive turbines to generate electricity.
- Biomass – this is organic material from plants and animals that can be burned or fermented to generate electricity.
- Geothermal – this is heat energy that comes from within the earth. This can be found in hot springs in some countries where the hot water can

be directly used – in other places, deep wells can be drilled to access the heat.

- Waves – tidal and wave energy can be found, either in tidal areas where the movement of the water can be used to drive turbines, or where tidal barrages can be used.

100% RENEWABLES

1.3 This refers to where, within an energy system, all energy is resourced from 100% renewable energy sources. There is an important distinction between having 100% renewable energy and carbon neutrality.

Carbon neutral

1.4 Carbon neutrality, or having a zero carbon footprint, refers to having a net carbon dioxide emission. This requires a balance between carbon emissions and carbon removal (sometimes referred to as 'carbon offsetting'). To do this, carbon neutrality is achieved by balancing the total carbon footprint of a country (not just emissions from energy and fuel) with carbon dioxide removal and carbon projects abroad.

As climate change is a problem caused by carbon dioxide released from the burning of fossil fuels such as oil, coal and gas, going carbon neutral is seen as an important way to offset this. If an organisation adds polluting emissions to the atmosphere, it can then subtract this by purchasing a carbon offset. The carbon offsets are simply a credit for emission reduction achieved by projects such as windfarms, solar installation or energy efficiency retrofitted solutions.

The following are examples of going carbon neutral (sometimes referred to as 'climate neutral'):

- Rock bands like the Rolling Stones, Coldplay and the Dave Matthews Band have offset the emissions associated with their concerts and albums. Coldplay announced that they would not be touring to promote their album *Everyday Life*.
- Conferences (eg United Nations World Climate Research Programme) and conventions have offset their emissions.
- The World Bank has committed to being carbon neutral[1].
- Some utilities are offsetting their emissions and allowing their customers to purchase carbon neutral energy.
- Airlines and travel agents are starting to offer customers the option to offset their flights, and some airlines are offsetting all of their flights.

1 See www.worldbank.org/en/topic/climatechange/overview.

100% renewable grid

Iceland

1.5 Renewable energy provided almost 100% of the country's electricity production, with about 73% coming from hydropower and 27% coming from geothermal power. Most of the hydropower plants are owned by Landsvirkjun (the National Power Company) which is the main supplier of electricity in Iceland. Iceland is the world's largest green energy producer per capita and largest electricity producer per capita, with approximately 55,000kWh per person per year.

Share of energy from renewable sources – EU countries

1.6 According to Eurostat[2] the share of renewable energy of the EU is up by 18%. There are 12 states which have already reached their share equal to or above their national 2020 binding targets:

- Bulgaria
- Czechia
- Denmark
- Estonia
- Greece
- Croatia
- Italy
- Latvia
- Lithuania
- Cyprus
- Finland
- Sweden.

In 2018, the share of renewable sources in gross final energy consumption increased in 21 of the 28 Member States compared with 2017, while remaining stable in one Member State and decreasing in six. Since 2004, it has significantly grown in all Member States. Sweden had by far the highest share in 2018, with more than half (54.6%) of its energy coming from renewable sources, ahead of Finland (41.2%), Latvia (40.3%), Denmark (36.1%) and Austria (33.4%). The lowest proportion of renewables was in the Netherlands (7.4%). Others with a low share (less than 10%) were also recorded in Malta (8.0%), Luxembourg (9.1%) and Belgium (9.4%).

National Grid

1.7 According to the National Grid, 2019 was the cleanest year on record for the UK as it was the first time that the amount of zero carbon power outstripped that from fossil fuels in 12 months – at a point mid-way between 1990 and 2050, which is when the UK has committed to have a 100% reduction in emissions based on the 1990 level. There is a mixture of energy from wind farms, solar and nuclear power, as well as energy imported

2 Eurostat – news release 23 January 2020: https://ec.europa.eu/eurostat/documents/2995521/10335438/8-23012020-AP-EN.pdf/292cf2e5-8870-4525-7ad7-188864ba0c29.

from subsea connectors. This delivered 48% of the UK's electricity in 2019, compared to 43% generated by fossil fuels.

Energy Sources National Grid

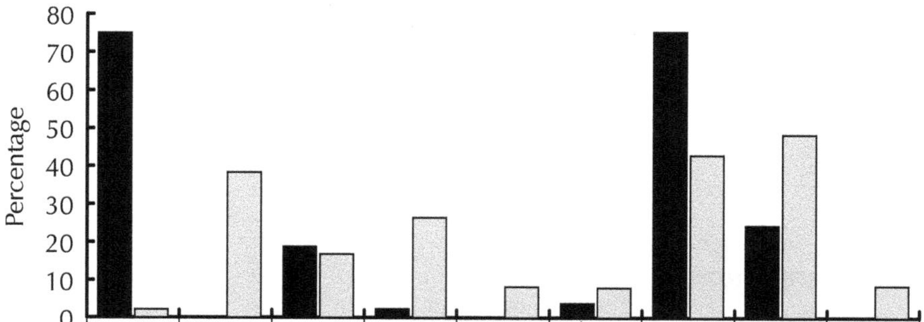

	Coal + other	Gas	Nuclear	Wind + Solar + Hydro	Biomass + Waste	Imports	Fossil Fuel	Zero Carbon	Biomass + Waste
1990	75.0%	0.1%	18.8%	2.3%	0.0%	3.8%	75.5%	24.4%	0.1%
2020	2.1%	2.1%	16.8%	26.5%	8.2%	8.0%	43.0%	48.5%	8.5%

CLIMATE CHANGE

1.8 There is overwhelming scientific evidence that highlights serious change to the climate, which is largely due to greenhouse gases, which is the result of human activities such as the combustion of fossil fuels and changing patterns of land use. In 1992, the UN Framework Convention on Climate Change (UNFCCC) had the objective of 'stabilisation of greenhouse gas concentrations in the atmosphere at a level that would prevent dangerous anthropogenic interference with the climate system'.

The Kyoto Protocol, which aims to reduce greenhouse gas emissions by 'Annex I' parties (a number of industrialised countries including the UK, other EU Member States, the Russian Federation, Canada, Australia and Japan), was agreed in December 1997. Under this Protocol, the parties agreed to reduce their collective greenhouse gas emissions to 5.2% below base 5-year levels between 2008 and 2012[3].

The IPCC report and the 2006 Stern Review demonstrated that international cooperation needed to go much further than to stabilise greenhouse gas concentrations at levels which will avoid dangerous climate change. At the 2008 Hokkaido summit, the G8 endorsed the target of reducing global greenhouse gas emissions by 50% by 2050.

At the December 2008 European Council meeting, agreement was reached on a package of legislation to achieve the unilateral 20% reduction in emissions by 2020. This included:

3 Kyoto protocol to the United Nations Framework Convention on Climate Change: https://unfccc.int/sites/default/files/resource/docs/cop3/l07a01.pdf.

- a strengthening of the EU Emissions Trading Scheme (EU ETS);
- national emissions reduction targets for those sectors not covered by the ETS;
- national targets for the proportion of energy supplied by renewable sources (to ensure that 20% of the EU's energy is supplied by renewables in 2020); and
- provisions to construct demonstration plants for carbon capture and storage (CCS) technology.

These measures received final agreement from the European Parliament in December 2008.

Paris agreement

1.9 The Paris Agreement sets out a global framework to avoid climate change by limiting global warming to well below 2°C and pursuing efforts to limit it to 1.5°C. It also aims to strengthen countries' ability to deal with the impacts of climate change and support them in their efforts. The Paris Agreement[4] is the first-ever universal, legally binding global climate change agreement, adopted at the Paris climate conference (COP21) in December 2015.

The EU and its Member States are among the 190 or so Parties to the Paris Agreement. The EU formally ratified the agreement on 5 October 2016, and it came into force on 4 November 2016. For the agreement to enter into force, at least 55 countries representing at least 55% of global emissions had to deposit their instruments of ratification.

Key elements

Mitigation: reducing emissions

1.10

- a long-term goal of keeping the increase in global average temperature to well below 2°C above pre-industrial levels
- to aim to limit the increase to 1.5°C, since this would significantly reduce risks and the impacts of climate change
- on the need for global emissions to peak as soon as possible, recognising that this will take longer for developing countries
- to undertake rapid reductions thereafter in accordance with the best available science, so as to achieve a balance between emissions and removals in the second half of the century.

As a contribution to the objectives of the agreement, countries have submitted national climate action plans, known as nationally determined contributions (NDCs). These are not yet enough to reach the agreed temperature objectives, but the agreement points the way to further action.

4 The Paris Agreement: https://unfccc.int/process-and-meetings/the-paris-agreement/the-paris-agreement.

Transparency and global stocktake

1.11 Governments agreed to:

- come together every five years to assess the collective progress towards the long-term goals and inform parties in updating and enhancing their NDCs;
- report to each other and the public on how they are implementing climate action; and
- track progress towards their commitments under the Agreement through a robust transparency and accountability system.

Adaptation

1.12 Governments agreed to:

- strengthen societies' ability to deal with the impacts of climate change; and
- provide continued and enhanced international support for adaptation to developing countries.

Loss and damage

1.13 The Agreement also:

- recognises the importance of averting, minimising and addressing loss and damage associated with the adverse effects of climate change; and
- acknowledges the need to cooperate and enhance the understanding, action and support in different areas, such as early warning systems, emergency preparedness and risk insurance.

Climate Change Act 2008

1.14 The Climate Change Act 2008[5], which put into legislation the UK's approach to tackling and responding to climate change:

- introduced a legally binding target, by 2050, to reduce greenhouse gas emissions by at least 80% relative to 1990 levels;
- introduced 'carbon budgets' which cap emissions over successive five-year periods and must be set 12 years in advance;
- requires the UK to produce a UK Climate Change Risk Assessment (CCRA) every five years – this assesses current and future risks and opportunities for the UK from climate change;
- requires the Government to produce a National Adaptation Programme (NAP) to respond to risk assessment; and
- gives the Government powers to require certain organisations to report on how they are adapting to climate change (the Adaptation Reporting Power).

In addition to the UK Act, there are also Climate Change Acts in Wales and Scotland, since action is needed at a devolved level. The UK's share of a global effort consistent with the G8 and EU goals equates to at least an 80% reduction

5 Climate Change Act 2008: www.legislation.gov.uk/ukpga/2008/27/contents.

in UK emissions from 1990 levels by 2050. Other developed countries have responded to the threat of climate change by adopting similar long-term targets.

Climate Change (Scotland) Act 2009

1.15 This legalisation has been introduced to set targets in Scotland. Scotland aims to set a target date for zero emissions of all greenhouse gases by 2045. They have also updated a Climate Change Plan to reflect the targets which have been set within the Climate Change (Emissions Reduction Targets) Act 2019.

The aims are to:

- reduce greenhouse gas emissions through a Just Transition to a net-zero economy and society;
- drive Scotland's adaptation to climate change;
- support decarbonisation in the public sector;
- engage with business and industry on decarbonisation;
- listen to the people of Scotland through the Big Climate Conversation and encourage individuals to move towards low-carbon living;
- lead international action on climate change;
- support communities to tackle climate change through the Climate Challenge Fund; and
- support developing countries to tackle climate change through the Climate Justice Fund.

Environment (Wales) Act 2016

1.16 This Act sets out the approach for the sustainable management of natural resources in Wales. The aims are to:

- set a 2050 greenhouse emission target to ensure that the Welsh emissions account 2050 is at least 80% lower than the baseline;
- set interim targets for 2020, 2040 and 2050; and
- set five-yearly carbon budgets for the limits on total emissions that can be emitted in Wales.

RENEWABLES STATISTICS

1.17 The UK Government produces data on the UK's sources of renewable energy, which includes capacity, electricity and heat generation and transport fuels[6].

Key results are:

- Provisional results show that renewable energy generation increased by 8.5% compared to 2018, which is 110TWh to 119TWh, and was largely due to increased capacity.

6 Renewable Statistics: www.gov.uk/government/collections/renewables-statistics.

- The renewables share of energy generation was a record 36.9%, which is an increase of 3.8% on the 33% share in 2018, reflecting higher renewable and lower overall electricity generation in 2019 compared to 2018.
- In 2019, on the 2009 Renewable Energy Directive basis (normalised to account for variable weather and with the addition of generation from biogas within the gas supply grid), renewable generation was a record 34.6% of gross electricity consumption, an increase of 2.9% on 2018's share.
- Renewable electricity capacity was 47.4GW at the end of 2019, a 6.9% increase (3.0GW) on a year earlier; around half of this increase was in offshore wind.

UK PASSES NET ZERO EMISSIONS LAW

1.18 In June 2019 the UK became the first major economy to pass a net zero emissions law. This means that the UK will need to bring all greenhouse gas emissions to a net zero target by 2050, compared to the previous target of 80%. The new target was recommended by the Committee on Climate Change, the UK's independent climate advisory body. The net zero emissions means that any emissions would be balanced by a scheme to offset an equivalent amount of greenhouse gases from the atmosphere, such as planting trees or using technology like carbon capture and storage.

Net zero

1.19 Net zero refers to achieving a balance between the amount of greenhouse gas emissions produced and the amount removed from the atmosphere. There are two different routes to achieving net zero, which work in tandem: reducing existing emissions; and actively removing greenhouse gases.

If the UK opted for a gross zero target, that would mean the reduction of all emissions to zero, which is not realistic. A net zero target recognises that there will be some emissions and that these will need to be fully offset.

UK's greenhouse gas emissions

1.20 The Climate Change Act 2008 named six major greenhouse gases[7]:

- carbon dioxide;
- methane;
- nitrous oxide;
- hydrofluorocarbons;
- perfluorocarbons; and
- sulphur hexafluoride.

Carbon dioxide, which makes up the bulk of these, comes mainly from burning fossil fuels in eg coal power stations. The main sources of other greenhouse

7 The government also tracks and reports on emissions of nitrogen trifluoride.

gases include industrial processes and waste management, such as agriculture and landfill sites. Together, these accounted for around 19% of all UK emissions in 2018. The UK's emissions of all greenhouse gases have been falling steadily over the past 30 years, though levels have risen globally. In 2018, UK emissions stood at 57% of their 1990 levels.

Legal status of the net zero target

1.21 The Climate Change Act 2008 committed the UK to an 80% reduction in carbon emissions relative to the levels in 1990, to be achieved by 2050. In June 2019, secondary legislation was passed that extended that target to 'at least 100%'. Whilst the amended Climate Change Act imposes a legal obligation on the Government, it is not clear how this could or will be enforced. The proposed Office for Environmental Protection would have enforcement powers. The courts have already shown that they will intervene where they do not think the Government has taken proper account of its climate change commitments.

Heathrow expansion ruled unlawful

1.22 This happened in February 2020, for example, when the UK Court of Appeal ruled that the Government's policy statement in favour of Heathrow expansion was unlawful. In *R v Secretary of State for Transport* [2020] EWCA Civ 213, the Court of Appeal ruled that the UK Government had failed to take into account the commitments it made under the 2016 Paris Agreement on climate change when assessing Heathrow's expansion plan and, as a result, it ruled that the Government's Airports National Policy Statement was unlawful. The Court's decision is part of a global trend of successful climate change litigation that shines a light on the requirement for governments to consider their obligations under the Paris Agreement.

Following the Heathrow decision, all projects must now be aligned with the Paris Agreement.

Stansted airport expansion

1.23 Uttlesford District Council's planning committee resolved in January 2020 to reject Stansted airport's planning application to increase its maximum number of passengers from 35 million to 43 million a year. A statement from the council said the reasons for the refusal were made in relation to 'noise, air quality and climate change, matters that the committee agreed were material planning changes since the approval was granted'.

Bristol airport expansion

1.24 Plans to increase capacity at Bristol Airport by two million passengers a year were thrown out by councillors, on noise and climate grounds, against the advice of planning officers.

There were concerns over increases in greenhouse gas emissions, North Somerset Council's planning committee refused to grant outline planning permission for the airport expansion, which included plans to build a 2,150-space multi-storey car park, extensions to the terminal building, changes to flight times and three additional aircraft spaces.

Devon gas-fired plant

1.25 East Devon District Council rejected plans to build a 40MW peaking plant, built around a series of gas engines. It said its commitment in its local plan to promote renewables and low-carbon energy was a reason to go against the advice of a planning officer, adding that it would be inconsistent with the emergency it had declared the previous month. Applications to build power stations able to generate up to 50MW of electricity are handled by local authorities, rather than under the Nationally Significant Infrastructure Projects (NSIP) regime.

South Oxfordshire local plan

1.26 In April 2019, South Oxfordshire District Council declared a climate emergency and, in May 2019, a Liberal Democrat-Green Party coalition, running on a climate ticket against the existing draft local plan and the Oxford to Cambridge Expressway, took office. However, plans to scrap the local plan have been criticised by the Housing Secretary, who has asked Oxfordshire County Council to prepare the plan instead of the district council.

Hereford bypass

1.27 Herefordshire Council granted planning permission for a major bypass to the south of Hereford in July 2018. However, following a change of control to an independent/Green coalition in May 2019, it decided to pause the development and considered whether it may be incompatible with the climate emergency that it declared in March 2019. This has disrupted plans to build more than 3,000 homes around it. The Marches Local Enterprise Partnership has warned that it would ask for the £3.8 million that it provided for the project to be paid back.

Arun local plan

1.28 Arun District Council voted to adopt a motion tabled by a group of independent councillors warning that future housing set out in the local plan, which proposes building about 20,000 new homes up to 2031, should not be carried out until the risk of flooding as a result of climate change has been properly considered. The motion stated that the district was 'uniquely unsuitable' for large-scale development because it is 'particularly vulnerable' to the risks arising from climate change.

Uganda Foundation v State of the Netherlands

1.29 In *Uganda Foundation v State of the Netherlands*, a case brought by an environmental group and nearly 900 Dutch citizens in 2015, the Dutch supreme court mandated that the government achieve a 25% reduction in greenhouse gas emissions from 1990 levels by the end of 2020 to protect its citizens from the harms of a warming climate system.

Demanda Generaciones Futuras v Minambiente

1.30 In *Demanda Generaciones Futuras v Minambiente*, Colombia's Supreme Court ordered the government to implement protective measures to halt deforestation in the Amazon. This case was brought by 25 young Colombians. The cases rested on the idea that the right to life is endangered by threats to the environment. Their success suggests that there will be more suits brought by citizens against their governments.

Rocky Hill

1.31 The Rocky Hill coalmine in the Hunter Valley in Australia will not go ahead after a ruling in the land and environment court that cited the impact it would have had on climate change. The judge dismissed an appeal by Gloucester Resources, which was seeking to overturn a New South Wales government decision to reject an open-cut mine because of its impact on the town of Gloucester, north of Newcastle. The Environmental Defenders Office joined the case in April 2019, arguing on behalf of its client, Groundswell Gloucester, that the mine's detrimental impact on climate change and on the social fabric of the town should be considered as part of the merit appeal. In his judgment, the judge explicitly cited the project's potential impact on climate change, that an open-cut coalmine in the Gloucester Valley 'would be in the wrong place at the wrong time'.

In his judgment, he noted that while there was 'no proscription' on the approval of new emissions sources such as coalmines under the agreement, approval of the project 'cannot assist in achieving the rapid and deep reductions in GHG emissions that are necessary' to meet the goals of the Paris Climate Agreement. The judgment also rejected the mine on the grounds of its visual impact and the social impact of factors such as dust and noise on the surrounding community.

Adani

1.32 The Australian Government granted the Indian mining company Adani the final approvals it needed to start work on a huge coalmine in Queensland. The project would open up the Galilee Basin, one of the last-known untapped coal reserves on earth. Adani's plan has become a source of bitter debates over climate change and the economic struggles of regional Australia. The proposal for an open-cut coalmine in central Queensland and a rail line connecting it to the port of Abbot Point, near the Great Barrier Reef, has faced years of opposition from activists and required multiple state and federal environmental assessments.

UK Budget 2020 – growing a greener economy

1.33 The UK has already cut carbon emissions by more than any other G7 country and, in 2019, it was the first major economy to legislate for a target of net zero greenhouse gas emissions by 2050. Increasing the UK's use of clean energy is an essential part of reducing carbon emissions. The Budget made a number of points in favour of renewable energy:

- It announces a Carbon Capture and Storage (CCS) Infrastructure Fund to establish CCS in at least two UK sites – one by the mid-2020s, and a second by 2030.
- To encourage more environmentally friendly ways of heating homes and other buildings, the Government will introduce a Green Gas Levy to help fund the use of greener fuels, increase the Climate Change Levy that businesses pay on gas, and reopen and extend the Climate Change Agreement scheme by two years.
- Road transport is responsible for 91% of domestic transport emissions, and around a fifth of overall UK emissions. To support drivers to move away from polluting vehicles, the Budget announces investment in electric vehicle charging infrastructure, which will ensure that drivers are never more than 30 miles from a rapid charging station, provides £532 million for consumer incentives for ultra-low emission vehicles, and reduces taxes on zero emission vehicles.
- The Government will promote air quality improvement by removing the entitlement to use red diesel except for agriculture, fish farming, rail and non-commercial heating. The Government will tackle air pollution by providing £304 million to help local authorities reduce nitrogen dioxide emissions and improve air quality.
- To encourage businesses to operate in a more environmentally friendly way, the Government is raising the Climate Change Levy on gas in 2022–23 and 2023–24 (whilst freezing the rate on electricity) and reopening and extending the Climate Change Agreement scheme by two years.
- The Government will invest in the natural environment, planting enough trees to cover an area the size of Birmingham, restoring peatlands, and providing more funding to protect the UK's unique plants and animals.
- The Government will go further to tackle the scourge of plastic waste by introducing a Plastic Packaging Tax, as well as providing further funding to encourage producers to make their packaging more recyclable.
- The Budget sets out ambitious action on tree planting, ultra-low emission vehicles, heat decarbonisation, and carbon capture and storage. Further climate policy measures will follow in the coming months.
- HM Treasury will also publish two reviews in 2020 – one into the economic costs and opportunities of reaching net zero, and the other (led by Professor Sir Partha Dasgupta) into the economics of biodiversity.
- The Budget announces the Nature for Climate Fund which will invest £640 million in tree planting and peatland restoration in England, increasing the rate of tree planting by over 600% and covering an area greater than Birmingham over the next five years. In addition, the Budget announces

the Nature Recovery Network Fund, which will partner with businesses and local communities to protect, restore and support existing habitats and wildlife. The Government will also introduce the Natural Environment Impact Fund to help prepare green projects that could be suitable for commercial investment in order to encourage private-sector support for environmental restoration.

The UK was due to host the COP26 Climate Summit, in 2020, but this is now postponed until November 2021.

Is the 2050 target achievable?

1.34 The UK is currently not on track to meet its previous, less ambitious, target of 80% emissions reductions by 2050. The Committee on Climate Change (CCC) has said that getting to net zero (ie meeting the 100% target) is 'technically feasible but highly challenging'. To do so will require sustained policy interventions across several sectors, many of which will be complex, costly and time-consuming.

And the initial signs are not positive: in its July 2019 progress report, the CCC said the UK Government's policy actions '[fell] well short of those required for the net-zero target'. The UK is also not on track to meet some of its pre-existing future carbon budgets, set before the net zero target was adopted. The Government has announced some policy changes in response, such as bringing forward the ban on the sale of new petrol and diesel cars from 2040, but more is needed.

Scotland

1.35 The Scottish Government has set itself a target of net zero by 2045, in line with recommendations by the CCC. It has plenty of land, with potential for afforestation (planting trees to create forests, which are natural carbon sinks), which means it has more potential capacity to remove emissions from the atmosphere than the rest of the UK. The Scottish Government is also updating its Climate Change Plan[8] to reflect the increased ambition of new targets set in the Climate Change (Emissions Reduction Targets) (Scotland) Act 2019[9].

It is taking the following actions:

- reducing greenhouse gas emissions through a Just Transition to a net-zero economy and society;
- driving Scotland's adaptation to climate change;
- supporting decarbonisation in the public sector;
- engaging with business and industry on decarbonisation;

8 Climate Change Plan targets: www.gov.scot/policies/climate-change/reducing-emissions.
9 Climate Change (Emissions Reduction Targets) (Scotland) Act 2019: www.legislation.gov.uk/asp/2019/15/contents.

- listening to the people of Scotland through the Big Climate Conversation and encouraging individuals to move towards low-carbon living;
- leading international action on climate change;
- supporting communities to tackle climate change through the Climate Challenge Fund; and
- supporting developing countries to tackle climate change through the Climate Justice Fund.

Scotland has a target of an 80% reduction in gas emissions by 2050 (Climate Change Plan, 2018), and forestry has a significant role to play by:

- locking up carbon in growing trees and creating more woodland;
- supporting the use of wood fuel and renewable energy as a substitute for fossil fuels;
- promoting the use of wood in place of more carbon-intensive materials; and
- promoting sustainable forest management.

The Scottish Government has an ambitious target to increase woodland cover in Scotland from around 19% to 21% of the land area by 2032. These new woodlands will absorb and store carbon and will provide a wide range of environmental, economic and social benefits.

Wales

1.36 Wales has a much more difficult path to reach net zero, even by 2050, in part because it has high agricultural emissions. The CCC recommended that Wales aim for a 95% reduction by 2050, which the Welsh Government accepted. This would not stop the UK as a whole from being net zero by 2050. Apart from the Environment Act (Wales) 2016, there is also the Well-being of Future Generations (Wales) Act 2015[10] which aims to improve the social, economic, environmental and cultural well-being of Wales, protecting the country's assets for the future, and sets out the seven well-being goals. The Act also details five ways of working (long-term, integration, involvement, collaboration, prevention) which public bodies must follow in developing policy and delivery of services.

Northern Ireland

1.37 Northern Ireland's second Climate Change Adaptation Programme (NICCAP2) was published in September 2019 and it covers the period 2019–2024. It contains the NICS Departments' response to the risks and opportunities relevant to Northern Ireland, as identified in the UK Climate Change Risk Assessment 2017 ('CCRA 2017') and focuses on key priority areas identified as requiring urgent adaptation action over the next five years.

10 Well-being of Future Generations (Wales) Act 2015: www.legislation.gov.uk/anaw/2015/2/contents.

It sets the policies, strategies and delivery plan actions by which NICS Departments will deliver outcome objectives so as to achieve the vision of 'A resilient Northern Ireland which will take timely and well-informed decisions to address the socio-economic and environmental impacts of climate change'.

NICCAP2 contains a chapter which sits outside government, titled 'Civil Society and Local Government Adapts'. The chapter is written by Climate NI, in conjunction with outside government stakeholders, and provides adaptation outcome objective delivery plans and actions that will be undertaken by Civil Society and Local Government sectors which will contribute to achieving NICCAP2's vision. Publication of the CCRA 2017 in January 2017 delivered on the UK Government's statutory requirement under the Climate Change Act, in a five-yearly cycle, to publish and lay before Parliament a UK-wide CCRA.

CCRA 2017 was informed by an independent 'Evidence Report' from the Adaptation Sub-Committee of the Committee on Climate Change (CCC), which was commissioned by the UK Government and Devolved Administrations. The assessment is known as 'UK Climate Change Risk Assessment – 2017 Evidence Report'. The report contained national summaries for each of the UK administrations, including a summary with climate change risks specific to Northern Ireland.

The NICCAP2 identifies key priority areas:

- **NC:** Natural Capital, including Terrestrial/Coastal/Marine/Freshwater ecosystems, soils;
- **IF:** Infrastructure Services, and biodiversity;
- **P:** People and the environment;
- **B:** Disruption to Businesses & Supply Chains; and
- **I:** Food Security/Global Food Production.

It also states:

> 'The scale and rate at which this change will happen in the future is difficult to predict due to various factors and inherent complexity. Such factors include, the success of the world implementing international mitigation agreements (such as the Paris Agreement) to cut GHG emissions, advancements in technology and the growth in populations or energy needs.'

Northern Ireland's 2010–2020 Strategic Energy Framework includes a target for 40% of its power to be generated from renewable sources by 2020. Statistics published by the Department for the Economy (DfE) in early September 2019 show that, for the 12-month period from July 2018 to June 2019, 44% of total electricity consumption in Northern Ireland was generated from renewable sources located in Northern Ireland – compared to 2005, when the Northern Ireland Renewables Obligation (NIRO) incentive scheme was first introduced, the figure stood at just 3%. The NIRO was designed to incentivise renewable electricity generation across the country.

Between July 2018 and June 2019, 85.3% of total renewable generation came from wind, with biogas the second largest contributor with just 5.5% consumption. The Office of Gas and Electricity Markets found that wind turbines under 250kW accounted for a third of onshore wind Renewables Obligation Certificates (ROCs), and anaerobic digestion stations with a declared net capacity (DNC) of less than 500kW accounted for over half of fuelled ROCs, and 92% of all solar ROCs were issued to stations with a capacity of 50kW and below.

Which business sectors will be affected the most?

1.38 The four highest-emitting sectors are:

- transportation, energy supply (generating electricity from burning fuels such as coal, oil and natural gas);
- business (commercial use of electricity); and
- residential (heating homes).

These account for around 78% of current emissions. Since 1990, the UK has achieved emissions reductions in the energy-supply sector, historically the worst offender, particularly in the last eight years as a result of phasing out coal and increasing the use of renewables, such as wind and solar. In other areas such as transport, homes and agriculture, the emissions remain largely unchanged. Decarbonising these areas will be more difficult.

Some regions of the UK will find getting to net zero more achievable than others.

Carbon budgets

1.39 The Climate Change Act 2008 requires the Government to set five-yearly carbon budgets, after taking advice from the CCC. These run until 2032. The budgets are fixed in advance and set five-year caps on the total greenhouse gas emissions allowed to ensure the UK meets its emissions reduction commitments. The UK is on track to meet its third carbon budget (the current one, covering 2018–22) but is not on track to meet its fourth (2023–27) and fifth (2028–32). The CCC will advise the Government on the sixth carbon budget (2033–37) in September 2020. This will be the first to take the net zero target into account. Carbon budgets currently exclude emissions from international aviation and shipping (those produced by planes and ships while in UK territorial waters and airspace). Accurately measuring the UK's share of these is difficult, but the advice from the CCC is that the final net zero target should account for such emissions.

How can the UK reach its target?

1.40 The carbon budgets allow for the use of international carbon units traded outside the EU's Emissions Trading System (ETS). Participating in this system means that the UK may produce more emissions than are accounted for, as some can be offset by trading 'carbon credits' with other countries. The Government has stated that the UK will remain a part of EU ETS until January 2021.

Costs and benefits

1.41 Reaching net zero will bring the UK important benefits but will also incur large costs. Estimating either of these with any accuracy is difficult, given the level of uncertainty around new and emerging technologies, and changes in the economy and people's behaviour. In 2019, the CCC estimated that the total costs of getting to net zero would be £50 billion per year, less than 1% of projected GDP over that period. The Treasury and the Department for Business, Energy and Industrial Strategy (BEIS) put the figure at £70 billion per year, or over £1 trillion by 2050. The economic analysis of net zero is now uncertain, following the coronavirus pandemic.

Models that attempt to calculate costs have a degree of uncertainty because the underlying economics are constantly shifting. One example is the changing price of offshore wind, whose cost fell by over 30% in 2019 alone, greatly exceeding expectations. Net zero could also bring wider societal benefits, for instance to human health as a result of improved air quality and a better-protected natural environment. The CCC says these could 'partially or fully offset costs', for instance by reducing hospital admissions, and enabling people to be more productive. In November 2019, the Treasury launched a review into the costs and opportunities of reaching net zero, and this is due to report in late 2020.

Which other countries have a net zero target?

1.42 Six nations have passed laws formally establishing net zero targets: Sweden and Scotland by 2045, and the UK (as a whole), France, Denmark and New Zealand by 2050. Similar legislation has been proposed in the EU, Spain, Chile and Fiji.

Many other countries have set targets, most at 2050 (Norway is aiming for 2030), but are yet to propose or pass legislation formalising these into law. The only countries which are currently net negative are Bhutan and Suriname.

Carbon capture and storage

1.43 Carbon capture and storage (CCS) is a technology that can capture up to 90% of the carbon dioxide emissions produced from those of fossil fuels in electricity generation and industrial processes and prevent the carbon dioxide from entering the atmosphere. CCS has three parts:

- capturing carbon dioxide;
- transporting carbon dioxide; and
- storing the carbon dioxide emissions.

Capture technologies

1.44 These allow the separation of the carbon dioxide from the gases that are produced by one of three methods:

- Pre-combustion capture – this involves converting the solid, liquid or gaseous fuel into a mixture of hydrogen and carbon dioxide, using a process such as:
  - reforming – which is a well-established process already used at scale at refineries and chemical plants around the world; or
  - gasification – which is widely practiced around the world and is similar in some respects to the process that is used to make town gas.

- The hydrogen produced by these processes may be used to fuel electricity production, but also it may, in the future, be used to power cars and heat homes with near zero emissions.
- Post-combustion capture – here, carbon dioxide can be captured from the exhaust of a combustion process by absorbing it in a suitable solvent. The absorbed carbon dioxide is released from the solvent and is compressed for transportation and storage. Other methods for separating carbon dioxide include high pressure membrane filtration, adsorption/desorption processes and cryogenic separation.
- Oxyfuel combustion – in this process the oxygen required is separated from air prior to combustion and the fuel is combusted in oxygen diluted with recycled flue-gas rather than by air. This oxygen-rich, nitrogen-free atmosphere results in final flue-gases consisting mainly of carbon dioxide and water, which produce a more concentrated carbon dioxide stream for easier purification.

Transporting the carbon dioxide

1.45 Carbon dioxide is then transported by pipeline or by ship for storage. Millions of tonnes of carbon dioxide are transported annually for commercial purposes by road tanker, ship and pipelines.

Storage of carbon dioxide

1.46 Once the carbon dioxide has been transported, it is stored in porous geological formations that are typically located several kilometres under the earth's surface, with pressure and temperatures such that carbon dioxide will be in the liquid or 'supercritical' phase. Suitable storage sites include former gas and oil fields, deep saline formations (porous rocks filled with very salty water), or depleting oil fields where the injected carbon dioxide may increase the amount of oil recovered.

At the storage site the carbon dioxide is injected under pressure into the geological formation; the carbon dioxide then moves up through the storage until it reaches an impermeable layer of rock (which cannot be penetrated by carbon dioxide). This layer is known as the cap rock and traps the carbon dioxide in the storage formation. This storage mechanism is called 'structural storage'.

Structural storage is the main storage mechanism in CCS and is the same process that has kept oil and natural gas trapped under the ground for millions of years. As the injected carbon dioxide moves up through the geological storage site towards the cap rock, some of it is left behind in the microscopic pore spaces of the rock. This carbon dioxide is tightly trapped in the pore spaces by a mechanism known as 'residual storage'.

The stored carbon dioxide in a geological formation will begin to dissolve into the surrounding salty water, which makes the salty water denser and it will begin to sink down to the bottom of the storage site. This is known as 'dissolution storage'.

Finally, 'mineral storage' occurs when the carbon dioxide held within the storage site binds chemically and irreversibly to the surrounding rock.

MEETING THE 2050 PATHWAYS

1.47 The UK is committed to reducing its greenhouse gas emissions by at least 80% by 2050, relative to 1990 levels. In order for this to take place, there needs to be a transformation the UK economy whilst ensuring secure, low-carbon energy supplies to 2050. This guidance[11] has been produced to look at how the UK can meet the 2050 emissions reduction target. In order for the UK to do this, there will be some choices and trade-offs. The pathway process which is proposed looks at the process system-wide, covering all parts of the economy and all greenhouse gas emissions released in the UK. It has its basis in scientific and engineering principles and looks at what is thought to be physically and technically possible in each sector.

The original calculator was released by DECC (now BEIS) and is available in three versions to allow a range of people to explore the question of how the UK can best meet energy needs while reducing emissions:

- the new-look web-tool version of the calculator, for a detailed look at the issue with a user-friendly interface;
- the 'classic' version of the web tool, that allows the user to see all of their options in one view; and
- the full Excel version of the calculator, for experts who want to look at the underpinning model.

The 2050 Pathways work presents a framework through which to consider some of the choices and trade-offs that will have to be made over the coming years.

Organisations can try out different ways of securing a low-carbon future for the UK by creating their own pathway using the calculator.

On the supply side, it is possible to choose how the UK produces its energy – for example, the building of up to 40,000 offshore wind turbines or up to 50 3GW nuclear power stations; the user can allocate up to 20% of the UK's land to growing bio crops, and can reduce the UK's use of landfill sites.

For each choice, four trajectories have been developed, ranging from little or no effort to reduce emissions (level 1), to extremely ambitious changes that push towards the physical or technical limits of what can be achieved (level 4). The assumptions behind these trajectories are explained. The toolkit is also available as a version for schools.

GLOBAL TRENDS

1.48 The Frankfurt School FS-UNEP Collaborating Centre has produced a detailed analysis of trends in global renewable energy investment[12]. The International Renewable Energy Agency (IRENA) has analysed renewable trends in energy costs. It found that, in 2018, around 0.5GW of new concentrating solar power was commissioned – predominantly from China,

11 2050 Guidance Pathways: www.gov.uk/guidance/2050-pathways-analysis.

12 Global Trends in Renewable Energy Investment 2019, Frankfurt School FS-UNEP Collaborating Centre: https://wedocs.unep.org/bitstream/handle/20.500.11822/29752/GTR2019.pdf.

Morocco and South Africa. The global weighted average of Levelised Cost of Energy (LCOE) concentrating on solar power in 2018 was USD0.185/kWh – 26% lower than in 2017 and 46% lower than 2010.

IRENA[13] also provides information by renewable energy technologies within countries.

Taking all the global data for 2019:

- 44.7% is hydropower;
- 23.4% onshore wind energy;
- 22.9% solar photovoltaic;
- 3.4% solid biofuels;
- 2.2% mixed hydro plants;
- 1.1% offshore wind energy;
- 0.8% biogas;
- 0.6% renewable municipal waste;
- 0.5% geothermal;
- 0.2% solar thermal energy; and
- 0.1% liquid biofuels.

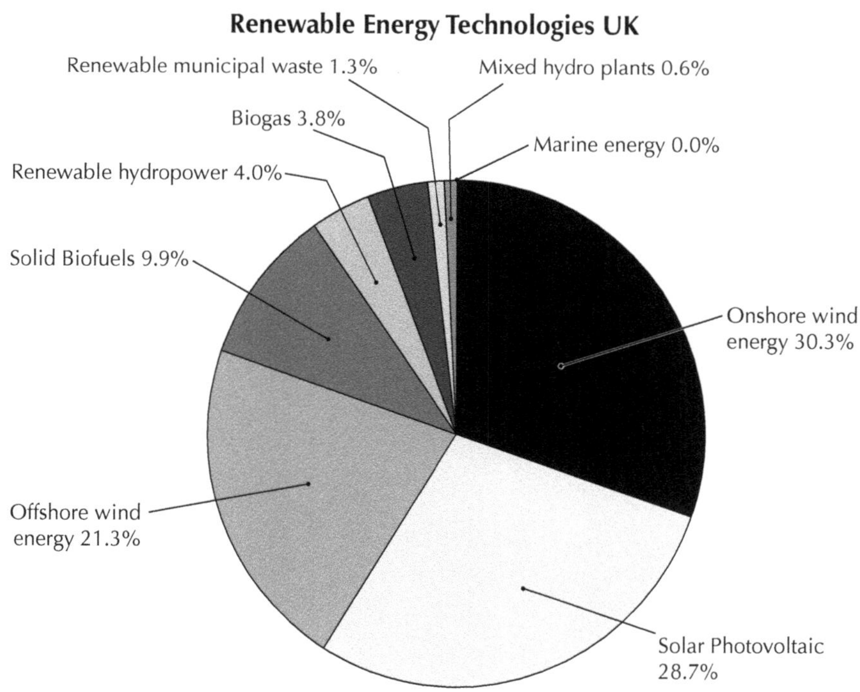

Data Source: IRENA

13 IRENA renewable energy data.

Chapter 2

Incentives to Invest in Renewable Energy

INTRODUCTION

2.1 In order for companies and domestic properties to invest in renewable energy technology with a view to reducing greenhouse gas production, the Government has provided various legally binding targets. As a result of this, there has been a significant increase in investing in renewable energy technology which has driven innovation since 1990. The UK infrastructure has been built around a centralised power network, with the majority of the energy coming from large fossil fuel plants connected to a large transmission network.

In 2016, coal, gas and oil accounted for 54% of the UK's total energy generation, with nuclear 20% and renewable energy 24%[1]. In 2016, many of the coal power stations in the UK were approaching the end of their life, and these stations could be decommissioned or regenerated. Fossil fuel stations can be converted into renewable energy plants with capital investment. Renewable technology has the potential to replace some of the existing infrastructure, substituting traditional fossil fuel plants with low-carbon alternatives. The UK's commitment to carbon reductions is set out in the 2009 EU Renewable Energy Directive[2], which imposes the requirement to achieve 15% of its energy consumption from renewable energy sources by 2020, including 30% of all electricity generation from renewables. In June 2019, Parliament passed legislation[3] requiring the Government to reduce the UK's net emissions of greenhouse gases by 100% relative to 1990 levels by 2050. Doing so would make the UK a 'net zero' emitter. Prior to this, the UK was committed to reducing net greenhouse gas emissions by at least 80% of their 1990 levels, also by 2050.

PAYMENTS FOR ELECTRICITY GENERATION

2.2 The Feed-in tariff (FIT) was announced in October 2008 as part of the Energy Act 2008[4], and came into effect in April 2010. However, FIT has been closed to new applicants since 31 March 2019. The effect of FIT has been to incentivise investment into small-scale renewable electricity generation. Where the generator is less than 5MW, it can install renewable energy technology and export energy to the grid. The energy exported is paid for by FIT. Between 2010 and 2016 almost 6,000MW of capacity was added and confirmed on the FIT scheme[5].

1 Energy-UK (2017) Electricity Generation: https://assets.publishing.service.gov.uk/government/uploads/system/uploads/attachment_data/file/695626/Press_Notice_March_2018.pdf.
2 Directive 2009/28/EC: https://eur-lex.europa.eu/legal-content/EN/ALL/?uri=CELEX%3A32009L0028.
3 Climate Change Act 2008 (2050 Target Amendment) Order 2019: www.legislation.gov.uk/uksi/2019/1056/contents/made.
4 www.legislation.gov.uk/ukpga/2008/32/contents.
5 Chapter 6 Renewable sources of energy: https://assets.publishing.service.gov.uk/government/uploads/system/uploads/attachment_data/file/840014/Chapter_6.pdf.

Application of FIT

2.3 FIT applies to small-scale generation of electricity using renewable technologies, subject to the following conditions:

- renewable sources producing up to 5MW of power;
- generators greater than 5MW were eligible for Renewables Obligation Certificates within an existing renewables obligation quota mechanism;
- other qualifications requirements include certification under a Micro-generation Certification Scheme (MCS) and the REAL code (Renewable Energy Assurance Limited) for up to 50MW;
- use of specific metering standards;
- system being installed no earlier than July 2009; and
- energy efficiency requirements added in March 2012 for buildings fitting PV systems under GF+FIT.

The contract term is 20 years and 25 years for solar panel projects. From 2010, providers of wind energy, hydropower, and energy from biomass and anaerobic digestion were eligible for the FIT scheme and would have had a guaranteed tariff. The tariff is subject to a degression, so that the tariff level available for new generators will decrease annually and programme costs are paid for by the energy suppliers.

Smart Export Guarantee[6], which came into force in 1 January 2020, is not a direct replacement for FIT but an initiative to reward solar generators for electricity exported to the grid. Where an energy supplier has more than 15,000 domestic customers, it will be obliged to provide at least one export tariff, and this must be greater than zero. Export will be measured by smart meters which will be installed free of charge by the energy supplier.

A scheme similar to FIT, called the Renewable Heat Incentive, was introduced in 2011 for renewable heat.

Climate Change Act 2008

2.4 In 2008, when approximately 80% of the UK's electricity came from fossil fuels, the Climate Change Act[7] became law. This Act sets up the framework for the UK to achieve its long-term goals of reducing greenhouse gas emissions and to ensure steps are taken towards adapting to the impact of climate change. It has the following main elements.

Setting emissions reduction targets in statute and carbon budgeting

2.5 The Act establishes an economically credible emissions reduction pathway to 2050 and beyond, by putting into statute medium- and long-term targets. In addition, the Act introduces a system of carbon budgeting which constrains the

6 www.gov.uk/government/consultations/the-future-for-small-scale-low-carbon-generation.
7 Climate Change Act 2008: http://www.legislation.gov.uk/ukpga/2008/27/contents.

total amount of emissions in a given time period. Carbon budget periods will last five years, beginning with the period 2008–2012, and must be set three periods ahead. The Secretary of State is required to give indicative ranges for the net UK carbon account in each year of a budgetary period, to set a limit on use that can be made of international carbon credits in each budgetary period, and to develop and report on his proposals and policies for meeting carbon budgets.

A new reporting framework

2.6 The Act provides for a system of annual reporting by the Government on the UK's greenhouse gas emissions. The new Committee on Climate Change will have a specific role in reporting annually on progress, with the Government required to lay before Parliament a response to this progress report.

The creation of an independent advisory body

2.7 The Act creates a new independent body, the Committee on Climate Change, to advise the Government and devolved administrations on how to reduce emissions over time and across the economy and, on request, on any other matter relating to climate change, including adaptation to climate change. This expert body will advise on the optimum trajectory to 2050, the level of carbon budgets, and on how much effort should be made by the part of the economy covered by trading schemes and by the rest of the economy, as well as reporting on progress.

Trading scheme powers

2.8 The Act includes powers to enable the Government and the devolved administrations to introduce new domestic trading schemes to reduce emissions through secondary legislation. This increases the policy options which the Government could use to meet the medium- and long-term targets in the Act.

Adaptation

2.9 The Act sets out a procedure for assessing the risks of the impact of climate change for the UK, and a requirement on the Government to develop an adaptation programme on matters for which it is responsible. The programme must contribute to sustainable development. The Act also gives powers to direct other bodies to prepare risk analyses and programmes of action, and advisory and progress-reporting functions to the Committee on Climate Change.

Policy measures which reduce emissions

2.10 The Act will be used to support emissions reductions through several specific policy measures: amendments to improve the operation of the Renewable Transport Fuel Obligations; a power to introduce charges for single-use carrier bags; a power to pilot local authority incentive schemes to encourage household waste minimisation and recycling; amendments relating to the Certified Emissions Reductions Scheme; powers and duties relating to the reporting of emissions by companies and other persons; and a duty to make annual reports on the efficiency and contribution to sustainability of buildings on the civil estate.

In order to promote the deployment of small-scale renewable energy installations in homes and business, the UK Government introduced the FIT scheme that required participating licensed energy supplier to make payments on both generation and export from eligible installations. It was closed to new applicants on 31 March 2019, except for some exemptions. There was also a complementary scheme for heat generation called the Renewable Heat Incentive[8].

FIT scheme

2.11 The FIT scheme was available for anyone who had installed or was looking to install technology of capacity up to 5MW (or 2kW for CHP) for:

- solar photovoltaic (solar PV);
- wind;
- micro combined heat and power (CHP);
- hydro; or
- anaerobic digestion (AD).

FIT payments are made quarterly (at least) for the electricity that the installation has generated and exported. Payments are made based on the meter reading submitted to the energy supplier (the FIT licensee). FIT payments are made by the energy supplier from the date of eligibility to be in the scheme.

FIT roles and responsibilities

Generators

2.12 Generators are the owners of installations who apply to the FIT scheme.

Licensees

2.13 FIT licensees are energy suppliers who process applications submitted for small installations and make FIT payments to all installations. Under the Ofgem safety net, the energy supply of customers of a licensee which has had its licence revoked continues as normal. The process is different for FIT customers whose payments were made by the licensee whose licence has been revoked.

8 Renewable Heat Incentive (RHI) is a UK Government scheme set up to encourage uptake of renewable heat technologies amongst householders, communities and businesses through financial incentives.

History of the FIT scheme

2012

2.14 On 1 December 2012, a number of changes were implemented to the scheme, which include:

- introduction of ROO-FIT (Renewables Obligation Order Feed-in Tariff) preliminary accreditation;
- the introduction of a degression mechanism to reduce generation tariffs; and
- the introduction of pre-registration for community energy and school installations, which provided the benefits of a tariff guarantee and relaxation of the energy efficiency requirement.

From 1 April 2012 onwards, solar PV installations with a capacity of 250kW and below have to meet an energy efficiency requirement. This, along with the introduction of the multi-installation rule, introduced the high, middle and lower tariff rates for PV installations.

2013

2.15 On 1 July 2013, the following provisions were introduced to the FIT scheme:

- the process of mutualisation was introduced in the event of a licensed electricity supplier being unable to make the whole or part of a levelisation payment into Ofgem's Levelisation Fund; and
- the introduction of instructions to deal with the treatment of FIT generators and FIT payments in the event of their FIT licensee having their electricity supply licence revoked or suffering an insolvency event.

2014

2.16 From 14 July 2014, provisions were made to withdraw ROO-FIT preliminary accreditation of certain hydro generating stations.

2015

2.17 On 1 April 2015, an amended definition of 'community organisation' and additional benefits available to community energy installations were introduced.

On 1 October 2015, the following changes were made to the FIT scheme:

- the removal of the tariff guarantee for community energy installations applying for pre-registration; and
- the removal of preliminary accreditation for ROO-FIT installations.

2016

2.18 The FIT scheme was paused from 15 January to 7 February 2016 (inclusive). This suspended new applications received during the pause from MCS registration or ROO-FIT accreditation.

Extensions to existing accredited FIT installations are no longer eligible for the FIT scheme where they are commissioned on or after 15 January 2016.

A number of changes were introduced to the scheme on 8 February 2016. This included:

- deployment caps for all technologies and capacities (with the exception of micro-CHP);
- changes to the default and contingent degression mechanisms which reduce generation tariff rates;
- the re-introduction of preliminary accreditation for ROO-FIT installations; and
- amendments to the energy efficiency requirement (EER) for solar PV installations.

From 9 May 2016, the EER was further amended to require solar PV installations (<250kW) to have an Energy Performance Certificate issued before the commissioning date in order to receive the higher tariff rate.

2017

2.19 On 1 April 2017, the following changes were introduced to the FIT scheme:

- the introduction of six-monthly 5MW deployment caps and contingent degression for micro CHP (combined heat and power) installations; and
- amended future generation tariff rates for anaerobic digestion (AD) installations and the introduction of default degression mechanism for AD.

All AD installations that made an application after 1 May 2017 are required to comply with sustainability criteria and will have their FIT generation payments limited according to feedstock type (referred to as 'feedstock restrictions').

2018

2.20 On 18 December 2018, the following changes were introduced to the FIT scheme:

- closure of the scheme to new applications from 1 April 2019, barring exceptions for a grid or radar delay grace periods and MCS installations which were commissioned before this date.

Impact of the FIT scheme

2.21 The DECC document 'Performance and Impact of the Feed-in Tariff Scheme: Review of Evidence[9], published in 2015, stated:

> 'The FIT has already succeeded in meeting the top three of its original objectives. The deployment of small-scale (<5MW) low-carbon electricity generation under the FIT has exceeded projections in terms of numbers of installations (column 2

9 DECC Performance and Impact of the Feed-in Tariff Scheme: Review of Evidence: https://assets.publishing.service.gov.uk/government/uploads/system/uploads/attachment_data/file/456181/FIT_Evidence_Review.pdf.

and 3, Table 1). In terms of cumulative capacity (indirectly specified in column 4 of Table 1) it is rapidly catching up with original projections, while actual generation appears on track to reach projected targets (column 5 and 6, Table 1).

Achievement of the FIT compared to objectives laid out in the 2010 Impact Assessment

	Cumulative number of FIT installations [2]	Cumulative number of domestic installations [3]	Generation per installation [4]	Total electricity generation [5]	Share of final UK electricity consumption [6]
2010 Impact Assessment	780,000 by 2020	450,000 by 2015	7.7MWh/a in 2020	6,000GWh in 2020	1.6% in 2020
Achievement	682,511 end of March 2015	640,344 end of March 2015	5.4MWh/a in Year 4 (2013/14)	2,645GWh in Year 4 (2013/14)	0.84% in Year 4 (2013/14)'

Legal challenge following the closure of the FIT scheme

2.22 The FIT scheme was introduced to encourage low-carbon generation of electricity. In 2009, the Department of Energy and Climate Change (DECC) held a consultation on the incentives to encourage renewable energy generation[10].

The Government's response[11] to this stated '... any individual installation, once starting to receive a tariff at a certain level, will continue to receive the same generation tariff level throughout its entire support period under the FIT scheme. This tariff will however be increased annually for inflation'.

There were concerns that the support scheme was too generous and DECC proposed in the consultation paper that the eligibility date by which installations had to be commissioned should be brought forward from the original specified date of 1 April 2012 to 12 December 2011. It was then 18 months since the FIT scheme had been introduced and had encourage people to get involved in green energy generation.

Former Energy Secretary Chris Huhne's 2011 announcement on proposed cuts in environmental subsidies led to many organisations and individuals dropping plans to install solar power with FIT equipment that feeds electricity generated by small-scale solar panel systems. This is turn led to an action through the courts against the DECC by a number of organisations which had been affected by these changes.

In its ruling, the High Court established that pre-existing contracts to supply solar micro-generation equipment constitute 'property' for the purposes of the protection of property rights under the European Convention on Human Rights (ECHR). Chris Huhne's announcement, which proposed bringing forward the reduction in the subsidised payment, constituted interference with those property rights and should potentially be compensated.

10 Department of Energy and Climate Change, Consultation on Renewable Electricity Financial Incentives 2009: www.fitariffs.co.uk/library/regulation/090715Consultation.pdf.

11 Department of Energy and Climate Change, Feed-in-tariffs, Government's response to the 2009 consultation, para 21: www.fitariffs.co.uk/library/regulation/100201FinalDesign.pdf.

The 31 October announcement amounted to a retrospective change in legislation without passing new legislation through Parliament. This damaged businesses and also consumers who had planned to install equipment on the basis of the higher payments. This then breached the ECHR Article 1 protocol[12] on protection of property rights regarding contracts concluded on or before the day of the announcement.

In a legal ruling in the High Court[13] the Government was found to have fallen foul of the principle that the law cannot be retrospectively changed if it damages people's interests[14].

Breyer Group plc, HomeSun Holdings and Touch Solar were among installers and potential micro-generators bringing the case against the DECC – which established the principle that the Government can be held monetarily responsible for the effects of its announcement, even if it was a mere proposal. The Government had argued that a mere proposal cannot amount to interference with property for the purpose of A1P1 claims.

Chris Huhne and the DECC thought that the initial rates were too generous to generators of solar electricity. Chris Huhne announced that the date by which the installations had to be commissioned/registered in order to qualify for the highest FIT rate would be brought forward, from 1 April 2012 to 12 December 2011 – prompting many people to drop plans. This happened even though Chris Huhne had 10 days earlier told Parliament that 'this Government is very committed to not having retrospection in legislation and legislative changes'.

Article 1 Protocol 1 states:

> 'Every natural or legal person is entitled to the peaceful enjoyment of his possessions. No one shall be deprived of his possessions except in the public interest and subject to the conditions provided for by law and by the general principles of international law.'

Mr Justice Coulson noted:

> 'The claimants [potential energy generators, solar panel suppliers and others] argued that, if the Government could avoid the devastating consequences of its own actions by saying that the change to the date was merely a proposal, then the way would be open for the Government to cause huge financial losses to its citizens without regard to the consequences, by claiming that a mere proposal cannot amount to interference for A1P1 purposes. On the other hand, the defendant [DECC] maintains that, if the claimants' claims were allowed, no Government would be able even to propose modifications to policy in future without risking huge losses, even if those proposals were never actually implemented. They say this would give rise to a limitless field of potential liability far beyond anything envisaged by A1P1'[15].

Coulson J favoured the claimants' view. He ruled that, in principle, signed or concluded contracts constituted 'property' in terms of A1P1, citing Lewison J in *Murungaru v Secretary of State for the Home Department* [2008] EWCA Civ

12 EHCR Article 1: www.coe.int/en/web/conventions/full-list/-/conventions/treaty/009.

13 *Breyer Group and Other v Department for Energy and Climate Change* [2014] EWHC 2257 (QB).

14 *R (Reilly) v Secretary of State for Work and Pensions* [2013] UKSC 68.

15 *Breyer Group and Other v Department for Energy and Climate Change* [2014] EWHC 2257 (QB) at paras 41–42.

1015: 'A claim justiciable in domestic law can amount to a possession for the purposes of A1P1 only if it is sufficiently established to be enforceable'. The contracts were sufficiently established and hence have a value, even if not yet realised before the work is done: 'They were tangible; they were assignable; on the face of it they had a present economic value' (Coulson J, para 51). Contracts not signed would not count as property unless the work had commenced without signing and with details of the contract yet to be agreed.

There is no property in loss of potential future income for A1P1 purposes nor in continuing to enjoy a particular level of trade since 'a possible contract in the future is, on the European analysis, no more than a hope or aspiration, and cannot be regarded as an asset or possession' (para 60).

However, financial goodwill in a company may be covered: 'Whilst loss of future income is not protected by A1P1, marketable goodwill may be, although sensibly distinguishing between the two is a Herculean task' (para 45). Goodwill represents work put into a business to establish it. It has a market value which is transferable so constitutes property – which governments should not interfere with.

The Government argued that the number of FIT schemes had increased more than was anticipated, in part because of the reduced costs of setting up the equipment. Rates of returns on investment rose above the 5–8% on which the scheme was based. The 'subsidy' actually comes from all other consumers of electricity, so it was fair to curb the scheme. The change would save £1.6bn. Coulson J nevertheless ruled that the Government's behaviour could not be justified. An earlier Court of Appeal hearing had established that 'Section 41 [of the Energy Act 2008] makes no reference whatever to the power to decrease the rate of return, other than in accordance with a formula' – in other words, there was no power to retrospectively cut the rate of return (*Secretary of State for Energy and Climate Change v Friends of the Earth and Others* [2012] EWCA Civ 28, para 50).

This suggests that the interference was unlawful *per se* but, even if it were not, any positive effects of intervention (lower subsidies borne by consumers at large) were outweighed by losses – including (significantly) damage to the environment. The claimants were entitled to damages 'to put them back in the position they would have been in had the violation not occurred' (para 156). The amounts would depend on looking at each individual contract.

Coulson J concluded: 'Although the entitlement to damages will ultimately depend on the facts, as a matter of general principle, the claimants have demonstrated an entitlement to damages assessed by reference to the loss of those possessions for which recovery is permissible, namely signed/concluded contracts and/or the marketable goodwill referable to such contracts.'

Note: The High Court originally found the Government's actions unlawful in 2011, though not on an A1P1 basis. Mitting J took the view that the Government action was *ultra vires* of the Act and inconsistent with the statutory purpose. The DECC went on to lose an appeal in January 2012: *Secretary of State for Energy and Climate Change v Friends of the Earth and Others*. Here the court held that the action was *ultra vires* on grounds of retrospectivity.

The 2014 High Court case, as a hearing on preliminary issues, has not concluded matters between the solar panel installers and the Government, but it has laid down the legal basis so that the sides can either come to agreement or test the issues on the individual facts at a future hearing.

The DECC lost a further stage of the legal action at the UK Supreme Court (May 2015), where the court confirmed that 'A possession within the meaning of A1P1 does not include a right to acquire possessions and a mere prospective loss of future income is not a possession'. However, marketable goodwill may be a possession. Crucially, it is based on past work building up a reputation rather than mere expectation of future profits. The judge said: 'The fact that the Proposal had no legal effect (because it was no more than a proposal) does not mean that it did not affect and interfere with the claimants' A1P1 rights. In short, I reject the submission that a mere proposal cannot, as a matter of law, amount to an interference'. In general, 'It will almost always be possible for the authority in question to justify the interference as being "in the public interest" and subject to the conditions provided for by law' – and hence be lawful.

SMART EXPORT GUARANTEE

2.23 The Smart Export Guarantee (SEG) is an obligation set by the Government for licensed electricity suppliers to offer a tariff and make payments to small-scale low-carbon generators for electricity exported to the National Grid, provided that certain criteria are met. It replaces the FIT scheme which pays many solar panel owners for the electricity that they generate.

The SEG came into force on 1 January 2020.

SEG applies to

2.24 The SEG is an opportunity for anyone who has installed one of the following technology types up to a capacity of 5MW (or 50kW for Micro-CHP):

- solar photovoltaic (solar PV);
- wind;
- micro combined heat and power (CHP);
- hydro; or
- anaerobic digestion (AD).

These installations must be located in Great Britain.

The SEG Licensee is required to put processes in place to pay for the electricity exported by the eligible installation and to report to Ofgem on installations under the SEG arrangements. SEG Licensees determine the rate they will pay, contract length and other terms.

However, whilst wholesale electricity prices can sometimes fall below zero, SEG Licensees must always offer a tariff that remains above zero. SEG payments must be calculated by SEG Licensees using Export Meter Readings.

SEG only pays for the excess electricity that is generated and all that's generated. Companies will set their own SEG tariff prices and just pay more than zero. All companies with more than 150,000 customers can offer an SEG tariff. The

SEG is not a price guarantee, the only guarantee is that the price will be greater than zero pence (p/kWh) at all times of the export over the period.

SEG tariffs

Fixed rate

2.25 SEGs have a set amount that they pay per kilowatt hour of electricity exported to the grid, regardless of the time that it is exported. Most of the SEG tariffs on offer at the moment follow this pattern.

Flexible rate

2.26 SEGs pay varying amounts depending on how valuable the electricity is to the system at different times. For example, the rates may be tied to day-ahead wholesale prices. So, more could be paid for exporting electricity at a time when there is a high demand for it (in the evening, for instance). Octopus Energy's Outgoing Agile tariff is this type.

SEG – summarised

2.27

- The SEG is for new generators of clean energy. It is most relevant for those not already benefiting from the FIT scheme, unless a generator is adding additional generation to an existing FIT registered scheme, in which case the new element will not quality for FIT but could qualify for the SEG.
- Technologies up to a capacity of 5MW, including:
  - solar PV;
  - onshore wind;
  - anaerobic digestion;
  - hydro; and
  - micro-combined heat and power (with an electrical capacity of 50kW or less),

  are eligible to receive payment for exported electricity under the SEG.
- Storage will be eligible to receive export payments, although suppliers will be allowed to exclude 'brown' electricity from those payments and require the generator to put metering in place that isolates 'green' exports.
- The exported power must be metered on a half-hourly basis and the meter must be registered for settlement under the Balancing and Settlement Code. This applies even if the tariff is not half-hourly (the SEG is flexible and does not necessarily require half-hourly readings).
- Suppliers must be satisfied that export installations are suitably safe. This could mean that exporters must show evidence that the installation is certified to the Microgeneration Certification Scheme (MCS), or equivalent, standards.
- Suppliers must be satisfied that anaerobic digestion installations meet sustainability criteria and feedstock requirements as verified by Ofgem.

There is no requirement for other schemes to meet any sustainability or energy efficiency standard.

- There is no specified minimum export floor price, and suppliers can set their own rate. The only guarantee is that the export tariff must always be greater than zero pence.
- Licensed suppliers with 150,000 or more domestic customers must provide at least one export tariff. Other suppliers can join voluntarily.
- The law was passed on 10 June 2019, and energy suppliers affected must offer at least one tariff by 1 January 2020.

CONTRACTS FOR DIFFERENCE

2.28 The Contracts for Difference (CfD)[16] scheme is the Government's main mechanism for supporting low-carbon electricity generation. A CfD is a long-term contract between an electricity generator and the Low Carbon Contracts Company (LCCC). The LCCC is a private company owned by the Department for Business, Energy and Industrial Strategy (BEIS). The LCCC is the other party in the contracts awarded in CfD rounds (auctions) and its primary role is to issue the contracts, manage them during the construction and delivery phase, and make payments. The National Grid is the delivery body for the CfD and is responsible for running the allocation process. Ofgem is responsible for hearing certain appeals.

The contract enables the generator to stabilise its revenues at a pre-agreed level (the 'strike price') for the duration of the contract. Under the CfD, payments can flow from the LCCC to the generator, and from the generator to the LCCC.

Under a CfD, when the price for electricity in the market or a CfD generator (reference price) is below the strike price set out in the contract, payments are made by the LCCC to the CfD generator to make up the difference. If, however, the reference price is above the strike price, the CfD generator pays the LCCC the difference. This way the CfD generator has a guaranteed return for its electricity generation.

Allocation rounds

2.29 There have been three rounds of CfD allocation to date, and the next is expected to open in 2021, subject to any required state aid approval of planned changes:

- first CfD allocation round (AR1): October 2014 to March 2015;
- second CfD allocation round (AR2): March 2017 to September 2017; and
- third CfD allocation round (AR3): May 2019 to September 2019.

16 Contracts for Difference (Allocation) Regulations 2014: www.legislation.gov.uk/uksi/2014/2011/contents/made.

Supplier Obligation and Operational Costs Levy

2.30 The obligation to make payments to CfD generators under the CfD is funded by a statutory levy on all UK-based licensed electricity suppliers ('Supplier Obligation'). Also, the operational costs of the LCCC is funded by a statutory levy on all UK-based licensed electricity suppliers ('Operational Costs Levy'). The LCCC is responsible for collecting and funds that are due from suppliers under the Supplier Obligation and the Operational Costs Levy. The Supplier Obligation and Operational Costs Levy are set out in secondary legislation.

CfD settlement services

2.31 The DECC uses EMR Settlement Limited to provide settlement services on behalf of the LCCC in relation to CfD. It runs the system and operates the processes that enable the CfD payments to be calculated and settled.

This includes:

- collecting metering data for CfD generators;
- maintaining the systems that allow it to collect, securely store and, where appropriate, securely transmit the data necessary for CfD settlement;
- managing settlement of payments by generators and suppliers;
- holding and managing reserve funds;
- calculating payments and charges; and
- invoicing and collecting payments due.

EMR Settlement Limited also acts on behalf of the Electricity Settlements Company (the Capacity Market settlement body). It manages the payments on behalf of the Electricity Settlement companies to and from the Capacity Providers and Suppliers.

This includes:

- collecting metering data for Capacity Market providers;
- setting up and maintaining the systems that allow it to collect, securely store and, where appropriate, securely transmit the data necessary for Capacity Market settlement;
- managing settlement of payments by capacity providers and suppliers;
- calculating payments and charges; and
- invoicing and collecting payments due.

RENEWABLES OBLIGATION

2.32 Where smaller-scale generation is mainly supported through the FIT scheme and latterly through the Smart Export Guarantee (see para **2.23**), the Renewables Obligation (RO) is one of the main support mechanisms for large-scale renewable electricity projects in the UK.

The RO came into effect in England, Scotland and Wales in 2003 and in Northern Ireland in 2005, and it places an obligation on UK electricity suppliers to source an increasing proportion of the electricity that they supply from renewable sources. The RO closed to all new generating capacity on 31 March 2017.

Renewable Obligation Certificates

2.33 Renewable Obligation Certificates (ROCs) are certificates issued to operators of accredited renewable generating stations for eligible electricity that they generate. Operators can trade ROCs with other parties. The ROCs are used by suppliers to demonstrate that they have met their obligation. If a supplier did not present a sufficient number of ROCs to meet their obligations in the reporting period, they must pay an equivalent amount into a buy-out fund. The cost of administrating this scheme is recovered from the fund and the rest distributed back to suppliers in proportion to the number of ROCs they have produced.

Annual obligation levels

2.34 This is set each year by the DECC. The RO scheme policy is set by the Department for Business, Energy and Industrial Strategy (BEIS) and, in Northern Ireland, the Department for the Economy (DfE), but the scheme is administered by Ofgem, who assess and, where appropriate, accredit RO applications that have been submitted to them. Assessments are made based on the evidence submitted with the application and the circumstances specific to the generating station.

Applicants must meet the eligibility criteria to be granted accreditation under the RO. It is not the role of Ofgem to interpret legislation on their behalf, and people are encouraged to seek legal and technical advice to help understand how the legislation applies to them. Ofgem are unable to comment on future policy amendments or on speculative applications and scenarios.

NON-FOSSIL FUEL OBLIGATION (NFFO)

2.35 This process operated from 1990 and was replaced by the RO. It was a series of orders which required the electricity distribution network operators for England and Wales to purchase electricity from the nuclear power and renewable energy sectors. In Scotland a similar system was the Scottish Renewables Obligation (SRO) and, in Northern Ireland, the Northern Ireland Non-Fossil Fuel Obligations.

The NFFO was put in place under the Electricity Act 1989[17] which privatised the generation of electricity in the UK. The original intention was support for nuclear power generators, but the scope was widened to include the renewable energy sector.

17 Electricity Act 1989: www.legislation.gov.uk/ukpga/1989/29/contents.

Funding

2.36 Funding for the NFFO was generated form the Fossil Fuel Levy, which was placed on all electricity consumption in the UK. It was collected by Ofgem, which paid the Non-Fossil Purchasing Agency, which was created in 1990 by the public electricity suppliers to purchase on the suppliers behalf.

EU EMISSIONS TRADING SYSTEM

2.37 The EU Emissions Trading System (EU ETS) is a cornerstone of the EU's policy to combat climate change and its key tool for reducing greenhouse gas emissions in a cost-effective manner. It is the world's first major carbon market and remains the biggest one. It is another policy based on a 'cap and trade' principle, which drives emissions down over time and promotes investment in green energy.

The EU ETS:

- operates in all EU countries plus Iceland, Liechtenstein and Norway;
- limits emissions from more than 11,000 heavy energy-using installations (power stations & industrial plants) and airlines operating between these countries; and
- covers around 45% of the EU's greenhouse gas emissions.

The EU Climate Action group identifies that 'robust policies' at EU and country level and the application of low-carbon technologies have contributed to carbon reductions. Evaluations confirm that innovation on renewable energy and energy efficiency has been the main driver behind the emission reductions in recent years, while the shift between economic sectors has had a marginal effect.

'Cap and trade' principle

2.38 The EU ETS works on the 'cap and trade' principle. A cap is set on the total amount of certain greenhouse gases that can be emitted by installations covered by the system. The cap is then reduced over time so that total emissions fall. Within the cap, companies receive or buy emission allowances, which they can trade with one another as needed. They can also buy limited amounts of international credits from emission-saving projects around the world. The limit on the total number of allowances available ensures that they have a value.

After each year a company must surrender enough allowances to cover all its emissions, otherwise heavy fines are imposed. If a company reduces its emissions, it can keep the spare allowances to cover its future needs or else sell them to another company that is short of allowances.

Trading aims to bring flexibility that ensures emissions are cut where it costs least to do so. A robust carbon price also promotes investment in clean, low-carbon technologies.

Sectors and gases covered

Carbon dioxide

2.39

- power and heat generation;
- energy-intensive industry sectors including oil refineries, steel works and production of iron, aluminium, metals, cement, lime, glass, ceramics, pulp, paper, cardboard, acids and bulk organic chemicals;
- commercial aviation;

Nitrous oxide

2.40

- from production of nitric, adipic and glyoxylic acids and glyoxal;

Perfluorocarbons (PFCs)

2.41

- from aluminium production.

Participation in the EU ETS

2.42 Participation is mandatory for companies in these sectors, but:

- in some sectors, only plants above a certain size are included;
- certain small installations can be excluded if governments put in place fiscal or other measures that will cut their emissions by an equivalent amount; and
- in the aviation sector, until 31 December 2023 the EU ETS will apply only to flights between airports located in the European Economic Area (EEA).

Key features of Phase 3 (2013–2020)

2.43 The EU ETS is now in its third phase, which is significantly different from Phases 1 and 2.

The main changes from the previous two phases are:

- a single, EU-wide cap on emissions applies in place of the previous system of national caps;
- auctioning is the default method for allocating allowances (instead of free allocation), and harmonised allocation rules apply to the allowances still given away for free;
- more sectors and gases included; and

- 300 million allowances set aside in the New Entrants Reserve to fund the deployment of innovative, renewable energy technologies and carbon capture and storage through the NER 300 programme.

Key features of Phase 4 (2021–2030)

2.44 The legislative framework of the EU ETS for its next trading period (Phase 4) was revised in early 2018 to enable it to achieve the EU's 2030 emission reduction targets and as part of the EU's contribution to the Paris Agreement.

This focuses on:

- strengthening the EU ETS as an investment driver by increasing the pace of annual reductions in allowances to 2.2% as of 2021 and reinforcing the Market Stability Reserve (the mechanism established by the EU in 2015 to reduce the surplus of emission allowances in the carbon market and to improve the EU ETS's resilience to future shocks);
- continuing the free allocation of allowances as a safeguard for the international competitiveness of industrial sectors at risk of carbon leakage, while ensuring that the rules for determining free allocation are focused and reflect technological progress; and
- helping industry and the power sector to meet the innovation and investment challenges of the low-carbon transition via several low-carbon funding mechanisms.

Impact of the EU ETS on renewable energy

2.45 A study of the interaction between the EU ETS and the Renewable Energy Directive was carried out[18] and looked at the co-existence of the EU ETS and other policy instruments, such as the Renewable Energy Directive (RED), and found that it could be justified as it was able to:

- correct market failures;
- correct policy failures;
- improve the design of the system; and
- meet multiple targets and objectives.

The key findings were as follows:

- The combination of policy instruments for energy efficiency improvement, renewable energy support and the EU ETS can be justified based on the fact that each of them has its own target under the EU Climate and Energy Package (such as 20% energy efficiency improvement, achieving a 20% market share for renewable energy, and a 20% GHG emission reduction for 2020, which have recently been updated for the year 2030.

18 Interaction between EU ETS and the Renewable Energy Directive – Transition Pathways – sustainable low-carbon societies, Europa website: www.pathways-project.nl/interaction-between-eu-ets-and-renewable-energy-directive.

- Detrimental effects of renewable energy support measures on the EU ETS have been among the major concerns of EU stakeholders in the power and energy trading sectors. The overachievement of the RE target meant that, in the power production sector, demand for ETS allowances decreased, resulting in a lower ETS market price. In terms of efficiency, this resulted in a loss as emission reductions delivered by RE support measures such as FIT schemes have higher abatement costs than those through 'cap and trade' systems such as the EU ETS.
- While interactions between the policy instruments were foreseen, the overachievement of the RE target was not anticipated. This success has been driven by policy objectives other than GHG emission reductions (eg energy security and air pollution reductions). The current EU policy framework in this field, the Energy Union, aims at an increase in RE share for multiple reasons.
- It is important to understand how the RES Directive affects the ETS, and to identify the conditions under which this effect will become detrimental to undermining the purpose of the latter, and how this can be prevented. For that, the case study analysis concludes on three key measures: (a) the effects of policies such as renewable energy support need to be fully accounted for when the ETS cap is set at the start of each ETS Phase through the review of the Linear Reduction Factor; (b) greater transparency in information is needed to assess the adequacy of the ETS cap and to monitor impacts of abatement delivered through complementary policies such as RE; and (c) the Market Stability Reserve is the only and most effective instrument in place to mitigate the impacts of complementary policies, which were unpredictable or/and unavoidable, during the phase.

European Union 2020 – Energy Policy Review

2.46 The International Energy Agency (IEA) conducted a peer review of countries' energy policies[19]. The new IEA report sets out recommendations to help the EU meet its 2030 targets for greenhouse gas emissions, renewables and energy efficiency as well as its longer-term decarbonisation goals. It finds that stronger policies than those currently in place will be needed to deliver on these ambitions and that the energy sector needs to be at the heart of those efforts, as it accounts for 75% of EU greenhouse gas emissions. As EU Member States have different energy policies and approaches to decarbonisation, the IEA report concludes that strong cooperation will be needed under the framework of the National Energy and Climate Plans. It also recommends that the EU build on the bloc's integrated energy market and cross-border trade and develop stronger carbon price signals.

This report on the EU discusses the energy challenges facing the continent and recommends possible solutions to help it achieve a secure and sustainable energy future. In relation to the EU ETS, it found:

- other policy drivers are the plans of 16 Member States to phase out coal use in the next decades (coal still accounted for 20% of the EU electricity

19 European Union, 2020 Energy Policy Review, June 2020: www.iea.org/reports/european-union-2020#executive-summary.

mix in 2018) and the successful reform of the EU ETS with a market stability reserve (MSR), which adapts to the economic development. In 2019, the EU saw a price for allowances of EUR28, up from only EUR8 in 2014. In 2020, the EU ETS withstood the oversupply from the Covid-19 crisis, thanks to the MSR;

- the industry sector is covered under the EU ETS, with free allowances for those industries that are at risk of carbon leakage. Industry does not have any specific target for energy efficiency or renewables, and its inclusion under the EU ETS has not yielded substantial reductions in emissions; and
- the EU ETS system has been, and can be, a strong enabler of fuel switching. The European Commission should examine the opportunity of strengthening the carbon price signal under the non-ETS and the EU ETS to incentivise innovation in low-carbon industrial development.

Chapter 3

Wind Power

INTRODUCTION

3.1 In 2019, renewable energy generation was increased by 8.5% compared to 2018, from 110TWh to 119TWh. This was largely due to an increase in capacity[1]. Record generation was seen in both offshore and onshore wind generation. Capacity at the site in Hornsea gradually increased and stood at 1,218MW by the end of 2019, which makes it the largest offshore wind farm in the world. The success of wind power generation has, in part, been based on the incentives that have been offered (see Chapter 2).

The industry has come a long way since the first known wind turbine was installed in 1887 and used to produce electricity in Scotland. The wind turbine was created by Professor James Blyth of Anderson's College, Glasgow (now known as Strathclyde University):

> 'Blyth's 10 m high, cloth-sailed wind turbine was installed in the garden of his holiday cottage at Marykirk in Kincardineshire and was used to charge accumulators developed by the Frenchman Camille Alphonse Faure, to power the lighting in the cottage, thus making it the first house in the world to have its electricity supplied by wind power. Blyth offered the surplus electricity to the people of Marykirk for lighting the main street, however, they turned down the offer as they thought electricity was "the work of the devil".'

1 https://assets.publishing.service.gov.uk/government/uploads/system/uploads/attachment_data/file/875410/Renewables_Q4_2019.pdf.

WIND POWER DEPLOYMENT

Planning policy for wind

3.2 In March 2012 the Government published the National Planning Policy Framework (NPPF). The NPPF sets out the Government's planning policies for England and how it expects these to be applied. It must be taken into account in the preparation of local and neighbourhood plans and is a material consideration for local planning authorities (LPAs) considering planning applications.

The NPPF replaced much of the former planning policy statements, and the Localism Act 2011 and subsequent orders made under it have abolished all but a few remaining policies of the Regional Spatial Strategies. This now means that LPAs no longer have to adopt targets for wind farms set at regional level. They may, however, choose to adopt their own targets if they wish to do so.

The NPPF directs that, when determining planning applications for renewable energy development, LPAs should:

- not require applicants for energy development to demonstrate the overall need for renewable or low carbon energy and also recognise that even small-scale projects provide a valuable contribution to cutting greenhouse gas emissions; and
- approve the application if its impacts are (or can be made) acceptable. Once suitable areas for renewable and low carbon energy have been identified in plans, LPAs should also expect subsequent applications for commercial-scale projects outside these areas to demonstrate that the proposed location meets the criteria used in identifying suitable areas.

The NPPF makes clear that renewable energy development is not normally considered appropriate development for Green Belt land. If located in the Green Belt, elements of many renewable energy projects will comprise of inappropriate development. In these cases, developers need to demonstrate very special circumstances for a project to proceed. These circumstances may include the wider environmental benefits associated with increased production of energy from renewable sources.

The NPPF also encourages LPAs to develop a strategy to promote renewable energy developments and identify suitable sites for them. It is important that the LPAs recognise the responsibility on all local communities to contribute to energy generation from renewable carbon resources.

They should:

- have a positive strategy to promote energy from renewable and low carbon sources;
- design their policies to maximise renewable and low carbon energy development while ensuring that adverse impacts are addressed satisfactorily, including cumulative landscape and visual impacts;
- consider identifying suitable areas for renewable and low carbon energy sources, and supporting infrastructure, where this would help secure the development of such sources;

- support community-led initiatives for renewable and low carbon energy, including developments outside such areas being taken forward through neighbourhood planning; and
- identify opportunities where development can draw its energy supply from decentralised, renewable or low carbon energy supply systems and for co-locating potential heat customers and suppliers.

In determining planning applications for such developments, planning authorities should follow the approach set out in the National Policy Statement for Renewable Energy Infrastructure[2], July 2011. This sets out the general principles that should be applied in the assessment of development consent applications for onshore wind (as well as other renewable energy technologies). Section 2.7 covers onshore wind.

Consideration should be given to:

- predicted wind speed;
- proximity of site to dwellings;
- capacity of a site, and access;
- grid connection issues;
- biodiversity and geological conservation;
- historic environment impacts;
- landscape and visual impact;
- noise and vibration;
- shadow flicker; and
- traffic and transport issues.

In July 2013 the Government published planning practice guidance for renewable and low carbon energy, which was replaced in March 2014 by online planning practice guidance on renewable and low carbon energy. The guide makes it clear that the need for renewable energy did not automatically override environmental protections and the planning concerns of local communities. It also aimed to ensure sufficient weight was given to landscape and visual impact concerns. The guidance sets out particular planning considerations that relate to wind turbines, which includes guidance on how LPAs should assess impacts such as noise, safety, interference with electromagnetic transmission, ecology, heritage, shadow flicker, energy output, and cumulative landscape and visual impacts.

Local policy

3.3 At a local level, an individual LPA may produce renewable energy studies in order to inform the evidence base for their local plans. The NPPF says that each LPA should produce a local plan which will contain policies relating to renewable energy in that particular area. Some LPAs also produce supplementary planning guidance to accompany the local plan, with more detail about policy in a particular area.

2 National Policy Statement for Renewable Energy Infrastructure (EN3): https://assets.publishing.service.gov.uk/government/uploads/system/uploads/attachment_data/file/37048/1940-nps-renewable-energy-en3.pdf.

Recovered appeals for Secretary of State determination

3.4 In October 2013 the Secretary of State announced that he would temporarily expand the criteria for recovering planning appeals for his own determination, for six months, to include appeals for renewable energy development[3]:

> 'This new criterion is added to the recovery policy issued on 30 June 2008 and will be applied for a period of six months from today after which it will be reviewed ... this does not mean that all renewable energy appeals will be recovered, but that planning Ministers are likely to recover a number of appeals in order to assess the application of the planning practice guidance at national level.'

Community engagement in the planning process

3.5 In October 2014 the Government published a document giving guidance on community benefits and engagement for onshore wind farm developers[4]. In January 2014 the Government published a community energy strategy, which set out Government policies for helping communities to produce, reduce, manage and purchase energy.

Separation distances

3.6 In England, there are no national minimum separation distances set between wind turbines and housing, and there are no proposals from Government to introduce them. In some specific circumstances, it may be possible for an LPA to set its own separation distance in its own local area.

In July 2014, Allerdale Borough Council became the first council to successfully introduce a separation distance between wind turbines and housing in its local plan for the area[5]. In the Allerdale Borough Council Local Plan, which was adopted earlier in July 2014, a policy on separation between wind turbines and residential housing of 800 metres was included. The policy is worded so that this separation distance does not have to apply rigidly, and it gives flexibility to decision makers not to have to use it in all cases.

Any local plans must be examined by an independent planning inspector before they can be adopted, to test that they meet legal requirements, that they comply with Government policy and that they are based on robust evidence. The policy on wind farm separation distances in the Allerdale Borough Council was scrutinised in depth by the planning inspector, who concluded that there

3 'Calling-in planning applications (England)', House of Commons Library No 00930, 31 January 2019.

4 'Community engagement for onshore wind developments: Best practice guidance for England': https://assets.publishing.service.gov.uk/government/uploads/system/uploads/attachment_data/file/364244/FINAL_-_Community_engagement_guidance_-06-10-14.pdf.

5 Allerdale Borough Council Local Plan (Part 1), Wind Turbine Separation Distance Topic Paper: www-cloudfront.allerdale.gov.uk/media/filer_public/78/86/78861921-f655-4d28-83a0-224d1dfff188/tp5_wind_turbine_separation_distance.pdf.

was nothing in the Government's planning policy which would exclude the principle of a minimum separation distance.

Disadvantages of wind power

Reliability

3.7 Wind power generation is governed by the weather and can therefore be unreliable and inconsistent, with onshore wind farms suffering from inconsistent wind patterns. Offshore wind is more consistent, but the infrastructure requirements and costs are much higher. The inconsistency in supply relies on processes such as battery storage to try and even out supply.

Initial high investment

3.8 The costs of wind projects are such that many rely on Government subsidy. This also means that a long period of energy generation is needed before the initial costs can be recovered.

Local residents

3.9 Some people dislike the appearance of wind farms, and people living nearby can complain about the noise that the turbines make whilst they generate electricity.

OFFSHORE

3.10 Britain has the largest installed offshore wind capacity in the world, with 9.8GW installed, which is set to rise to 19.5GW by the mid-2020s. In March 2019 the UK Government published the Offshore Wind Sector Deal[6], which set out a partnership between the Government and industry to raise the productivity and competitiveness of UK companies.

The Sector Deal set up a number of targets and commitments from the sector and the Government which are aimed at delivering the benefits to the UK economy of ongoing offshore wind. It is consistent with the Clean Growth Challenge (see para **14.13**).

It aims to do this by:

- providing forward visibility of future Contracts for Difference rounds;
- committing to increase UK content to 60% by 2030, including increases in the capital expenditure phase;

6 'Offshore Wind Sector Deal one year on', March 2020: www.gov.uk/government/publications/offshore-wind-sector-deal/offshore-wind-sector-deal.

- increasing the representation of women in the offshore wind workforce to at least a third by 2030;
- setting an ambition of increasing exports fivefold to £2.6 billion by 2030; and
- investing up to £250 million in building a stronger UK supply chain, establishing the Offshore Wind Growth Partnership (OWGP) to support productivity and increase competitiveness.

With the UK having the largest installed offshore wind capacity in the world, and the prices that consumers pay for the energy that the sector generates falling significantly, the OWGP aims to encourage innovation by bringing together industry, academic and public sector representatives, by developing regional clusters for collaboration between developers and the regional supply chain, and public sector and education bodies.

They are:

- Deep Wind (North Scotland);
- Forth & Tay Offshore;
- North East England;
- Humber;
- East Anglia;
- Solent;
- Celtic Sea Cluster; and
- North West & North Wales.

Offshore consents and licensing

3.11 As the UK offshore renewable industry has expanded, there have been changes to the consenting regimes and the introduction of legislation designed to facilitate the development of these schemes.

The Planning Act 2008[7] introduced a new consenting regime for offshore windfarms generating over 100MW. This means that the entire planning process for a project is overseen by one body and this is intended to streamline the process to enable the Nationally Significant Infrastructure Projects to be determined more efficiently.

In addition to this, the provision of advice and guidance for offshore renewables was transferred to the Marine Management Organisation[8] which was established under the Marine and Coastal Access Act 2009[9].

Case law – liability for foundation adequacy

3.12 In the cases of the offshore windfarms at Robin Rigg and Solway Firth, the Supreme Court ruling changed the legal landscape surrounding offshore

7 Planning Act 2008: www.legislation.gov.uk/ukpga/2008/29/contents.

8 Marine Management Organisation: www.gov.uk/government/organisations/marine-management-organisation/services-information.

9 Marine and Coastal Access Act 2009: www.gov.uk/government/organisations/marine-management-organisation/services-information.

wind farm design and construction. In August 2017 the Supreme Court handed down a judgment in the case of *MT Højgaard v E.ON Climate & Renewables and others*[10]. The case involved the foundation of the two offshore windfarms at Robin Rigg and Solway Firth, which were designed and installed by MT Højgaard. It was found that, after installation, there were grouted connection problems in each foundation at Robin Rigg and this was the result of fundamental problems with the industry design standard.

The legal dispute was over the cost of remediation costs of about €26.25 million ($30.6 million). The Supreme Court said that MT Højgaard were responsible as they had failed to deliver foundations that were fit for purpose, even though the clients had specified a standard.

ONSHORE

3.13 The UK Government reduced the subsidies available for onshore wind farms which then made new installation unfeasible. This led to an 80% decrease in new onshore wind farms. The government has now changed this, and the onshore wind farm schemes can compete for subsidies with other schemes such as solar. The Government has said it would cut emissions to virtually zero by 2050, which is something that experts have said will require the UK's wind-power capacity to triple in the next 15 years.

The new auction will take place in 2021.

Windfarm developers will need to comply with the proposals for community consent to qualify for the auction process. This means they need the consent of the local community through the existing planning codes.

Planning process for onshore wind turbines

3.14 Most onshore wind turbines require planning permission granted by the relevant local planning authority (LPA) for that area. Recently, larger onshore wind turbines of above 50MW were treated as Nationally Significant Infrastructure Projects (NSIPs). This meant that they had to obtain development consent granted by the Secretary of State under the rules provided for in the Planning Act 2008, rather than obtaining planning permission from the LPA.

The Energy Act 2016[11] together with the Infrastructure Planning (Onshore Wind Generating Stations) Order 2016[12] changed this position. This legislation removed onshore wind farms of over 50MW in size from the NSIP regime and returned the decision-making powers to LPAs. The LPAs make planning decisions in accordance with the policies set out in the NPPF[13] and by following

10 [2017] UKSC 59.
11 Energy Act 2016: www.legislation.gov.uk/ukpga/2016/20/contents.
12 Infrastructure Planning (Onshore Wind Generating Stations) Order 2016: www.legislation.gov.uk/uksi/2016/306/contents/made.
13 National Planning Policy Framework: www.gov.uk/government/collections/revised-national-planning-policy-framework.

the procedure set out in the Town and Country Planning Act 1990[14] and the Town and Country Planning (Development Management Procedure) (England) Order 2015[15] (SI 2015/595). The time period for planning determination under these rules will therefore depend on the size of the site for the proposed wind turbine development.

Planning policy for onshore wind is contained in a number of documents, principally the Government's National Planning Policy Framework, the National Policy Statement for Renewable Energy Infrastructure and online Planning practice guidance for renewable and low carbon energy. Local authorities will have policies on onshore wind development in any up-to-date local plan for a particular area. While there are no nationally set minimum separation distances between wind turbines and housing in England, one council has successfully set guidelines for a minimum distance for its area in the Allerdale Borough Council Local Plan.

The former Government temporarily expanded the planning appeals recovery criteria to allow the Secretary of State to take the final decision on onshore wind appeals. This expired in April 2015 and the current Government has not renewed it.

In its online Planning Practice Guidance, the former Government's aim was to make clear that the need for renewable energy did not automatically override environmental protections and the planning concerns of local communities. Compulsory pre-application engagement exists for 'more significant onshore wind', which is for any development involving more than two turbines or any turbine exceeding 15 metres height.

Section 106 agreements

3.15 Concerns about new infrastructure are sometimes met by the local council imposing planning obligations on developers. New developments in a particular area may bring with them wider impacts on the local area – for example, construction of a new wind farm might bring more people to the area who use local public facilities and infrastructure. New facilities may therefore need to be built or upgraded to cope with this extra demand and this needs to be paid for. Section 106 of the Town and Country Planning Act 1990 (as amended) allows developers to enter into 'planning obligations' with a local authority in order secure planning permission for a development.

Section 106 agreements are legally binding, and the obligations may be either in cash or kind, to undertake works, provide affordable housing, or provide additional funding for services.

Planning obligations to support new development must help meet the objectives of the local plans and neighbourhood plans for a particular area. The amount available from section 106 obligations is a matter for negotiation between a developer and the local council. Therefore, there is no standard amount given

14 Town and Country Planning Act 1990: www.legislation.gov.uk/ukpga/1990/8/contents.
15 Town and Country Planning (Development Management Procedure) (England) Order 2015: www.legislation.gov.uk/uksi/2015/595/contents.

for renewables projects. Many councils, however, issue their own planning obligations supplementary planning document (SPD). These documents explain a Council's approach to planning obligations, its aims for the types of planning obligations that may be sought, and the methodology for calculating the amount of these obligations. Having this document helps a local council refute allegations that planning permission can be 'bought' if it sets out in advance how much money will be required in what circumstances.

Business rate retention

3.16 In England, under the Local Government Finance Act 2012 and the Non-Domestic Rating (Renewable Energy Projects) Regulations 2013 (SI 2013/108), from April 2013, all of the business rates income from new renewable energy projects, including onshore wind farms, can be retained by the local planning authority (ie the decision maker for the relevant renewable energy project at county or district level).

Goodwill payments

3.17 There are also community benefits (in addition to section 106 obligations) provided by industry, rather than Government. In some cases, wind farm developers have made what they call 'goodwill payments' to a local community. These payments are offered outside of the planning system but have led to criticisms that planning permission for windfarms can be bought and sold. The Campaign to Protect Rural England (CPRE) has criticised this practice.

These payments range from grants to carry out immediate one-off improvements to local amenities (eg new playgrounds for children) through to annual funding to support longer-term projects which could have a wider and more lasting legacy (eg environmental enhancement schemes and energy efficiency programmes).

A community fund

3.18 One way for wind energy developments to provide community benefits is for money to be paid into a fund for the use of the community. This is where the owner of a wind farm distributes funds directly to community projects, often on an annual basis. This can be linked to the output of the wind turbine or can be linked to the financial revenue generated by the wind farm. An example of this is the Wadlow Wind Farm Community Fund in Cambridgeshire.

Contribution to energy efficiency schemes

3.19 Some wind energy projects contribute funds to sustainable energy initiatives within the local community, often through a third party specialising in providing these services. This could include, for example, improving home insulation levels and heating efficiency, or installing small-scale renewable energy equipment such as solar water heating. Energy advice and education activities might also be included.

Wider environmental and societal benefits

3.20 A wind developer may also choose to directly deliver local improvements. Examples are improvements to local facilities, environmental improvements, tourism or recreational provision.

Provision of cheaper electricity

3.21 According to the Government, some developers have explored ways to offer reductions to electricity bills for local communities in the vicinity of wind farms. An example of this is the Renewable Energy Systems (RES) Local Electricity Discount Scheme, which offers an annual discount on the electricity bills of those properties closest to an RES wind farm.

The Community Benefit Protocol

3.22 In February 2011 the trade association RenewableUK brought together some of the different sorts of benefits into a scheme called the Community Benefits Protocol. The Protocol was originally a benefit package worth a minimum of £1,000 per megawatt (now worth £5,000 per megawatt), per year of installed wind power during the lifetime of the wind farm (typically 25 years). The Protocol was designed to account for the fact that not all communities are the same, and they will not all necessarily want the same sorts of benefits, so it contains flexibility to tailor schemes to match the wishes of communities and covers financial payments and/or benefits in kind and profit sharing or community ownership.

The change in the value of the community benefit package was made by the renewables industry following a Government response to a consultation on community engagement and benefits of onshore wind. In the Government's response, it recommended that the wind industry should increase the value of its Community Benefit Protocol.

In response to the Government report, DECC announced a revision to their existing Community Benefit Protocol to increase the current recommended community benefit package value in England fivefold from £1,000/MW of capacity per year to £5,000/MW of capacity per year for the lifetime of the windfarm (usually around 25 years). To put this in context, £5,000/MW for a 20MW windfarm (or around eight turbines) would mean £100,000 per year that could be used to fund programmes to roll out energy efficiency measures, employ neighbourhood energy advisors, establish local skills and training projects, and provide meaningful electricity bill offsets for many individual households or other community initiatives that local people might want.

The previous Government said that it would not put the requirements of a community benefit package in legislation, in order to allow for a degree of flexibility in the types and levels of benefit packages offered. A revised Community Benefit Protocol was subsequently published by RenewableUK in October 2013 to reflect the recommended changes.

PLANNING ISSUES

Some reasons for rejection

3.23 These are some examples of refusals by planning inspectors or the Secretary of State, since the start of 2009, for onshore wind developments.

Landscape harm and adverse effect

3.24 A site in North Yorkshire had a plan for five 100-metre-high wind turbines rejected due to landscape harm and a serious adverse effect on residential amenity at a nearby farm. An inspector held that the landscape contributed to the area's distinctive character.

A proposal to site seven wind turbines in the Grampian foothills was rejected on the grounds that it would have a significant adverse effect on landscape character and harm visual amenity.

A proposal for a 127-metre wind turbine at a sewage treatment works in Staffordshire was turned down following findings that it would diminish Lichfield Cathedral's visual dominance in views from the south-west.

On the Northumbrian coast a proposal for four 125-metre-high wind turbines was dismissed because it would undermine landscape character and local residents' amenities.

A proposal for 12 145-metre-high wind turbines and a permanent meteorological mast in the Trent Valley was rejected, although the site lay within one kilometre of eight power stations and was crossed by pylon lines. The inspector held that the turbines would still have a significant effect on the surroundings.

A 75-metre-high wind turbine in Southern Scotland was rejected because of its harm to the setting of an historic hill fort 500 metres away.

The Secretary of State refused planning permission for two wind turbines at a farm in Staffordshire, stating that local concerns about the effects on the landscape and townscape quality had not been addressed.

Harm to animals

3.25 A proposal for two wind turbines with a hub height of 24 metres, close to a racecourse in Somerset, was blocked partly due to the adverse effect on the horses.

Air traffic control

3.26 A proposal for a turbine with a blade tip of 25 metres in Somerset was rejected because it would affect an air traffic control centre. Other refusals have related to air safety at an airfield.

Some reasons for acceptance

Landscape mitigation

3.27 On the Solway coast, four 121-metre wind turbines were allowed, after limited landscape and tourism harm were outweighed by the need to combat global warming and improve energy security.

In granting consent for a 126-metre-high 2MW wind turbine in Lancashire, the inspector agreed that such structures were not uncommon and could become an accepted part of the landscape.

The Secretary of State approved a wind farm in Northumberland because of the landscape's low quality.

Two 15kW wind turbines were approved at a school in Plymouth because their visual impact would be acceptable and there would be educational benefits.

In the Cotswolds Area of Outstanding Natural Beauty, a turbine was approved after an inspector found that it would be seen as part of a farm complex and would be partly hidden in the landscape.

A Leicestershire council withdrew noise and cultural heritage objections to a wind farm of 125 turbines, 80 metres high, after English Heritage withdrew an objection. The Judge recognised that the quality of view could be eroded but this was not considered so harmful as to justify refusing permission. Noise would be within nationally accepted limits, and suggested conditions were reasonable and enforceable.

Nine 125-metre wind turbines were approved in Essex after an inspector found that they would not dominate the landscape because, since they were built on low-lying arable land, they would be viewed against the broad expanse of the sky. The inspector's opinion was most local properties had various views and the wind turbines would not make them unattractive places to live.

Two turbines, up to 35 metres high, were allowed at a farm in the Lincolnshire Wolds Area of Outstanding Natural Beauty on the basis that they would not undermine its character or be seen as dominant features.

Permission was granted for 18 wind turbines in south-west Scotland after a report found that the council had not fully explained its concerns about the scheme's visual impact.

A 15-metre high turbine was allowed at a farm in West Yorkshire after an inspector held that potential harm to a protected bat species would be small and the adverse landscape impact slight.

A wind turbine in the East Riding of Yorkshire was approved by the Secretary of State. In his decision letter, Greg Clark said he felt that 'the planning concerns of the parish councils, representing the local community, have been addressed'. He also gave 'significant weight' to his finding that the proposal would help to reduce greenhouse gas emissions.

Number of applications approved or rejected

3.28 Information about decisions is held on the database 'Energy infrastructure development applications: decisions'[16].

A parliamentary question answered in the House of Lords on 22 July 2014 sets out the number of onshore wind farms that have been through the planning system and either accepted or rejected each year since January 2009. A written statement from 12 May 2014 gives this information showing the numbers on monthly basis and also providing the installed capacity.

In a recent case, the Supreme Court found that the Forest of Dean District Council[17] had given planning permission for a wind farm unlawfully, as it took into consideration a donation to a local community fund. The permission was for the change of use of farmland in Gloucestershire from agricultural use to the erection of a turbine. Resilient Energy had proposed that the turbine would be built and run by a community benefit society, which would make an annual donation to a local community fund.

Forest of Dean District Council took this donation into account when deciding to grant permission. In doing so, it had regard to government policy to encourage community-led wind turbine developments.

Mr Wright argued that the donation was not a material planning consideration and that the Forest of Dean District Council had acted unlawfully. He succeeded in the High Court and the Court of Appeal.

In the case of Wood Farm, Shipdham, Norfolk an appeal was lodged under the Town and Country Planning Act 1990 against a refusal to grant planning permission. The main issue was the proposed turbines and the noise they may impose on nearby residents and the impact of the turbines on the character and nature of the area. Considering the pros and cons of the scheme and in the light of new evidence about noise, the appeal was dismissed.

TYPES OF WIND TURBINE

3.29 Wind turbines are categorised by the method of generating electricity and the types of electricity they can generate.

One relevant factor is the ways the blades are connected to the generator.

16 www.gov.uk/government/collections/energy-infrastructure-development-applications-decisions.

17 *R (on the application of Wright) v Resilient Energy Severndale Ltd and Forest of Dean District Council* [2019] UKSC 53.

Horizontal axis

3.30 These are the most common type, where all of the components (blades, shaft and generator) are on the top of a tall tower and the blades face the wind. The shaft is horizontal to the ground and the wind hits the blades of the turbine that are connected to a shaft, causing rotation. The shaft has a gear on the end which turns a generator. This generator produces electricity which can then be used by the power grid.

Vertical axis

3.31 On a vertical axis generator, the shaft to which the blades are connected is vertical to the ground and all the components are close to the ground. These are subdivided into lift-based and drag-based.

Ducted wind turbines

3.32 This type is positioned at the edge of a roof of a building and uses the air flow along the side of a building. The air flows upwards and enters the front of the duct.

WIND TURBINES FOR DOMESTIC USE

3.33 Under permitted development rights, in some cases it is possible to install domestic wind turbines without the need for an application for planning permission, so long as specified limits and conditions, detailed in the following paragraphs, are met.

In other cases, it is necessary to apply for planning permission from the local authority to add a domestic wind turbine to a house, or grounds surrounding the home.

Building-mounted wind turbines

3.34 The installation, alteration or replacement of a building-mounted wind turbine can be considered to be permitted development, not needing an application for planning permission, provided that *all* of the limits and conditions listed below are met:

- Permitted development rights for building-mounted wind turbines apply only to installations on detached houses (not blocks of flats) and other detached buildings within the boundaries of a house or block of flats. A block of flats must consist wholly of flats (ie it should not also contain commercial premises).
- Development is permitted only if the building-mounted wind turbine installation complies with the Microgeneration Certification Scheme Planning Standards (MCS 020) or equivalent standards.

- The installation must not be sited on safeguarded land.
- Only the first installation of any wind turbine would be permitted development, and only if there is no existing air-source heat pump at the property. Additional wind turbines or air-source heat pumps at the same property require an application for planning permission.
- No part (including blades) of the building-mounted wind turbine should protrude more than three metres above the highest part of the roof (excluding the chimney) or exceed an overall height (including building, hub and blade) of 15 metres, whichever is the lesser.
- The distance between ground level and the lowest part of any wind turbine blade must not be less than five metres.
- No part of the building-mounted wind turbine (including blades) must be within five metres of any boundary.
- The swept area of any building-mounted wind turbine blade must be no more than 3.8 square metres.
- In Conservation Areas, an installation is not permitted if the building-mounted wind turbine would be on a wall or roof slope which fronts a highway.
- Permitted development rights do not apply to a turbine within the curtilage of a Listed Building or within a site designated as a Scheduled Monument or on designated land* other than Conservation Areas.

In addition, the following conditions must also be met. The wind turbine must:

- use non-reflective materials on blades;
- be removed as soon as reasonably practicable when no longer needed for microgeneration; and
- be sited, so far as practicable, to minimise its effect on the external appearance of the building and its effect on the amenity of the area.

Applicants may wish to discuss with the LPA for their area whether all of these limits and conditions will be met.

* 'Designated land' includes national parks and the Broads, Areas of Outstanding Natural Beauty, and World Heritage Sites.

Stand-alone wind turbines

3.35 The installation or alteration of a stand-alone wind turbine (ie not a building-mounted wind turbine within the boundaries of a house or block of flats) can be considered to be permitted development, not needing an application for planning permission, provided that *all* of the limits and conditions set out below are met. The block of flats must also be only flats and not contain any commercial premises.

Development is permitted only if the stand-alone wind turbine installation complies with the Microgeneration Certification Scheme Planning Standard (MCS 020)[18] or equivalent standards (see para **3.38**).

18 https://mcscertified.com.

The following limits and conditions must be complied with:

- The installation must not be sited on safeguarded land.
- Only the first installation of any wind turbine would be permitted development, and only if there is no existing air-source heat pump at the property. Additional wind turbines or air source heat pumps at the same property requires an application for planning permission.
- The highest part of the stand-alone wind turbine must not exceed 11.1 metres.
- The distance between ground level and the lowest part of any wind turbine blade must not be less than five metres.
- An installation is not permitted if any part of the stand-alone wind turbine (including blades) would be in a position which is less than a distance equivalent to the overall height of the turbine (including blades) plus 10 per cent of its height when measured from any point along the property boundary.
- The swept area of any stand-alone wind turbine blade must be no more than 3.8 square metres.
- In Conservation Areas, development would not be permitted if the stand-alone wind turbine would be installed so that it is nearer to any highway which bounds the curtilage (garden or grounds) of the house or block of flats than the part of the house or block of flats which is nearest to that highway.
- Permitted development rights do not apply to a turbine within the curtilage of a Listed Building or within a site designated as a Scheduled Monument or on designated land* other than Conservation Areas.

In addition, the following conditions must also be met. The wind turbine must:

- use non-reflective materials on blades;
- be removed as soon as reasonably practicable when no longer needed for microgeneration; and
- be sited, so far as is practicable, to minimise its effect on the external appearance of the building and its effect on the amenity of the area.

* 'Designated land' includes national parks and the Broads, Areas of Outstanding Natural Beauty, and World Heritage Sites.

ENVIRONMENTAL IMPACTS OF WIND TURBINES

Noise limits

3.36 The closest that a wind turbine would be placed to a home is 300 metres; at that distance, the turbine has a sound pressure level of 343 dB, similar to a refrigerator and, at 500 metres, this drops to 38 dB.

A recent study by the World Health Organisation (WHO) recommended reducing noise levels produced by wind turbines to below 45 dB, as wind turbine noise above this level is associated with adverse health effects.

The number of people exposed to wind turbine noise is far lower than for many other sources of noise (such as road traffic). Therefore, the WHO estimated the burden on health from exposure to wind turbine noise to be low, concluding that any benefit from specifically reducing population exposure to wind turbine noise in all situations remains unclear.

As the evidence on the adverse effects of wind turbine noise was rated 'low quality' by the WHO itself, it made a 'conditional' recommendation. The WHO recommends 'suitable measures' to reduce noise exposure to wind turbines. In most European countries, citizens can also address their concerns post-construction and request additional mitigation measures from the project developers[19].

Variability and related issues

3.37 Wind-generated power is a variable resource, and the amount of electricity produced at any given time by a given plant will depend on wind speeds, air density and turbine characteristics (among other factors). If wind speed is too low (less than about 2.5 m/s), the wind turbines will not be able to make electricity, and if it is too high (more than about 25 m/s), the turbines will have to be shut down to avoid damage. If this happens other power sources must have the capacity to meet demand.

While the output from a single turbine can vary greatly and rapidly, as local wind speeds vary, as more turbines are connected over larger and larger areas, the average power output becomes less variable.

MICROGENERATION CERTIFICATION SCHEME

3.38 To support the development of the microgeneration industry and to drive the quality and reliability of installations, a Microgeneration Certification Scheme has been developed in partnership with the industry and other organisations representing consumer interests.

The Microgeneration Certification Scheme includes clear standards to support the installation of wind turbines and air-source heat pumps. The main purpose of the scheme is to build consumer confidence in microgeneration technologies and to help move the industry to a sustainable position.

It includes certification for products and installer companies, and a code of practice based on the Office of Fair Trading Consumer Code. Permitted development rights for wind turbines and air-source heat pumps will only be granted for equipment installed by an installer who has been certificated through the scheme using a certificated product. The installer is therefore responsible for ensuring that the installation meets permitted development noise standards at the time of installation.

19 'Noise Regulations and Wind deployment in EU member states': https://publications.jrc.ec.europa.eu/repository/bitstream/JRC93792/d1_regulatory_framework_wind_energy_in_ms_march_2015%20(2).pdf.

WIND POWER IN THE UK

3.39 In March 2019, the Government announced an 'offshore wind energy revolution to provide a third of all electricity by 2030[20]' when launching a new joint Government-industry Offshore Wind Sector Deal. The main points of the deal are:

- industry to invest £250 million, including new Offshore Wind Growth Partnership to develop the UK supply chain, as global exports are set to increase fivefold to £2.6 billion by 2030;
- a third of British electricity set to be produced by offshore wind power by 2030; and
- part of the Government's ambition to make the UK a global leader in renewables, with more investment potential than any other country in the world as part of the modern Industrial Strategy.

The deal aims to see more electricity form renewables than fossil fuel, with 70% of British electricity predicted from low carbon sources by 2030 and an infrastructure investment of over £40 billion. The deal also aims to increase the sector target for the amount of UK content of home-grown projects to 60%, making sure that the £557 million pledged by the Government in July 2018 for further clean power auctions over the next 10 years directly benefits communities from Wick to the Isle of Wight; and also making sure that UK companies in areas like the North East, East Anglia, Humber and the Solent continue to be competitive and are leaders internationally in offshore wind innovations in areas such as robotics, advanced manufacturing, new materials, and floating wind and larger turbines.

Vattenfall's offshore windfarm expansion blocked

3.40 In June 2020, the Government refused to grant development consent for Vattenfall's 340MW windfarm extension off the coast of Kent, and it also delayed two other planning decisions in the South East. There were concerns that the extension would hinder shipping navigation in their approach to the Thames Estuary. Planning decisions on Vattenfall's 1.8GW Norfolk Vanguard offshore wind project and for Ørsted's 2.4GW Hornsea Three offshore wind project were also delayed.

The Norfolk Vanguard offshore wind farm is being developed by Swedish energy company, Vattenfall. The 1.8GW capacity project is to be located more than 47km from the Norfolk Coast. Vattenfall originally submitted an application for consent in June 2018, which has now seen a number of delays.

The Hornsea Three wind farm is being developed by Danish offshore wind energy giant, Ørsted, and is to be located in the North Sea off the coast of North Norfolk. The project is to have a maximum capacity of 2.4GW and, if

20 'Offshore wind energy revolution to provide a third of all UK electricity by 2030': www.gov.uk/government/news/offshore-wind-energy-revolution-to-provide-a-third-of-all-uk-electricity-by-2030.

approved, will be the world's largest offshore wind farm, featuring up to 300 wind turbines and expected to power approximately 2 million UK homes.

These delays put at risk the Government's target of reaching 40GW of offshore wind capacity by 2030.

UK renewables (October to December 2019[21])

England

3.41 In 2019, renewable energy generation was 77.0TWh which is an increase of 5.8% (4.2TWh) on 2018; of this, 3.1TWh came from offshore wind due to increased capacity.

Scotland

3.42 Generation in 2019 was 30.5TWh, an increase of 15% (4.1TWh) on 2018, with 2.0TWh of additional generation from offshore wind and a further 1.4TWh from onshore wind.

Wales

3.43 Generation in 2019 was 7.6TWh, an increase of 12% (0.8TWh) on 2018. Most of this change (74%) was due to increases from onshore wind.

Northern Ireland

3.44 Generation in 2019 was 4.2TWh, an increase of 5.6% (0.2TWh) on 2018; most of this increase was from wind, and the remainder was from bioenergy.

INTERNATIONAL COMPARISON FOR WIND GENERATION

3.45 According to a report published by Power technology, where it lists the top 10 countries by wind generation capacity, the UK was situated at number 6 in 2019.

China

3.46 China, with an installed capacity of 221GW, has over a third of the world's capacity; the largest onshore windfarm, in Gansu Province, has a capacity of 7,965MW. The farm is currently operating at 40% of its capacity,

21 UK Renewable electricity capacity and generation, October to December 2019: www.gov.uk/government/statistics/energy-trends-section-6-renewables.

with a further 13,000MW to be installed, leading to a grand total of 20,000MW (20GW) in 2020. This expansion is expected to cost $17.5bn.

US

3.47 The US has 96.4GW of installed capacity and is particularly strong in onshore wind power.

Six of the largest 10 onshore windfarms are based in the US. These include the Alta Wind Energy Centre in California (the world's second largest onshore wind farm with a capacity of 1,548MW), Shepherd's Flat Wind Farm in Oregon (845MW) and Roscoe Wind Farm in Texas (781.5MW).

The state of Texas produces a quarter of the US's wind power, with 24.9GW, providing more wind power than 25 other US states together.

Germany

3.48 Germany has the highest installed wind capacity in Europe with 59.3GW. Its largest offshore windfarms are the Gode Windfarms (Phases 1 and 2), which have a combined capacity of 582MW. Germany has the Nordsee One offshore wind farm, with a capacity of 382MW, which provides energy for 400,000 homes. According to Wind Europe, Europe installed 11.7GW of wind energy in 2018. Of this, Germany led the way with 29% of this capacity at a total of just under 3.4GW, with 2.4GW of this onshore and just under 1GW offshore.

India

3.49 India has the second highest wind capacity in Asia, with a total capacity of 35GW.

The country has the third and fourth largest onshore wind farms in the world, at the Muppandal windfarm in Tamil Nadu, Southern India (1,500MW) and the Jaisalmer Wind Park in Rajasthan, Northern India (1,064MW). The Indian government set a target of installing 60GW of wind energy by 2022, with 25GW to be installed in the next three years.

Spain

3.50 Spain has a capacity of 23GW, accounting for 18% of Spain's electricity supply, with none of its onshore or offshore wind farms being in the top 20 largest by capacity.

United Kingdom

3.51 The UK is the third European country on the list, with a total capacity of just over 20.7GW.

The UK has six of the 10 highest-capacity offshore wind projects in the world. One of these is the Walney project off the coast of Cumbria, North West England. This is the largest offshore wind project in the world, with Walney 1 & 2 (367MW) and Walney Extension (659MW) forming a grand total of 1,026MW. The Walney installation was set to be overtaken by the 1,218MW Hornsea One project in the North Sea.

France

3.52 France, with 15.3GW of installed capacity, is currently moving away from nuclear power, which previously delivered 75% of the country's energy needs, and will be increasing its renewables budget to €71bn for the period 2019–2028. This will allow it to triple its onshore wind capacity by 2030. However, there is opposition to wind energy in France, as many consider wind turbines to be ugly and noisy.

Brazil

3.53 Brazil has the largest wind capacity in South America, with 14.5GW, and it is expanding. The most recent figures show that wind power had increased by 8.9% year-on-year in February 2019. Wind power is fourth place in Brazil's total energy mix, forming about 8% of Brazil's total energy capacity of 162.5GW.

Canada

3.54 Canada's renewable energy capacity stands at 12.8GW, with 566MW of new installed capacity added in 2018. This energy is generated by a total of 299 wind farms with 6,596 turbines. Ontario has the largest amount of wind energy, with just over 5GW installed, including the 230MW Niagara Region Windfarm and the 199.5MW Amaranth Windfarm, north of Toronto. The largest wind farm in Canada is the Rivière-du-Moulin project in Quebec, which has a total capacity of 300MW. Wind accounts for about 5% of Canada's renewable energy supply, with hydroelectric at 67.5%.

Italy

3.55 In tenth place is Italy, which reached just over 10GW in wind energy capacity in 2018.

Italy's wind power was entirely generated from onshore wind, but a German wind turbine manufacturer has signed a deal to build the first offshore farm off the coast of Puglia, Southern Italy.

Chapter 4

Hydropower

INTRODUCTION

4.1 Hydroelectric energy is energy which is derived from the movement of water. The water falls and moves downwards due to gravity and this provides kinetic energy which can be used. For this to happen, a power plant needs to be installed in an area of flowing water such as at a dam which blocks or diverts water.

HYDROPOWER DEPLOYMENT

4.2 During the industrial revolution of the 1800s, hydroelectric power was important as it provided mechanical power for textile and machine industries. In 1831 the first electric generator was invented by Michael Faraday and this was the foundation for hydroelectric power in 1878. The first ever hydroelectric plant was located in Appleton Wisconsin and began to generate electricity in 1882, with a power output of 12.5kW.

Throughout the nineteenth century these plants became larger and they were built in suitable areas around the world. In 1936 the largest hydroelectric power plant was opened, the Hoover Dam, and this generated 135MW (later increased to 2,080MW) from the Colorado River. In the first half of the twentieth century, hydroelectric power became the world's most important source of electricity. China built the Three Gorges Dam in 2007 and this can generate 22,500MW which added to China's installed capacity of 196.79GW (2009).

The UK has used water generation since 1879, when a 4.5kW generator was installed to provide electricity for a single incandescent lamp. Over the past 30 years the proportion of electricity generated by hydroelectric power has remained at around 2 per cent of the total power generation.

HYDROELECTRIC SCHEMES

Storage scheme

4.3 This is where a large hydroelectric power plant uses a dam to store river water in a reservoir. The water that is released from the reservoir flows through a turbine, spinning it, which in turn activates a generator to produce electricity. The generation can be flexible, depending on demand, as the water can be released to meet needs or maintain a constant reservoir level. One of the world's best-know storage dams is the Hoover Dam. The largest storage hydropower scheme in the UK is the Dinorwig Hydro Power Station in north Wales.

Most of the hydroelectric schemes in the UK are in Scotland and Wales and are located within reservoirs and dams across the countryside.

Kielder Power Station

4.4 This is the largest hydroelectric plant in England, located in Northumberland, which can generate 6MW of electricity and has been generating since 1982. It can produce about 20,000MWh a year, which is sufficient to power 4,000 homes and offsets 8,600 tonnes of carbon dioxide per year. Kielder Water is the largest man-made lake in Northern Europe and the reservoir is used to regulate flow into the rivers Tyne, North Tyne, Derwent, Wear and Tees. It holds up to 200 million cubic metres of water and covers an area of 1,086 hectares, with a shoreline 43km long and at its deepest is 52 metres below water level. The releases of water for river regulation and hydroelectricity are controlled by the Environment Agency, with total water releases set at a maximum of 1.3 million cubic metres per day. The turbine house is situated just below the dam, with four turbines and a combined output of 12MW.

The dual turbines were refurbished in 2005–06. A 5.5MW Kaplan turbine generates electricity when water is released. An additional 500kW Francis turbine generates constant hydroelectricity from the compensating flow of water from the reservoir to the North Tyne. The scheme can be operated remotely from a control room in Dolgarrog, Wales.

Run-of-river scheme

4.5 This uses the natural flow of the river, where a weir can enhance the river flow. A portion of the river flows through a canal or penstock. It may not require the use of a dam but also has limited flexibility to follow peak variation in power demand. it is useful for base load capacity.

Beeston Hydro

4.6 This is a small hydroelectric scheme in Beeston, Nottinghamshire, and is located on the River Trent. It was built during 1999 by Hyder Industrial Limited and is the largest run-of-river scheme in the UK. It was commissioned in 2000 and later sold to United Utilities.

Hydropower scheme stopped by anglers

4.7 Fish Legal[1] won an historic injunction against a hydropower development on the River Trent at Sawley Weir and, in the process of doing so, exposed some major failings in the regulatory process. The membership association Fish Legal, acting for its member the Pride of Derby Angling Association (PDAA), secured an injunction to stop impending construction of a hydropower scheme at Sawley Weir on the River Trent. The case was heard at a four-day trial in Nottingham County Court against developers, the Small Hydro Company, and the Canal and River Trust (CRT, previously known as British Waterways).

Fish Legal's case was that the development would have destroyed the PDAA's 1,200 members' enjoyment of their prime stretch of river fishing on which they own the freehold rights. The Judge found that the developers and the CRT did not consult with the PDAA until very late in the planning process, and that they should have made much more careful enquiries about the fishing rights at the outset. The Judge recognised that they either ignored or were aware of the risks, both to the scheme and the fishing rights, but they pushed forward with their plans anyway.

Had the scheme gone ahead, the natural riverbanks would have been transformed into a 150 metre-long concrete and steel facility with floodlights and alarms sounding at intervals. Anglers were expected to access their fishing via a locked security gate into a fenced compound and to use a series of metal platforms suspended up to eight feet above the river. The developers' own health and safety witness conceded in court that this would put them 'at risk of death'. The Judge ruled that the club should not be forced against its will

1 Fish Legal is a membership organisation that is set up to use the law to protect their members' fishery interests.

to accept the proposal at the expense of its fishing rights, and that the scheme should not go ahead.

Angling rights to be sacrificed

4.8 The first hydropower scheme on Lancashire's River Lune has been given the go-ahead by the Environment Agency (EA) at Forge Weir, even though it may significantly harm the local recreational fishery by diverting the majority of the river's flows through the turbines during the fishing season. Salmon and sea trout will either no longer lie in the 'depleted' pool, or it will be almost impossible to fish as downstream will be subjected to the large artificial 'return flows' from the hydro. The scheme was approved just days before the EA published its revised 'Good Practice Guidelines', which would have prohibited the development from going ahead.

Pumped storage

4.9 Pumped storage uses two reservoirs. At times where there is low demand, electricity is used to pump the water from the lower to the upper basin. The water is then released to create power at a time when demand is high. Although this is not considered as renewable energy (because it relies on electricity), it is a good way of improving overall energy efficiency. There are currently four pumped storage projects in Scotland and Wales, the largest being at Dinorwig Power Station in Dinorwig Llanberis in Snowdonia National Park. In Scotland, the Cruachan Power Station in Argyll and Bute can generate 440MW of hydroelectric power and power up to 225,000 homes.

Cruachan Power Station

4.10 Cruachan is one of only four pumped storage power stations in the UK and works like an enormous rechargeable battery, temporarily storing energy by managing water resources between a reservoir in the Argyll hills and Loch Awe, 396 metres below. Using its reversible turbines, the station pumps water from Loch Awe to fill the upper reservoir at times when demand for electricity is low. When demand increases, the stored water can be released through the plant's turbines to generate power quickly and reliably.

It has been generating since 1965 and is often dormant, but it is used to provide back-up electricity to the National Grid when demand is high. The turbines can be operating at full capacity within 30 seconds of being activated. The plant usually runs for short periods to meet peaks in demand, but it can operate continuously at full output for around 15 hours if necessary. The idea was that of Sir Edward McColl in the 1930s. The scheme was eventually taken through Parliament in 1947 and, in 1950, the design was started in detail. Many working models of the turbines were built, and work tests were carried out on completed alternators before being delivered to the site. The construction took six years and a workforce of 1,300. A 275,000V transmission line was constructed to carry power from the top of the cable shaft just in front of the dam to Dalmally substation, five miles east of Cruachan, and then on to Windyhill, north of Glasgow. This line remains in place today, passing through rough terrain and reaching 550 metres above sea level at its highest point. The station was finally opened by Queen Elizabeth II in October 1965. It was the first reversible pumped storage hydro system on this scale built in the world.

Drax acquired Cruachan Power Station in 2019 as part of a £702m deal. Cruachan is part of a portfolio of hydro, pumped storage and gas power generation assets which were sold by the Spanish company Iberfola to Drax Group, which also owns Selby Power Station in North Yorkshire.

Ffestiniog pumped storage scheme

4.11 This was the first pumped storage scheme in Britain and has been operating since 1963. It is in continual use and has sufficient capacity to meet the power requirements of North Wales for several hours. The upper reservoir was created by enlarging an existing glacial tarn (Llyn Stwlan) and creating a new dam. The lower reservoir was formed by damming the Afon Ystradau south of the village of Tan y Grislau. Construction took place between early 1957 and March 1963 and was opened by Queen Elizabeth II. The scheme obstructed and submerged part of the Ffestiniog Railway between the 1844 Moelwyn Tunnel and Tan y Grisiau Station. The railway was awarded compensation and, in the 1970s, volunteers built a new tunnel and realigned section of narrow gauge track.

Dinorwig Hydro Power Station

4.12 This is situated in north-west Wales and is the largest hydropower plant within the UK with a capacity of 1,728MW which is sufficient to power 2.5 million home. It started generating electricity in 1984 and uses a pumped storage system that can provide back-up electricity at short notice in times of high demand.

Tidal and offshore hydropower

4.13 This involves harnessing the power of changing tides of the sea to generate energy to turn into electricity. Tidal power turbines are placed in shallow water off the coast and, as the tides flow in and out, the water flowing back and forth passes through large turbines, powering a generator. Since the tide changes multiple times a day in a reliable cycle, it is a consistent and sustainable source of energy generation.

Currently, tidal and offshore hydropower projects in the UK are few as it is a new technology. However, there are plans for many tidal power projects in the UK, which could potentially increase the UK's overall hydropower generation in the future.

The world's first 'tidal lagoon' project, the 'Swansea Bay Tidal Lagoon' project, could potentially generate enough power for 155,000 homes, and similar projects could also be established elsewhere along the UK's coastline.

Swansea Bay – Tidal Lagoon

4.14 The proposed scheme was to have a tidal lagoon in Swansea Bay that could operate 14 hours a day with a maximum output of 320MW, generating sufficient power for 155,000 homes. The project was named as part of the UK Government's 2014 National infrastructure Plan[2] and granted planning permission by the Department for Energy and Climate Change in June 2015. In June 2018 the Welsh Government offered to invest £200 million in the project's business case. In June 2018 the Department for Business, Energy and Industrial Strategy (BEIS) rejected a contract for difference electricity purchasing agreement necessary to fund the £1.3 billion proposal. The main reason given was that there was little cost reduction potential for future lagoons, and a series of lagoons would cost the average electricity consumer an additional £700 by between 2031 and 2050, compared to a mix of offshore wind and nuclear power projects.

Tidal stream generator

4.15 Some tidal stream generators can be built into the structures of existing bridges or are entirely submerged, therefore not impacting on the landscape. Land constrictions such as straits and inlets create high velocities at specific sites, which can be captured with the use of turbines. These turbines can be horizontal, vertical, open, or ducted. Stream energy can be used at a much higher rate than wind turbines, due to water being denser than air.

SeaGen – Strangford Loch

4.16 SeaGen was the world's first large-scale commercial tidal stream generator. It was four times more powerful than any other tidal stream generator in the world at the time of installation, and it was successfully decommissioned by SIMEC Atlantis Energy Limited in summer 2019, having exported 11.6GWh to the grid since 2008.

Micro hydropower

4.17 Hydroelectric power can be generated using a water mill. On a much smaller scale, hydroelectric energy can be generated by small turbines placed in rivers or by converting old water mills to be able generate electricity for individual homes, businesses or small communities. Micro hydropower projects are typically much cheaper to install and can generate a modest but reliable amount of electricity.

Homeowners who have a stream or river flowing past their property can often install micro hydropower turbines and generators to generate their own electricity.

2 National Infrastructure Plan 2014: https://assets.publishing.service.gov.uk/government/uploads/system/uploads/attachment_data/file/381884/2902895_NationalInfrastructurePlan2014_acc.pdf.

Osney Lock Hydro

4.18 Osney Loch Hydro is the first community-owned hydro scheme built on the River Thames. It was set up by a group of local residents to enable the development of a community-owned hydro scheme in the heart of Oxford. It is set on the banks of the River Thames at Osney Lock, opposite the site of Oxford's first electrical power station, and is one of only three sites suitable for hydro generation in the city. Work started in 2013 and the plant began generating electricity in 2015. It uses an Archimedean screw hydropower system, suggested by the Environment Agency for its efficiency, robust design and 'fish friendliness'[3]. The initial lease from the Environment Agency is for 40 years. The screw has a 25–40 year lifespan and is held within the concrete hydro casing which should only need to be replaced once during this time. Electricity generation depends on the flow of the river. The performance figures take into account restrictions imposed by the Environment Agency's abstraction licence.

Archimedean screw

Solar panels to boost generation

4.19 The generating capacity of the project has been maximised by the inclusion of 7.75kWp solar photovoltaic array panels on the roof of the building, generating an additional 6,665kWh of green electricity annually.

Flow management

4.20 The conditions of the Environment Agency's abstraction licence have been designed to allow careful flow management in the area. In particular, there can be no additional flow as a result of the scheme. There may also be a very localised effect that less water will flow over the main weir when operating, as it will be diverted down the Archimedean screw which will be directly adjacent to the buck gate.

Impact on fish

4.21 In order to secure planning permission and Environment Agency support for the scheme, an independent environmental study was commissioned to investigate any potential negative impact on local biodiversity, including impact on fish. The study concluded that:

> 'Currently the weir represents an impassable barrier to all fish species and therefore it is not anticipated that the proposed scheme will have any adverse impacts on the river from a fish upstream migration perspective. Installation of the fish pass associated with the proposed scheme is likely to significantly improve fish migration opportunities past the barrier.'

3 MannPower, 'UK's First supplier of Archimedean Screw Hydropower Turbines': www.mannpower-hydro.co.uk.

River Dart Country Park Hydro Scheme

4.22 The River Dart Country Park Hydro Scheme is located in a very public and attractive area within the Dartmoor National Park. Western Renewable Energy (WRE), now Renewables First, was brought in by the site owner to carry out the feasibility work and design of this hydro scheme. The issue that needed to be addressed was the fact that this was the first scheme using this technology, so the Environment Agency at that time was unfamiliar with it. The river is a sensitive salmonid river and so a fish-testing programme needed to be established.

MICRO-HYDROELECTRIC POWER AND THE HISTORIC ENVIRONMENT

4.23 English Heritage (now Historic England) commissioned a report[4] to consider whether buildings with historic significance, which have used water as a way of generating power for industry and agriculture in the past, could be used to produce electricity. Hydroelectric generation is often well-suited to sites with historic significance. These sites may contain:

- buildings such as watermills with existing mill wheels;
- buildings which were once mills but have since been converted to other uses, and so only remnants of the original use are visible;
- sites with existing infrastructure suitable for a hydroelectric scheme; or
- other sites where potential for hydroelectric generation has been identified.

Where a potential building has been identified, the new hydroelectric system attached to the building must be designed to ensure that the significance of the heritage asset is not substantially harmed. The new installation may be one of any number of different types of wheel or turbine. How the new scheme interacts with the existing environment is a key consideration. This includes, but is not limited to:

- how the wheel or turbine is attached to the ground;
- whether the building structure is strong enough to cope with the imposed forces;
- any ground works that will need to be undertaken;
- how the generator is attached to the ground or building;
- any places that a historic building is penetrated;
- where cables are laid under or above ground;
- where cables are laid within the building; and
- how any items such as electrical distribution boards are attached to the building.

4 Micro-Hydroelectric Power and the Historic Environment: https://historicengland.org.uk/images-books/publications/micro-hydroelectric-power-and-historic-environment/micro-hydroelectric-power/.

Consents and legislation

4.24 The Environment Agency will need to be consulted, as its approval is crucial for any project to go ahead. Permissions will also need to be sought if the site contains, is within or adjacent to a:

- Scheduled Monument;
- Listed Building;
- Conservation Area;
- World Heritage Site;
- Site of Special Scientific Interest (SSSI);
- Special Area of Conservation (SAC);
- Ramsar Site (wetland of international importance);
- Special Protection Area (SPA);
- National Nature Reserve;
- Area of Outstanding Natural Beauty (AONB); or
- National Park.

Listed building consent will be needed for all work that involves alteration, extension or demolition of a listed building affecting the character as a building of special architectural or historic interest. Contact the local planning authority to apply for listed building consent.

Work of any kind to a Scheduled Monument requires consent from the Secretary of State under the Ancient Monuments and Archaeological Areas Act 1979. This can be applied for through Historic England.

Linton Lock Hydro

4.25 Linton Lock was built in the eighteenth century on the north bank of the River Ouse in North Yorkshire. Its construction included a weir on the river's south bank to help control the flow of water; both the lock and weir are listed structures. It was in response to rising coal prices after the First World War that York Corporation decided to build a hydroelectric power plant, which was opened in 1923. After the implementation of the National Grid, power was increasingly sourced from larger generating stations fed mostly by coal, and Linton Lock Hydro was abandoned in 1962. In 2000, Linton Lock Hydro was designated a scheduled monument, as an early example of rural hydroelectric power generation. It was left to decay and was going to be added to the Heritage at Risk Register when developers JN Bentley asked Historic England's Yorkshire office about its possible conversion back into a working power station. Repair and conversion of the site's existing turbine house enabled it to produce electricity. The project has a commercial basis so the restored power plant would generate enough electricity to justify the investment in renovation. Reusing the original type of turbine could not produce enough power to be economical, and there is no commercially available modern replacement. The system has two Archimedes screws installed.

Gants Mill

4.26 The mill's history goes back to the Domesday survey of 1068. For a millennium the watermill has been modified, renovated and extended to suit whichever industry or process profited from the water-power. In the 1990s, it was becoming clear that the mill building was starting to deteriorate; in particular, the roof had started to sag and leak. After long discussions with builders, architects, local planners and conservation advisers, restoration work was put in hand. The repair was to retain, wherever possible, the elements of a building that had seen many changes over its history. In 2003 a new turbine and electricity generator were installed to complement the 1888 Armfield turbine. An initiative by South Somerset District Council led to the formation of the South Somerset Hydropower Group, a group of 10 mill owners working together to install electrical generating equipment in their mills. The new turbine was made by Valley Hydro of Cornwall, and the electronic mains connection unit by GP Electronics from Devon. Installation of the new turbine started in September 2003, and the staff of Hydro Generation tackled with enthusiasm the variety of engineering problems encountered.

The equipment is designed to produce up to 12kW of electricity in continuous operation, fed into the local grid. The automatic operation also adjusts water flow through the turbine to maximise power output while maintaining a reserve flow of water in the main river. The actual output of electricity depends very much on river flow, being naturally greater during winter than in the summer months.

ADVANTAGES AND DISADVANTAGES OF HYDROPOWER SCHEMES

Advantages

Efficient, reliable and sustainable

4.27 Hydropower generation relies only on a constant flow of running water and so could generate energy 24 hours a day when installed in rivers or waterways. It has a conversion rates of 90% of the kinetic energy of the water into electrical power, which makes it the most efficient source of renewable energy (a solar panel converts about 16.5% of solar energy into usable electrical power).

Cheap to generate

4.28 Whilst installing the infrastructure is costly, when it's generating it is a low-cost source of energy since water is a free and natural resource.

Long-lasting infrastructure

4.29 The infrastructure (hydroelectric dams, man-made reservoirs and hydropower stations) can last between 50 to 100 years, with only maintenance needed to keep them functional. In the UK, examples of this are Bonnington Power Station (1927) and Lochaber Hydroelectric Scheme (1929), both still in operation in Scotland.

Energy storage

4.30 Hydropower is the only renewable energy source that can be stored in large quantities, through pumped storage systems which store large bodies of water in reservoirs, with the water being converted into electricity when needed.

Quick generation during high demand

4.31 Hydropower plants located within reservoirs and dams can be switched on and off, to increase or decrease electricity generation as and when needed. As previously mentioned, the Cruachan Power Station can be up to speed and generating within 30 seconds. When there are major power shortages due to huge demand, hydropower can rapidly generate new electricity reserves and balance the grid.

Disadvantages

Not as 'clean' as expected

4.32 Although hydropower is often thought of as a clean source of energy, it can produce harmful greenhouse gases when generated from hydropower plants with dams and reservoirs. Decaying vegetation and other organic matter or run-off from surrounding farmland or logging sites, for example, can enter the dams and reservoirs. Over time, as the water levels rise and fall, gases from these pollutants are released into the atmosphere, containing methane and carbon dioxide which contribute to global warming.

Negative impacts on local communities and wildlife

4.33 Hydropower generation often involves making major changes to the environment that it is located in and can cause issues such as displacing the communities that rely on the river for fishing. Damming a river can also affect wildlife that previously relied on the river and its surrounding habitat for food or protection. Environmental disruption is usually the main reason for opposition to new hydropower projects around the world.

Construction costs

4.34 Construction of large-scale hydropower projects is expensive. The Swansea Bay Tidal Project currently being planned is estimated to cost £1.3 billion to construct. These costs often cause projects to be cancelled as the developers fail to find sufficient funding or government subsidies to make it financially viable. However, once the infrastructure has been built, the ongoing maintenance and running of hydropower projects is fairly minimal and only requires a handful of employees to keep it running.

Limited hydropower capacity in UK

4.35 Unfortunately, large-scale hydropower generation is restricted in Britain due to the lack of available and suitable sites that are not already using hydropower. To generate large-scale hydroelectric power requires large sources of water, limiting the suitable locations for constructing hydro projects. Inland hydropower capacity is fairly limited, restricting new hydropower to small-scale, micro-projects or to offshore and tidal projects.

PLANNING PERMISSION FOR A SMALL HYDRO SCHEME

England

Scheme design

4.36 Specialist advice on how to design a scheme can be obtained from the British Hydropower Association or the Micro Hydro Association. Technical information can also be obtained from the Environment Agency about how to design and operate a scheme and protect the environment. Proposals that are in sites of high environmental sensitivity are less likely to be accepted – for instance, those in areas where there are protected sites and species[5].

Permission from the Environment Agency to build will only be given if it can be shown how the scheme's design will prevent harm to the environment and other water users by ensuring that:

- it will not prevent the achievement of Water Framework Directive[6] objectives, eg it will not damage the ecological status of water or prevent the improvement of its status. Consideration may also need to be given to objectives for the local area[7];
- it will not affect protected and designated sites or species in unacceptable ways, eg it will not damage habitats that are important for protected species of fish;
- it will maintain or improve fish passage;
- it will not affect people's access to the water, eg anglers; and
- it will not have negative impacts on local communities, eg it must not increase the risk of flooding.

Rights of access

4.37 The Environment Agency will need to grant an abstraction licence, and there is then a need to show that there is right of access to the river at the point where it is planned to build the scheme.

5 Protected sites and Species: www.gov.uk/topic/planning-development/protected-sites-species.

6 Water Framework Objectives: https://ec.europa.eu/environment/water/water-framework/info/intro_en.htm.

7 River basin management plans 2015: www.gov.uk/government/collections/river-basin-management-plans-2015.

Weirs on upland watercourses

4.38 To build or reconstruct a weir on an upland watercourse, the proposal is likely to be rejected by the Environment Agency if it's higher than 1.5 metres.

For weirs up to about 1.5 metres, it is necessary to show that the scheme will not harm the watercourse and its ecology. This can be shown in the application by providing a report containing hydrological assessments that explain:

- any changes that the scheme will make to the watercourse; and
- how these changes will avoid causing harm to the environment.

Existing weirs on a lowland river

4.39 Check with the Environment Agency that there are not any existing plans to remove the weir.

Permission will not be given by the Environment Agency to use an existing weir on a lowland river if the scheme will increase the risk of flooding or disrupt:

- water level controls; or
- use of the river, eg it must not affect the movement of boats.

It is unlikely that permission will be given to raise the height of an existing weir unless it can be shown that a small increase in the height of the weir is needed because:

- the height is being raised to compensate for turbine drawdown; or
- the proposed work will improve fish passage.

Building or reconstructing weirs on a lowland river

4.40 The Environment Agency is unlikely to give permission for a proposal to build or reconstruct a weir in a lowland river. Permission might be given if it can be shown that there will not be significant impacts on the environment. The detailed design will need to include environmental and technical assessments showing that there will be no significant impacts on:

- fish migration;
- fisheries and conservation;
- targets and objectives for the river under the Water Framework Directive;
- sediment movement;
- flood risk;
- land drainage;
- navigation rights;
- designated habitats and species;
- other people's rights to, and uses of, water; and
- water ecology (for example, from the creation of a pond or a lake behind the weir).

These assessments will require specialist technical reports that will normally need to be prepared by experts in these areas.

Using existing weirs that are used to measure river flow

4.41 Some weirs and river structures are used by the Environment Agency to measure river flows. If the proposed scheme will change the flow of water across one of these structures, it must avoid affecting the accuracy of the data that the Environment Agency collects.

Information about whether the weir is used for measuring flows will be provided by the Environment Agency.

Advice before applying

4.42 Unless the hydropower scheme satisfies the Environment Agency that the scheme will not harm the environment, it is unlikely that a licence will be granted.

The Environment Agency will appoint a permitting officer, who may ask to visit the site. They will provide information about:

- what needs to be done to apply;
- what permissions are needed;
- what environmental assessments need to be carried out; and
- whether Natural England needs to be contacted about protected sites and species.

Consult local communities

4.43 Local people that might be affected by a scheme should be consulted before making the application. This can help gain the support of local communities for the scheme.

Consultation has no specific requirements, but consideration should be given to:

- people who use the river and the groups that represent them;
- environmental groups such as rivers trusts, wildlife trusts, the Royal Society for the Protection of Birds and people who manage any Areas of Outstanding Natural Beauty;
- the district network operator – that is, the company that distributes electricity in the area of your scheme; and
- neighbouring local planning authorities, if your proposal is on a river which is a local planning authority boundary.

Application for licences, consents and approvals

4.44 The Environment Agency will indicate which licences, consents or approvals are needed for the proposed scheme. The Environment Agency will need to be sent different documents and assessments, depending on the licences, consents or approvals that are needed. Applications for consents, licences or approvals should be made at the same time as applying for planning permission.

Application for an abstraction or impoundment licence

4.45 Most hydropower schemes will need an abstraction licence or an impoundment licence, and these are known as 'water resources licences'.

The following documents need to be sent to the Environment Agency:

- completed hydroelectric power schemes application form (WR317);
- completed water resources licence application forms – for abstraction licences, the WR330 form and the WR332 form, for impoundment licences, the WR334 form (the WR330 form guidance, the WR332 form guidance and the WR334 form guidance should be read before filling out these forms);
- hydrological assessment;
- environmental report with assessments of the impacts of the scheme on ecology, fish passage and Water Framework Directive objectives, including geomorphology and a weir pool assessment (only if the Environment Agency requests one);
- fish screen design proposal or an explanation of why there is not a proposal to include a fish screen in the scheme; and
- site plan.

The Environment Agency may ask for additional information.

Apply for fish pass approval

4.46 The Environment Agency needs to approve the design and size of any fish passes proposed, including eel passes.

The following documents need to be sent to the Environment Agency:

- completed hydroelectric power schemes application form (WR317);
- completed fish pass approval application form (FP002);
- fish pass design proposals;
- fish pass assessment;
- site plan; and
- hydrological assessment.

Apply for an environmental permit for a flood risk activity

4.47 An application for an environmental permit for a flood risk activity[8] must be made if the scheme plans to construct either:

- in, over or under the channel of a main river; or
- close to the bank of a main river.

A permit will be needed for both permanent and temporary work. Some activities are exempt from needing an environmental permit. This means that, although a permit is not needed for these activities, the exemption[9] must be registered with the Environment Agency.

8 Flood Risk Activities: www.gov.uk/guidance/flood-risk-activities-environmental-permits.

9 Exempt Activities: www.gov.uk/government/publications/environmental-permitting-regulations-exempt-flood-risk-activities.

The application is for a bespoke permit if the activities do not fit the conditions of the exemptions and before applying for a bespoke environmental permit:

- develop a management system;
- check whether a risk assessment needs to be completed;
- follow relevant technical guidance and any advice given by the Environment Agency in any pre-application discussions; and
- prepare plans and documents clearly describing the proposed activities, and any supporting information such as site surveys and method of work.

If the scheme is not on a main river but is on a river or stream designated as an ordinary watercourse, application must be made to the lead local flood authority for consent. This can be either the county council, unitary authority or internal drainage board.

Permit application

4.48 For a bespoke permit for a flood risk activity, the following need to be completed:

- hydroelectric power schemes application form (WR317);
- Part B10: bespoke permit for flood risk activities; and
- Part F3: charging and declarations.

An environmental permit is required for each individual flood risk activity.

Fees

4.49 These are payable to the Environment Agency:

- £1,500 if the scheme needs an abstraction licence or an impoundment licence; if both licences are required, the fee is only paid once; and
- a fee for each application for a permit for a flood risk activity in accordance with the Environment Agency charges for environmental permits.

These fees are payable whether or not consent is granted.

Some applications require the Environment Agency to advertise in local media such as newspapers. In this case, the Environment Agency requires:

- £500 for an environmental permit application;
- a £100 application fee and the cost of the advertisements for an abstraction or impoundment; and
- licence application.

Scotland

4.50 Whereas the opportunities for large-scale impoundment are likely to be limited, there is a potential for smaller impoundment and run-of-river projects in Scotland. There is a policy statement issued by the Scottish Ministers on balancing the benefits of renewable electricity generation from hydropower schemes and the protection of the water environment[10]. The

10 Renewable and Low Carbon Energy: www.gov.scot/policies/renewable-and-low-carbon-energy/.

emphasis will be on supporting hydropower developments which can make a significant contribution to Scotland's renewables targets whilst minimising any adverse impacts on the water environment. Following on from the Ministerial Statement, the Scottish Environment Protection Agency (SEPA), developed guidance on run-of-river hydro schemes.

In 2011 the Electricity Act 1989 (Requirement of Consent for Hydro-electric Generating Stations) (Scotland) Revocation Order 2011 came into force, which means that the threshold above which applications for hydroelectric generating stations are made to Scottish Ministers under the Electricity Act 1989 is increased to 50MW. Applications below that will be determined by planning authorities.

Planning authorities' focus

4.51 Planning authorities will:

- provide guidance on where there are greatest opportunities for hydro developments within the planning authority area and the type of hydro schemes that are likely to be the most appropriate;
- detail criteria to be applied in assessing hydro applications;
- establish a clear protocol for involving key consultees at spatial planning, policy making, pre-application and application stages;
- identify proportionate levels of information to service pre-application discussions and for assessing applications; and
- secure support from local communities, hydro operators and other stakeholders on policies and procedures.

Stage in planning process: spatial planning

4.52 Consideration will be given to:

- the adequacy of any existing spatial plans for hydro in the planning authority area;
- cumulative effects and optimisation of the resource, taking account of consented and operational hydro schemes, and consulting other stakeholders if necessary;
- working closely with consultees to ensure that spatial plans identify known sensitivities and potential constraints and identify areas of greatest opportunity,
- consulting with SEPA to ensure that spatial plans have regard to river basin management plans (spatial plans should not put in place a sequential approach to determining applications with areas of greatest opportunity);
- any spatial guidance prepared for hydro that helps to identify opportunities for new and restored hydro, including opportunities for particular scales or types of hydro; and
- ensuring that spatial guidance recognises the potential for cumulative impacts.

Stage in planning process: drafting development plan policy

4.53 Consideration will be given to:

- ensuring that hydro policies cover:
  - the range of potential scales and types of hydro;
  - construction, design, supporting infrastructure and management of schemes;
  - the restoration of former hydro schemes or the alteration of existing schemes (including dam raising);
  - landscape, nature conservation, cultural, fisheries, water quality, amenity and recreational interests; and
  - cumulative impacts and decommissioning;
- ensuring that only matters of detail and guidance are reserved for supplementary planning guidance (SPG);
- for Strategic Development Planning Authorities, providing strategic guidance to manage cross-boundary and cumulative impacts of hydro; and
- consulting key consultees for hydro at an early stage on the drafting of hydro energy policies.

Stage in planning process: development plan action programmes

4.54 Consideration will be given to selecting an action officer to take forward development plan objectives for hydro. Typically, this might involve sharing knowledge through a local hydro working group involving key consultees and landowners, producing a project plan to decide on focus and priorities, preparing local design guidance, development briefs and considering local solutions to local problems.

Stage in planning process: securing sufficient information to determine planning applications

4.55 Consideration will be given to:

- recognising that design statements are required for electricity generating stations producing 20MW or greater (including hydro), with design statements a voluntary measure for hydro schemes below that threshold; and
- developing Environmental Impact Assessment (EIA) scoping templates in conjunction with SEPA, SNH and Historic Scotland as necessary.

Stage in planning process: pre-application stage

4.56 Consideration will be given to:

- prioritising early engagement with SEPA at pre-application stage, as applicants will also be required to obtain a water use licence from SEPA under the Water Environment (Controlled Activity) Regulations 2011[11];

11 The Water (Controlled Activities) (Scotland) Regulations 2011: www.legislation.gov.uk/ssi/2011/209/regulation/8/made.

- ensuring that key consultees are given adequate opportunity to be involved in pre-application meetings/site visits;
- gauging where the most significant issues are likely to lie with the particular application – if these relate to impacts on the water environment, advise the applicant that securing a controlled activity regulations (CAR) licence first may be financially more prudent (SEPA's early stage checklist will assist with this);
- determining information needs for applications at an early stage, particularly if seasonal ecological surveys are required or if the development might affect designated areas, and providing early advice on whether schemes require an EIA; and
- identifying that works may need to be scheduled to avoid the breeding seasons of sensitive species

Stage in planning process: determining planning applications

4.57 Consideration will be given to:

- ensuring that key consultees are given early opportunity for meetings and site visits on the application, to help ensure that constraints are timeously overcome where possible;
- ensuring that planning authorities obtain and have particular regard to SEPA advice and expertise on matters relating to the protection of the water environment;
- ensuring that planning authorities, in balancing the environmental, social, cultural and economic considerations in determining applications, note that SEPA also has a statutory duty to consider social and economic matters under the 2011 Regulations, including to ensure compliance with the Water Framework Directive. Early joint discussion with applicants is advised on these matters;
- technical information and guidance on typical planning considerations associated with hydro, provided below, which planning authorities should draw upon in determining applications.

Technical information for hydro schemes

4.58 There are a wide range of hydro operations, of different scales and types. This diversity allows different volumes of water and flow rates to be captured, schemes to be positioned within different positions within the landscape, and for water courses flowing over different gradients to be used.

Typical considerations in determining planning applications for hydro

Environmental Impact Assessment (EIA) procedures

4.59 Some hydropower schemes will require an EIA. Planning authorities are recommended to work with other relevant organisations.

Siting in the landscape and design considerations

4.60 Whilst hydropower schemes are tied to the location of the water resource, there may be scope to adjust the siting to achieve good integration with the landscape. Elements of the works could be concealed using existing woodland or new planting or by carrying out land re-profiling works.

Habitats and species

4.61 The EIA would be expected to establish whether or not there are any significant impacts on the biodiversity of an area, including aquatic and terrestrial ecosystems, habitats and species, eg breeding birds or freshwater fish.

Social and economic considerations

4.62 Planning authorities are required to take into account social and economic considerations (alongside environmental and cultural considerations) in assessing planning applications. SEPA also has specific duties to consider the environmental, social and economic effects of proposed controlled activities when determining water use licence applications, to ensure that the requirements of the Water Framework Directive are satisfied. Planning authorities and SEPA have duties to co-operate and adopt an integrated approach, as far as practicable, in exercising their respective functions.

Where a proposed scheme is likely to have an adverse effect on the water environment, planning authorities are advised to have regard to the advice of SEPA on matters relating to the protection of the water environment. SEPA may be able to provide this advice in advance of an application for a water use licence being made. This depends on the scheme location and design. SEPA's guidance to developers of run-of-river hydropower schemes identifies the relevant circumstances.

Wales

4.63 For developing hydropower in Wales, there is information available on the Welsh Government website:

- 'Community energy: hydropower project guidance';
- 'Permitted development rights and small-scale, low risk hydropower'; and
- 'Non-domestic (business) rates support for hydropower projects 2020 to 2021'.

Northern Ireland

4.64 Further information specifically about Northern Ireland is available on the Planning Portal.

4.64 *Hydropower*

This covers many of the issues dealt with in other parts of the UK but with the emphasis on specific issues in Northern Ireland. It is found in 'Draft PPS18: Renewable Energy Annex I Small Hydro: Planning Issues'[12].

It covers:

- siting and landscape;
- design considerations;
- hydrological considerations;
- ecological considerations;
- fisheries interests;
- noise;
- construction disturbance;
- operations disturbance; and
- recreation and public access.

12 Draft PPS18: Renewable Energy Annex I Small Hydro: Planning Issues: www.planningni.gov.uk/de/index/policy/planning_statements_and_supplementary_planning_guidance/pps18/pps18_annex1/pps18_annex1_hydro/pps18_annex1_hydroissues.htm.

Chapter 5

Solar Power

INTRODUCTION

5.1 Solar power is the conversion of energy from sunlight into electricity, either directly using photovoltaics (PV), indirectly using concentrated solar power, or a combination of the two. Concentrated solar power systems use lenses or mirrors and solar tracking system to focus a large area of sunlight into a small beam.

Until the 2010s, solar power contributed little to the UK's energy production but, following the Feed-in tariff (FIT) subsidies and the falling cost of the solar panels, in 2019 the installed capacity was over 13GW. As of 2019, Shotwick Solar Park with a capacity of over 72.2MW is the largest in the UK.

The share of generation from renewables in the UK rose to a new high of 33.0% in 2018[1], driven by an increase in generation from wind and solar compared to 2017, up 11 and 2.6% respectively. Weather conditions for solar generators were particularly favourable, with 2018 reporting the greatest average sun hours since 2003.

1 Electricity generation and supply figures for Scotland, Wales, Northern Ireland and England, 2015–2018: https://assets.publishing.service.gov.uk/government/uploads/system/uploads/attachment_data/file/853557/Regional_Electricity_Generation_and_Supply_2015_to_2018.pdf.

Solar PV deployment

5.2 According to statistics produced by the Department of Business, Energy and Industry Strategy[2] from February 2020:

- At the end of January 2020, there were 13,409MW installed in UK solar capacity across 1,025,044 installations. This is an increase of 2.0% since January 2019.
- There has been a fall in new installations of 38%, which is due to the closure of the FIT scheme at the end of March 2019.
- 44.9% (6,020MW) of the total installed PV capacity comes from 646 large-scale installations (greater than 5MW).
- At the end of December 2019, 58% of capacity (7,695MW) came from ground-mounted or stand-alone solar installations.

Types of PV panel

5.3 There are currently three types of PV panel available:

- monocrystalline (black cells) – they appear black because the low light interacts with the pure silicon;
- polycrystalline – bluish hue due to the light reflecting off the silicon; and
- thin-film – cadmium telluride, indium gallium and gallium arsenide.

Monocrystalline and polycrystalline panels

5.4 These have cells made of silicon wafers. To build a panel, wafers are assembled in rows and columns to form a rectangle, covered in a glass sheet and framed together. Both of these types have cells made from silicon – the monocrystalline and polycrystalline vary in the composition of the silicon itself:

- monocrystalline – these solar cells are cut from a single, pure crystal of silicon; and
- polycrystalline – these solar cells are composed of fragments of silicon crystals that are melted together in a mould before being cut into wafers.

Thin-film panels

5.5 Thin-film solar panels are made from a variety of materials. The most common is a thin film made from cadmium telluride (CdTe). To make this type of panel, a layer of CdTe is placed between transparent conducting layers that help capture sunlight. This type of thin-film technology also has a glass layer on the top for protection.

Thin-film panels can also be made from amorphous silicon (a-Si), which is similar to the composition of the monocrystalline and polycrystalline panels.

2 www.gov.uk/government/statistics/solar-photovoltaics-deployment.

Though they are silicon in composition, they are not made up of solid silicon wafers, but non-crystalline silicon placed on top of glass, plastic or metal.

Copper Indium Gallium Selenide (CIGS) panels are another thin-film type. This type of panel has four elements placed between two conductive layers (ie glass, plastic, aluminium or steel) and electrodes placed on the front and the back of the material to capture electrical currents.

SOLAR PANELS – NON-DOMESTIC USE

5.6 Information about planning permission for non-domestic solar panels can be found on the Planning Portal website[3]. Guidance for non-domestic solar panels in Wales can be found on the Welsh Government website[4], and for Scotland on the Scottish Government website[5].

The installation of solar panels on non-domestic buildings and land may be 'permitted development' with no need to apply to the local planning authority for planning permission. There are important limits and conditions which will need to be followed.

Siting of solar panels on non-domestic dwellings

5.7 The equipment must be sited to minimise the effect on the external appearance of the building and the amenity of the area.

When the equipment is no longer needed, it should be removed as soon as is reasonably practicable.

The following conditions need to be met:

- solar panels that are installed on a wall or pitched roof should not project more than 200mm from the wall surface or roof slope;
- where panels are installed on a flat roof, the highest part of the equipment should not be more than one metre above the highest part of the roof (excluding the chimney);
- equipment mounted on a roof must not be within one metre of the external edge of that roof;
- equipment mounted on a wall must not be within one metre of a junction of that wall with another wall or with the roof of the building;
- panels must not be installed on a listed building or on a building that is within the grounds of a listed building, or on a site designated as a scheduled monument;
- if the equipment is on the roof of the building, the capacity for generation of electricity across the whole of the site cannot exceed 1MW;
- other than microgeneration solar thermal equipment or microgeneration solar PV equipment, if there is to be any other solar PV equipment installed

3 www.planningportal.co.uk/info/200130/common_projects/52/solar_panels_non_domestic.
4 https://gov.wales/planning-permission-solar-panels-non-domestic.
5 www.gov.scot/publications/permitted-development-rights-non-domestic-solar-panels-domestic-air-source/pages/4/.

on the roof of a building, the prior approval (56 days) of the Local Planning Authority is required. This will assess the design and external appearance of the development, particularly in respect of the impact of glare on occupiers of neighbouring land;
- if the building is on Article 2(3) designated land[6], the equipment must not be installed on a wall or a roof slope which fronts a highway.

'Article 2(3) designated land' comprises:

- an area designated as a conservation area under section 69 of the Planning (Listed Buildings and Conservation Areas) Act 1990[7] (designation of conservation areas);
- an area of outstanding natural beauty (AONB);
- an area specified by the Secretary of State for the purposes of section 41(3) of the Wildlife and Countryside Act 1981[8] (enhancement and protection of the natural beauty and amenity of the countryside);
- the Broads;
- a National Park; and
- a World Heritage Site.

Note: A leaseholder may need to get permission from their landlord, freeholder or management company.

Stand-alone solar panel installations in the grounds of a non-domestic building

5.8 Equipment should be sited, as far as is reasonably practicable, so that it minimises the effect on the amenity of the area. When the equipment is no longer needed, it should be removed as soon as is reasonably practicable.

The following conditions must be met:

- no part of the installation should be higher than 4 metres;
- the installation should be at least 5 metres from the boundary of the property;
- the size of the array should be no more than 9 square metres, or 3 metres wide by 3 metres deep;
- panels should not be installed within the boundary of a listed building or a scheduled monument; and
- if the property is in an Article 2(3) designated area (see previous paragraph), no part of the solar installation should be nearer to any highway bounding the grounds of the property than the part of the building that is nearest to that highway.

Note: A leaseholder may need to get permission from their landlord, freeholder or management company.

6 Town and Country Planning (General Permitted Development) (England) Order 2015.
7 www.legislation.gov.uk/ukpga/1990/9/contents.
8 www.legislation.gov.uk/ukpga/1981/69/contents.

Building Regulations

5.9 The installation of solar panels on a roof will normally be subject to Building Regulations.

The ability of the existing roof to carry the load (weight) of the panel will need to be checked and proven. Some strengthening work may be needed.

5.10 Building Regulations also apply to other aspects of the work such as electrical installation, fire protection and weather proofing. It is advisable to contact an installer who can provide the necessary advice, preferably one who belongs to the Competent Person Scheme[9].

There is general guidance on the performance expected of materials and building work in order to comply with the Building Regulations, and practical examples and solutions on how to achieve compliance for some of the more common building situations (see para **5.61**).

SOLAR FARMS

5.11 Harvesting solar energy on a commercial basis is through solar farming. These are large-scale applications of PV systems that provide a source of safe, locally produced renewable energy. The building of solar farms has both positive and negative aspects.

In order to get approval for solar farms in the UK, a series of rigorous planning procedures must be passed, taking into account the suitability of the site, any potential impact on the locality (such as whether the presence of solar farms will harm or endanger the environment, taking into consideration ecological as well as socio-economic factors) and the relevant renewable energy targets.

Advantages and disadvantages of solar farms

5.12 There are many advantages and disadvantages of solar energy; however, investing on a large scale can have different implications.

Advantages

5.13

- solar farms generate electricity locally and feed into the local electricity grid using energy from the sun to generate electricity;
- no moving parts, so assembly and maintenance is minimal;
- represent time-limited, reversible land use and provide an increased, diversified and stable source of income for landowners;

9 www.gov.uk/building-regulations-competent-person-schemes.

- no by-product or waste generated, except during manufacturing or dismantling;
- have lower visual and environmental impacts than other forms of power generation; and
- customer given the choice of buying green electricity and reduce reliance on fossil fuels.

Disadvantages

5.14

- to produce enough energy for most power grids, solar farms need to use thousands of panels which can take up a lot of land area and can potentially destroy wildlife and agricultural lands;
- sunlight limited due to excess shade or heavy cloud cover affects the amount of energy produced. The UK climate is changeable and so that can be a big factor in profitable use;
- public perception towards solar energy fields in some cases is that they are unattractive and can take away from the natural look of the land; and
- start-up solar farm costs are relatively high and often require an incentive programs to offset these costs such as government subsidies, which the UK governments granted for example to farmers willing to transform their lands into solar farms.

Solar farms in the UK

5.15 The presence of solar farms in the UK has been met with mixed feelings. One of the reasons is that the farms are taking the space of agricultural land, with farmers investing in solar farms which are located on the land used previously for agriculture. Food and farming are the number one manufacturing industry in the UK, and some feel it is a problem if productive agricultural land is converted into land for solar farm establishments. The UK Government officials are cutting subsidies to farmers for solar farms in an effort to stop the rapid expansion of these on farmlands.

Others argue that typically less than 5% of the land on which a solar farm is sited is taken up by fixings, leaving 95% available for other uses, and they disagree that solar farms are displacing food production; good practice in the industry now routinely combines solar with existing farming activities.

Cleve Hill Solar Park

5.16 Planning consent was granted at the end of May 2020 for the development of the UK's largest solar farm, Cleve Hill Solar Park, located outside Faversham close to the village of Graveney in Kent. Consent was granted by the Department for Business, Energy and Industrial Strategy (BEIS), which also confirmed that the 50MW electrical storage and connection infrastructure located on the site was approved. There were concerns raised by some groups that the 900-acre development could harm the natural environment in the area, partly because of the energy storage system. It is expected that the subsidy-free project will be underway in 2021 and electricity generation by 2023. The 350MW farm would feature almost 900,000 solar panels across 900 acres of farmland. The developers expect that the farm would generate enough renewable electricity to power 91,000 homes, reduce UK carbon emissions by 68,000 tonnes annually, and generate £1m annually for the Kent and Swale councils.

Cleve Hill Solar Park Ltd, a joint venture between Hive Energy Ltd and Wirsol Energy Ltd, made the application for a development consent order ('DCO')[10] under the Planning Act 2008 for a solar and energy storage generating station project, connecting to the National Electricity Transmission System ('NETS') at Cleve Hill Substation in Kent.

Planning permission refusals and appeals

Sandridge Solar Power

5.17 A proposed 44MW solar farm in Wiltshire was refused planning permission, even though it had been recommended for approval by planning officers. The proposal had received no objections from statutory consultees over the 80.5-hectare site, and three of the four local parish councils expressed their support. The strategic planning committee refused planning permission and said that the development would have an inverse visual impact on the site due to its large size. The proposal was for 170,000 solar panels spread over 199 acres and the accompanying control buildings. However, Sandridge Solar appealed the decision and this planning application was granted by a Government planning inspector in 2015.

Dunsmore Farm

5.18 An application to change the use of agricultural land to a solar farm and associated infrastructure, to generate up to 4.45MW with continued agricultural use, was turned down and this decision was subject to an appeal. However, the appeal was dismissed, based on the likely impact on the landscape, even though there was a revision to the plan which reduced the size of the solar farm.

Three Houses Lane

5.19 Local objectors succeeded in stopping this solar farm development. Planning permission was refused for the installation and operation of a solar farm on land south of Three Houses Lane, Codicote, Hertfordshire. The

10 Cleve Hill Solar Park – Statement of need: https://infrastructure.planninginspectorate.gov.uk/wp-content/ipc/uploads/projects/EN010085/EN010085-000432-7.3%20Statement%20of%20Need.pdf.

application was within the green belt and, at the inquiry, the council supported the application.

There were two fundamental objections to the application. The 8.4 hectare site was wholly within the Green Belt, and 3.8 hectares of it was grade 3a Best and Most Versatile (BMV) agricultural land. Therefore, the proposal was contrary to both national and local policy towards the Green Belt and loss of BMV land. Furthermore, the Rule 6 parties argued that it was for the Applicant and Council to demonstrate the existence of very special circumstances sufficient to outweigh the clear harm to the Green Belt by virtue of inappropriateness and any other identified harm.

HISTORIC BUILDINGS

5.20 Historic England has published a guide to energy efficiency in historic properties, in particular looking at the use of solar electric[11]. The document looks at how to view the options for solar energy and weigh this against a number of factors to avoid damaging both the significance of the building and its fabric. Consideration should be given to:

- the potential visual or physical impact on the building's historic fabric;
- carrying out an assessment of all renewables to ensure that photovoltaics are the right solution for an application;
- what energy is required (heating or electricity?);
- the amount of energy that could be generated and what the payback period would be;
- any technical risks associated with the measure; and
- whether consent is needed: consent will most likely be needed if the installation is located on or near a listed building or within a conservation area.

Consents

Planning permission

5.21 Planning permission is required for works which are 'development' and, broadly, it is given either after a formal application is made, or if it is considered to be 'permitted development' and can be carried out subject to compliance with any conditions or limitations set out. Solar PV and other forms of renewable energy can fall within the scope of permitted development. If the proposals do not fall within the permitted development or there are implications for the historic environment (listed buildings, conservation areas, scheduled monuments etc), or the ability to rely on permitted development has been removed, an application for planning permission will be required.

11 Energy Efficiency and Historic Buildings (Historic England): https://historicengland.org.uk/images-books/publications/eehb-solar-electric/heag173-eehb-solar-electric-photovoltaics/.

Listed building consent

5.22 This is required for the change to a listed building in any way which would affect its character as a building of special architectural or historic interest. The requirement applies to all types of works, and to all parts of buildings covered by the listing protection (possibly including attached and curtilage buildings or other structures). An application for listed building consent is made to, and determined by, the local planning authority. This is separate from any need for planning permission. The local planning authority must consult Historic England and the National Amenity Societies on certain listed building consent applications. If listed building consent is granted, conditions may be attached to the consent, such as how much the solar panels project above the roof, or how quickly they need to be removed at the end of their useful life.

Places of worship

5.23 Installation of a PV system on a listed place of worship needs permission from the denominational body and/or local authority. An Ecclesiastical Exemption will be needed from the Church of England Advisory Committee. The Ecclesiastical Exemption does not remove the need for planning permission. If a denomination is not exempt, it will need listed building consent and planning permission as set out above.

Scheduled monument consent

5.24 If the site where the solar panels are to be installed is a scheduled monument, any work will require scheduled monument consent from the Secretary of State, not the local planning authority. Historic England manages the process of scheduled monument consent on behalf of the Secretary of State. The protected site of a monument may also include any adjoining land essential for its support and preservation.

Building Regulations and other consents

5.25 When installing a PV system, consideration is also needed as to whether it will harm a nearby protected habitat or designated landscape area. The planning authority may not grant planning permission if the work will damage a protected site or area. Natural England provides advice about these protected sites.

NATIONAL TRUST AND SOLAR POWER

5.26 The National Trust aims to produce 50% of its energy requirements from renewable sources by 2021, using solar power to help achieve this. It currently has 58 places that use solar power which generates 256,384kWhs of energy and, under the Renewable Energy Investment programme, there are 10 green energy projects running, and others in the pipeline, which is expected to create an extra 11.5 million kWhs of energy.

CONCENTRATED SOLAR POWER

5.27 Concentrated solar power (CSP) technologies use mirror configurations to concentrate the sunlight energy into a receiver and convert it to heat. The heat can then be used to create steam to drive a turbine to produce electrical power or used as an industrial process heat.

A CSP plant can integrate thermal energy storage systems to use to generate electricity during cloudy periods or for hours after sunset or before sunrise. This function to store solar energy makes CSP a flexible source of renewable energy. CSP systems can be also combined with combined cycle power plants resulting in hybrid power plants which provide high-value power. They can also be integrated into existing thermal-fired power plants that use a power block like CSP, such as coal, natural gas, biofuel or geothermal plants.

CSP plants can also use fossil fuel to supplement the solar output during periods of low solar radiation. In that case, a natural gas-fired heater or a gas steam boiler/reheater is used.

Advantages and disadvantages of CSP

5.28 Since the system relies on the sun, it uses renewable resources and produces no pollution whilst generating power. CSP systems can store energy in batteries that can be tapped for energy on demand, which helps the systems to more consistently meet local power demands, especially during peak usage times.

CSP systems have low operating costs and produce power at a high efficiency rate. As the technology can also be integrated into fossil fuel power plants, it can be used to cut carbon emissions and maximise efficiency during the processing of both resources.

However, it can only operate during the daytime when the solar energy is available and, if it is a community's only power source, residents may experience intermittent blackouts if energy production is restricted by consistent overcast weather. Covering large surface areas with solar panels could damage wildlife habitats or promote deforestation. Also, manufacturing solar panels produces many potent greenhouse gases that can contribute significantly to global warming.

CSP and the UK

5.29 CSP systems require large areas of land as they cannot be situated on a roof, and they also have a requirement for energy storage which is inefficient. Given the area of land required and the UK climate, CSP plants may not be a suitable development for the UK.

Types of CSP technology

5.30 There are four types of CSP technologies, the earliest in use being trough, and the fastest growing being tower. There are also design variations or different configurations, depending on whether thermal energy storage is included and the method used to store solar thermally.

Parabolic trough

5.31 In a parabolic trough CSP system, the sun's energy is concentrated by parabolically curved, trough-shaped reflectors onto a receiver pipe, which is the heat absorber tube and runs along about a metre above the curved surface of the mirrors. The temperature of the heat transfer fluid flowing through the pipe, ie thermal oil, is increased from 293°C to 393°C, and the heat energy is then used in the thermal power block to generate electricity in a conventional steam generator.

A trough solar collector comprises multiple parabolic trough-shaped mirrors in parallel rows which are aligned to enable these single-axis trough-shaped mirrors to track the sun from east to west during the day, to ensure that the sun is continuously focused on the receiver pipes. According to the National Renewable Energy Laboratory (NREL), in the US in 2018, 90% of the CSP in commercial operation was trough[12].

Example of working parabolic trough

5.32 La Florida CSP Plant is located in Badajoz, Spain. This has been operational since 2010 and covers 200 hectares of land. It uses 2-tank indirect with a storage capacity of 7.5 hours and 29,000 tons of molten salt.

Power tower

5.33 A power tower or central receiver system uses sun-tracking mirrors (heliostats) to focus sunlight onto a receiver at the top of a tower. A heat transfer fluid which is heated in the receiver up to around 600°C is used to generate steam, which is used in a conventional turbine-generator to produce electricity.

Early power towers used steam as the heat transfer fluid, which does not lend itself to storage. Khi Solar One in South Africa and Ivanpah in California operate commercially by directly heating water to steam. Gemasolar (2011), Crescent Dunes (2013), and Noor III (2018) use molten salts because of their superior heat transfer and energy storage capabilities.

Example of working power tower

5.34 Greenway CSP Mersin Tower Plant is located in Mersin, Turkey. Operational since 2012.

12 NREL–CSP Projects database: https://solarpaces.nrel.gov.

CSP Crescent Dunes – no longer in use

5.35 The dispute over failures at the Crescent Dunes tower plant in Nevada is going through US law courts.

Developed by SolarReserve, the 110MW Crescent Dunes plant was the first solar tower project with molten salt storage. Nevada utility NV Energy terminated its offtake contract for Crescent Dunes after the plant failed to meet output expectations.

Crescent Dunes was brought online in October 2015, a year behind schedule. Output was below target during the first year of operation. A year after start-up, the plant was shut down for eight months due to a leak in the molten salt storage system. By 2018, the average capacity factor of Crescent Dunes was 20.3% compared with a planned factor of 51.9%, according to EIA data. SolarReserve blamed ACS Cobra, designer of the salt storage tanks, for the leak, but does not appear to have filed legal action against the company. ACS Cobra declined to comment on the matter. Since Crescent Dunes, CSP tower developers have improved reliability, but concerns remain.

Linear Fresnel systems

5.36 Similar to the long arrays of a parabolic trough CSP system, a linear concentrating collector field consists of a large number of collectors in parallel rows. These are usually aligned in a north-south orientation to maximise annual and summer energy collection. The mirrors are laid flat on the ground and reflect the sunlight to the pipe above. Like trough and tower, Fresnel can also incorporate storage in a power block, or generate steam for direct use.

Example of working linear Fresnel system

5.37 Dacheng Dunchuang 50MW Molten Salt Fresnel Project is located in Dunchuang, China. Operational since 2019.

Parabolic dish

5.38 A parabolic dish system consists of a parabolic-shaped point focus concentrator in the form of a dish that reflects solar radiation onto a receiver mounted at the focal point. These concentrators are mounted on a structure with a two-axis tracking system to follow the sun. The collected heat is typically used directly by a heat engine mounted on the receiver moving with the dish structure. Dishes can attain extremely high temperatures.

Example of parabolic dish system

5.39 Maricopa Solar Project is located in Peoria, Arizona, USA. Currently non-operational.

SOLAR PANELS – DOMESTIC USE

5.40 Since a change in legislation in April 2008, the installation of solar panels and equipment on residential buildings and land may be 'permitted development' and therefore planning permission IS NOT required, unless the building is listed, or in a conservation area.

Being in a conservation area does not in itself prevent the installation, but it is necessary to notify the council and the conservation team of installation.

Solar equipment mounted on a house or block of flats or on a building within a curtilage

5.41 Equipment on the building should be sited, as far as is reasonably practicable, to minimise the effect on the amenities and the appearance of the building. When the equipment is no longer required, it should be removed as soon as is reasonably practicable.

All of the following limits must be met:

- panels should not be installed above the highest part of the roof (excluding the chimney) and should project no more than 200mm from the roof slope or wall surface;
- the panels must not be installed on a building that is within the grounds of a listed building or on a site designated as a scheduled monument; and
- for a property that is in a conservation area, or in a World Heritage Site, panels must not be fitted to a wall which fronts a highway

Note: A leaseholder may need to get permission from their landlord, freeholder or management company.

Stand-alone solar equipment (panels not on a building but within the grounds of a house or a block of flats)

5.42 Equipment should be sited, as far as is reasonably practicable, to minimise the effect on the amenity. When the equipment is no longer required, it should be removed as soon as is reasonably practicable.

The following conditions must be met:

- only the first stand-alone solar installation will be permitted development. Further installations will require planning permission;
- no part of the installation should be higher than 4 metres;
- the installation should be at least 5 metres from the boundary of the property;
- the size of the array should be no more than 9 square metres, or 3 metres wide by 3 metres deep;
- panels should not be installed within the boundary of a listed building or a scheduled monument; and
- if the property is in a conservation area, or in a World Heritage Site, no part of the solar installation should be nearer to any highway bounding the house than the part of the house that is nearest to that highway.

Note: A leaseholder may need to get permission from their landlord, freeholder or management company.

Case law – solar panels have right to light

5.43 The case of *R (on the application of McLennan) v Medway Council*[13] involved an application from William McClennan for judicial review of a planning decision; the local authority had granted planning permission for an extension, even though it would block sunlight falling on a neighbour's solar panels. This went to court and the judge overturned the planning permission on the basis that the electricity generated by solar PV panels was helping to mitigate climate change.

ISSUES RELATED TO INSTALLING SOLAR PANELS

5.44 With many people now installing solar panels on domestic properties, the House of Commons has published a briefing paper that looks at some of the issues that need to be considered[14].

Lender requirements

5.45 The Microgeneration Certification Scheme (MCS, see para **3.38**) has become an installation standard and any installations made outside this scheme may be unacceptable to lenders. Only MCS installations are eligible for FIT payments (or their equivalent), so financial benefits from a non-MCS project are much lower.

In October 2011, the Council of Mortgage Lenders (CML) and the Building Societies Association (BSA) agreed guidance for their respective members[15]. They provided separate guidance for England and Wales[16] and Northern Ireland[17].

Leasing roof space for a panel installation has been triggered by government policies and people wanting to have renewable energy for their homes.

Consideration should be given to the following:

- agreeing to a lease of roof space for fitting PV panels – most lenders' mortgage conditions will require the lender's consent to be obtained for any lease;

13 [2019] EWHC 1738 (Admin).
14 'Q&A: solar panels' House of Commons Library, Briefing Paper (7 February 2020).
15 CML-BSA guidance from solar photovoltaic panels on roofspace: www.cml.org.uk/policy/guidance/all/cml-bsa-guidance-and-minimum-requirements-regarding-leases-of/.
16 Guidance for solar PV panels on roofspace in England and Wales: www.cml.org.uk/policy/guidance/all/cml-bsa-guidance-and-minimum-requirements-regarding-leases-of/.
17 Guidance for solar PV panels on roofspace in Northern Ireland: www.cml.org.uk/policy/guidance/all/cml-bsa-guidance-and-minimum-requirements-regarding-leases-of/.

- some lenders may also have in place protections (in the form of restrictions entered on the title at the Land Registry) which prevent the registration of a lease without the lender's written consent;
- borrowers may wish to consider contacting their lender at the earliest opportunity (prior to entering into any arrangements regarding panels) to check their requirements; and
- proceeding without a lender's consent, where required, may be a breach of the mortgage terms and conditions and, even if the lease can be registered, the lender may not be bound by it in the absence of their consent.

Re-mortgages or applications for mortgages on properties with existing leases

5.46 Where a borrower seeks to re-mortgage or purchase a property with an existing PV panel lease, it is likely that the lender will review the lease with reference to the minimum requirements set out here and with reference to any specific requirements they have. If the lender feels that the lease does not meet their requirements, they may request that the lease is varied, or may choose not to lend on the property.

Obtaining a lender's consent (England and Wales)

5.47 Consideration should be given to the following:

- The PV panel provider (with consent from the borrower) should contact the mortgage lender to request consent on behalf of the borrower to the registration of a lease of the airspace above a roof of a mortgaged property, in order to install the panels. The lender may advise the borrower that they have been contacted by the provider.
- The provider should supply the relevant information to lenders, to enable the lender to make a decision about whether to grant consent to the lease. The information includes:
  - evidence of accreditation which shows that the panels will be installed to a suitable standard;
  - evidence that the provider and installer are members of a Code of Practice for the renewable energy sector that is approved by the Chartered Trading Standards Institute;
  - evidence that there has been a valid contracting out of the security of tenure provisions under the Landlord and Tenant Act 1954, where the lease applies to a property in England and Wales. In order to validly contract out, the landlord (borrower) must serve notice on the tenant (provider) in the prescribed form and the tenant must sign a declaration that he has received the notice and that they accept the consequences of contracting out. The lease must also contain reference to the exclusion agreement, notice and declaration. In practice, this will mean that the lender will need to see the signed contracting out notice and sworn declaration;
  - signed confirmation by a suitably authorised representative that the provider satisfies the lender minimum requirements, and any specific requirements of the individual lender. The template letter contains the minimum requirements. The letter was developed to provide a way of certifying to lenders that providers, and their lease agreements, meet those minimum requirements;

- signed authorisation of borrower(s) for provider to contact lender directly with respect to the consent;
- contact details of the provider;
- copy of lease(s) or reference to where the lender may access a copy of the lease(s).

- The lender will either base their decision on satisfactory information from the provider, rather than case-by-case review, or review each consent individually, using provider information to fast-track the process.
- The provider should inform the lender of any changes to the lease which are likely to impact on the lender's decision to consent, in order for the lender to review whether they can continue to give consent. Lenders do not need to be advised of minor changes to the lease which do not conflict with the lender's minimum requirements. For example, where the provider amends the lease to remove the requirement for a maintenance fee to be charged to the borrower, this would remain within the spirit of the minimum requirements and the lender would not need to be advised of the change.
- The lender decision on consent will be communicated to the provider and/or borrower.

Obtaining a lender's consent (Northern Ireland)

5.48 Consideration should be given to the following:

- The PV panel provider (with appropriate consent from the borrower) should contact the mortgage lender to request consent on behalf of the borrower to the registration of a Lease of Rights in relation to the roof of a mortgaged property, in order to install the panels. The lender may advise the borrower that they have been contacted by the provider.
- The provider should supply the relevant information to lenders, to enable the lender to make a decision about whether to grant consent to the Lease of Rights. The information includes:
  - evidence of accreditation which shows that the panels will be installed to a suitable standard;
  - evidence that the provider and installer are members of the REAL Assurance Scheme;
  - signed confirmation by a suitably authorised representative that the provider satisfies the lender minimum requirements, and any specific requirements of the individual lender. The template letter, accessible here, contains the minimum requirements. The letter was developed to provide a way of certifying to lenders that providers, and their Lease of Rights agreements, meet those minimum requirements;
  - signed authorisation of borrower(s) for provider to contact lender directly with respect to the consent;
  - contact details of the provider;
  - copy of Lease(s) of Rights or reference to where the lender may access a copy of the Lease(s) of Rights.
- The lender will either base their decision on satisfactory initial up-front information from the provider, rather than case-by-case review, OR review each consent individually, using provider information to fast-track the process.

- The provider should inform the lender of any changes to the Lease of Rights which are likely to impact on the lender's decision to consent, in order for the lender to review whether they can continue to give consent. Lenders do not need to be advised of minor changes to the Lease of Rights which do not conflict with lender's minimum requirements. For example, where the provider amends the Lease of Rights to remove the requirement for a maintenance fee to be charged to the borrower, this would remain within the spirit of the minimum requirements and the lender would not need to be advised of the change.
- The lender decision on consent will be communicated to the provider and/or borrower.

Leasing space for solar panels

5.49 This is an option that people took to install expensive solar panels on their property for free in exchange for leasing the roof space. These providers offered the free installation and maintenance of solar panels in exchange for a 20- to 25-year lease of the roof and air space above it, sometimes taking a rent of all the money that would have been earned by the homeowner under the FIT scheme or the free electricity. The Government also introduced the Green Deal in January 2013, which was a scheme providing an initial loan to cover the installation of green technologies, including solar panels, with an arrangement for repayment through utility bills.

Ownership and maintenance

5.50 The solar panels should be clearly defined as forming part of (or being expressly excluded from) the property itself or the fixtures and fittings. Where solar panels have been installed by a solar panel provider, the provider will usually own and maintain them under the roof top lease. The lease should set out clearly the responsibilities for maintenance and removal of the panels where works are required to the roof. The lease also should make clear what happens with the panels at the end of the lease.

Purchasing a property with solar panels

5.51 In purchasing a property with solar panels, it is important to know:

- What year were the solar panels installed?
- Are the solar panels owned outright?
- How long is the lease of the roof space to the solar panel provider?

It is likely that a lease of the roof space to a solar panel provider will create a protected business tenancy under the Landlord and Tenant Act 1954. The homeowner, ie the landlord, will need to ensure they contract out of the 1954 Act so that they can regain possession of the roof space at the end of the term of the lease.

Solar panels and the mortgage lender

5.52 The lender's mortgage conditions will generally require the lender's consent to be obtained for the grant of a lease to a solar panel provider, and many lenders enter a restriction on the homeowner's title to the property at HM Land Registry, preventing the registration of a lease without their written consent. A failure to liaise with a lender before granting a lease can give rise to serious complications for a homeowner with both the lender and the solar panel provider. Proceeding without a lender's consent may be a breach of the mortgage terms and conditions and could trigger the lender's right to require repayment of the mortgage loan. Where a lease has been granted without consent, even if it can be registered, the lender may not be bound by its terms. Where a borrower is seeking to re-mortgage or purchase a property with an existing solar panel lease, the lender is likely to review the lease with reference to the minimum requirements set out in the guidance as well as their own specific requirements.

ENVIRONMENTAL IMPACTS OF SOLAR PANELS

Production of a functioning solar panel

5.53 The main raw material of which a solar panel is made is quartz, which is processed into silicon. Also, aluminium and copper or silver are materials which must be mined or obtained from recycled sources – but they are mainly mined, as the PV industry has expanded.

The life-time carbon emissions from solar panels is heavily front loaded; but then, after installation, the panels produce emission-free energy for 30 or more years.

The manufacturing of the solar panels requires more energy to produce than other forms of energy generation, which is due to the manufacturing process.

To produce solar-grade silicon, the processing of semi-conductors typically involves hazardous chemicals. Depending on the solar panel manufacturer, these chemicals may or may not be disposed properly. The Silicon Valley Toxics Coalition (SVTC) presents an annual report on the environmental records of major solar manufacturers. Like every industry, there are companies leading by example, and others which cut corners to save money. Not every company will dump chemicals, or recycle their by-products improperly, but there are a few bad apples out there fuelling the anti-green bandwagon.

Land use and ecological impacts

5.54 At the scale of a solar farm, this requires a large area of land and this can interfere with existing land uses and can impact on areas of wilderness or recreation.

Soil, water and air resources

5.55 The creation of land-based solar facilities can result in the clearing of land and changes to drainage and the potential for increased erosion.

Recycling

5.56 Although solar panel recycling has not become a major issue yet, it will in the coming decades as solar panels need to be replaced. Within two to three decades, there will be a need to recycle the existing solar panels. The International Renewable Energy Agency (IRENA) in 2016 estimated that there were 250,000 metric tonnes of solar panel waste in the world, and they projected that this would reach 78 million tonnes in 2050.

Monocrystalline and polycrystalline panels

5.57 These are approximately:

- 76% glass;
- 10% plastic;
- 8% aluminium;
- 5% silicon; and
- 1% metals.

Recycling consists of dismantling the aluminium and glass parts. 95% of the glass can be reused and 100% of the metal. Thermal processing causes the plastics to evaporate and this can be reused as a heat source. Then separation of the cell modules takes place and the silicon wafers are etched and the broken wafers provide 85% of the silicon for reuse. And 80% of the modules are reused.

Thin-film panels

5.58 These are approximately:

- 89% glass;
- 4% plastic;
- 6% aluminium; and
- 1% metals.

Recycling consists of shredding the PV panels into 4/5 mm pieces to remove the lamination. The solids and liquids are separated with a rotating screw, removing the film using peroxide and acid. Then, by using a precipitation and dewatering process, separation and processing of the metals is possible with 85% of the semiconductor metals used recovered. The removal of the interlayer materials is done by vibration, and the glass is rinsed, and 90% is ready for reuse.

Energy payback time of solar panels

5.59 The energy payback period for solar power depends on location and what the typical form of energy generation is. Only when compared to the form of energy displaced can the payback period be looked at. If a home is powered 100% by wind and hydro energy, then replacing that with solar will not provide much environmental benefit; however, if it is powered by fossil fuels, or energy derived from coal, gas or nuclear power, solar power will have a very short environmental payback period.

WORLD CAPACITY FOR SOLAR ENERGY

5.60 According to data from International Renewable Energy Agency (IRENA), in 2019 the ranking of the installed capacity of the top 10 countries was:

1) China – 205,492MW
2) USA – 62,298MW
3) Japan – 61,840MW
4) Germany – 48,962MW
5) India – 35,060MW
6) Italy – 20,906MW
7) Australia – 15,930MW
8) UK – 13,398MW
9) Spain – 11,065MW
10) France – 10,571MW.

RELATED DOCUMENTS

Building Regulations 2010[18]

5.61 The Building Regulations are the minimum standards for design, construction and alterations in virtually every building. The following Approved Documents, supplementing the Building Regulations in relation to specific topics, are available[19]:

- Regulation 7 – Materials and workmanship
- A – Structure
- B – Fire safety
- C – Site preparation and resistance to contaminants and moisture
- D – Toxic substances
- E – Resistance to the passage of sound
- F – Means of ventilation
- G – Sanitation, hot water safety and water efficiency
- H – Drainage and waste disposal
- J – Combustion appliances and fuel storage systems
- K – Protection from falling, collision and impact
- L – Conservation of fuel and power
- M – Access to and use of buildings
- P – Electrical safety – Dwellings
- Q – Security – Dwellings
- R – Physical infrastructure for high-speed electronic communications networks.

18 www.legislation.gov.uk/uksi/2010/2214/contents.
19 www.gov.uk/guidance/building-regulations-and-approved-documents-index.

Chapter 6

History of Photovoltaics

INTRODUCTION

6.1 A physical phenomenon allowing light-electricity conversion, the photovoltaic effect, was discovered in 1839 by the French physicist, Alexandre Edmond Becquerel; while experimenting with metal electrodes and electrolytes, he discovered that conductance rises with illumination. The photovoltaic effect in selenium was discovered by Willoughby Smith in 1873. In 1876, with his student Richard E. Day, William G. Adams discovered that illuminating a junction between selenium and platinum also has a photovoltaic effect. These two discoveries were the foundation for the first selenium solar cell construction, which was built in 1877.

The author of the most comprehensive theoretical work about the photovoltaic effect was Albert Einstein, who described the phenomenon in 1904. For this explanation, he was awarded a Nobel Prize in 1921. In 1918, a Polish scientist Jan Czochralski discovered a method for monocrystalline silicon production, which enabled monocrystalline solar cell production. The first silicon monocrystalline solar cell was constructed in 1941. In 1932, the photovoltaic effect in cadmium-selenide (CdS) was observed. CdS is among the important materials for solar cell production.

Space research provided a critical impetus to photovoltaic development and, from 1992 to 2018, there has been a worldwide growth in photovoltaics.

Large utility-scale photovoltaic systems

6.2 One of the first large-scale photovoltaic systems was installed in Germany in 1983. It had a capacity of 300kW and was built on the North Frisian Island of Pellworm. The first MW-ranged power plant was constructed in Hesperia, California with Atlantic Richfield Company (ARCO) modules in the early 1980s. Carrizo Plain, the largest photovoltaic array in the world at that time, was producing more than 6MWp power, and it remained in service until 1994.

Pilot PV power plants were constructed in other regions, including Japan, Africa and the Middle East. Among large-scale research facilities constructed in Japan is the MW-ranged plant in Saijo City. It was constructed in 1985. However, in Japan much attention was also given to residential PV rooftop programmes. Some residential PV systems had been generating power capacity in the MW range and were put into service in Japan last as a result of these early activities. In Saudi Arabia, a 350kW pilot power plant for three remote villages was constructed in the early 1980s.

In the early 1990s, research activities in Europe – especially in Germany, Italy, Spain, Switzerland and the Netherlands – resulted in several large-scale PV projects covering a wide range of applications, from wind-PV hybrid systems and noise barriers to a PV-powered hydrogen facility. Systems with fixed and tracking arrays have been constructed.

The 340kWp power plant in Kobern-Gondorf, Mosel Valley, in the 1990s was constructed by companies RWE and AEG. Some other projects, like the Lake Neurath PV plant, were also put into service almost at the same time.

In the 1990s, attention was paid to residential PV programmes and some other applications like PV noise barriers and BIPV applications. In the late 1990s, large utility-scale residential PV programmes in Germany, the Netherlands and Australia were successfully installed. The first utility-scale PV noise barrier was put into service in Switzerland.

Some other large utility-scale, roof-mounted PV power plants in the late 1990s clearly indicated the direction of future development. Technical obstacles for large utility-scale PV power plants were minimised, and MW-ranged, free-field PV power plants, as well as MW-sized, roof-mounted PV power plants, were no longer uncommon.

Solar cars

6.3 A year later, in 1983, the worldwide production of photovoltaic modules exceeded 21.3MW peak power. A Solar Trek vehicle with a 1kW photovoltaic system drove 4,000 km in the 20 days of the Australia Race. The maximum speed was 72 km/h and the average speed was 24 km/h. The same year, the vehicle surpassed the distance of 4,000 km between Long Beach, California, and Daytona Beach, Florida, in 18 days. Solarex Corporation bought amorphous cells production technology from cells producer RCA and built its own trial power plant in Newtown, Pennsylvania. ARCO Solar built a 6MW photovoltaic power plant as a subsystem of the public electricity grid for a Pacific Gas and Electric Company application in California. The system satisfied the demand of 2,000 to 2,500 households. Solar Power Corporation built four stand-alone photovoltaic systems for the needs of a village in Tunisia, with total peak power of 31kW per system. A 1.8kW photovoltaic system was built to satisfy the needs of a local hospital in Guyana. The applications, such as vaccine refrigerators, indoor lighting, ordination lighting and radio appliances, were powered by the system. The system was planned and built by NASA LeRC and Solarex. A similar, yet more powerful, photovoltaic system of 4kW was set up in Ecuador. A 1.8kW photovoltaic system was set up in Zimbabwe for the same purpose. Solarex Corporation merged with Amoco Solar Company, owned by Standard Oil Company.

In 1990, Energy Conversion Devices Inc (ECD) and Canon Inc established a joint company, United Solar Systems Corporation, for solar cell production. Siemens bought ARCO Solar and established Siemens Solar Industries. The Solar Energy Research Institute (SERI) was renamed the National Renewable Energy Laboratory (NREL). A year later, in 1991, BP Solar Systems was renamed BP Solar International (BPSI) and became an independent unit within the British Petroleum Group.

In 1992, a photovoltaic system of 0.5kW was placed in Antarctica for the laboratory, lighting, personal computers and microwave oven power requirements. A silicon solar cell with 20% efficiency was patented. In 1994, the Department of Energy (DOE) built several trial systems for the needs of agriculture, hospitals, lighting, water pumping, etc in Brazil. ASE GmbH, from Germany, purchased Mobil Solar Energy Corporation technology and established ASE Americas, Inc. A year later, in 1995, the first international fund for the promotion of photovoltaic system commercialisation was established, which supported projects in India.

Multi-MW utility-scale PV power plants

6.4 Mostly in Germany, some photovoltaic and renewable energy resources companies have shares listed on the stock exchange. Capital mergers in Germany led to the establishment of large photovoltaic corporations. During 2000 and 2001, production by Japanese manufacturers increased significantly. Sharp and Kyocera each produce modules with peak power equivalent to the annual consumption in Germany, the most demanding European market. Sanyo is close as well. After many years of research and trial flights, the HELIOS solar-powered plane, developed by NASA and AeroVironment Inc, broke the height record on 13 August 2001. HELIOS reached a height of almost 30,000 metres. During 2002 and 2003, several large power plants were built in Germany. On 29 April 2003 the world's largest photovoltaic plant at that time was connected to the public grid in Hemau near Regensburg (Bavaria), Germany. The peak power of the 'Solarpark Hemau' plant is 4MW. Due to the 'EEC' renewable energy law, many other large systems of up to 5MW were built in Germany in 2004, including the Geiseltalsee, Leipzig, Bürstadt and Göttelborn solar parks.

Solar cars

6.5 The first solar-powered car was made by General Motors and was showcased in a convention in Chicago in 1955. This solar car was made using a small Pooley electric motor and 12 selenium photovoltaic cells. The Pooley electric motor was responsible for turning a pulley that rotated the rear wheel shaft. It was the first-ever solar car, but it was too small to drive. However, Sion can be considered as the first hybrid electric vehicle that charges itself using solar energy. It has 248 solar cells that are integrated into its body, and it uses solar energy to charge itself.

Solar cars are electric cars that use solar energy. They use photovoltaic cells to convert energy from sunlight into electricity. These cars can store some solar energy and can also run smoothly at night or in the absence of direct sunlight.

Solar-powered cars not only help with environmental pollution but also noise pollution. However, solar cars have design limitations because aesthetics need to be considered as well so that they can accommodate solar panels. Therefore, most solar vehicles have been developed to run in solar car races so far, and not for regular use.

Some of the advantages of using solar cars:

- saves money on fuel;
- is sustainable and environment-friendly;
- no additional costs except battery replacement; and
- does not cause noise pollution or air pollution.

Disadvantages of solar powered cars:

- the solar panel itself, since current commercially operated solar panels have only 15–20% efficiency. So, to power a solar car, the car's body space would need to be packed with solar cells; but, in doing so, it creates two other problems: weight and cost;
- solar panels are not cheap, and they are not weightless either. Packing the car's body with solar panels means adding a lot of weight and cost to the car. Factoring in the weight of the battery, the idea of the solar-powered cars seems less and less feasible;
- on a clear day, the earth's surface receives approximately 1kW of solar energy per square metre; given that highly efficient 4-square metre PV panels can generate approximately 8kWh of energy per day, it will only power the car to drive about 25 miles (40 km);
- poor weather conditions, improper positioning of the panels and dirt would likely make the solar car struggle to even reach this distance;
- additionally, solar-powered cars aren't '100%' eco-friendly. Considering the way in which batteries and solar cells are made, especially how they are mined from the earth, it becomes clear that each vehicle comes with its share of carbon footprint.

All this does not mean that it is impossible. In future, research may create low-weight batteries and high-efficiency photovoltaic cells.

World Solar Challenge

6.6 The idea for the competition came from a Danish-born adventurer Hans Tholstrup. He was the first to circumnavigate the Australian continent in a 16-foot (4.9-metre) open boat. Later he became involved in various competitions with fuel-saving cars and trucks. Already in the 1980s, he became aware of the necessity to explore sustainable energy as a replacement for fossil fuels. Sponsored by BP, he designed the world's first solar car, called The Quiet Achiever, and traversed the 2,518 miles (4,052 km) between Sydney, New South Wales and Perth, Western Australia in 20 days. That was the precursor of the World Solar Challenge.

The race has to balance power resources and power consumption. The optimal driving speed is dependent on the weather and the remaining batteries. The team members in the escort cars will continuously remotely retrieve data from the solar car about its condition and use these data as input for prior developed computer programs to work out the best driving strategy. It is also important to charge the batteries as much as possible in periods of daylight when the car is not racing. In order to capture as much solar energy as possible, the solar panels are generally directed such that these are perpendicular to the incident sun rays. Sometimes the whole solar array is tilted for this purpose.

Solar car races – a new challenge for research laboratories

6.7 There are a number of solar power car races, for which the prize money is driving development of PV and cars. The ones with the most notable distances are the World Solar Challenge and the American Solar Challenge.

In the Pentax World Solar Challenge 1987 race through Australia, a General Motors Sunracer vehicle won with an average speed of 71 km/h. In 1988, the fourth Tour de Sol race of 350 km in Switzerland and Austria took place. The vehicle categories included photovoltaic supplied vehicles, additional pedal vehicles, commercial photovoltaic supplied vehicles and electric vehicles without photovoltaic supply. The overall award fund was worth SFR 140,000.

Solar Team Twente, which competes in the World Solar Challenge using only power from the sun to run the 3,000km course, has used power analyser technology to help boost its speed and chances of winning, using a lightweight, solar-powered car that can only harvest energy from the sun for propulsion. The biennial Bridgestone World Solar Challenge is a test of technology and precision. To be able to win the World Solar Challenge, a race car must generate as much solar energy as possible and convert the electricity it generates as efficiently as possible into mechanical power delivered to the wheels. At the same time, it must keep energy losses to a minimum. Attention is paid to minute details of aerodynamic design to keep wind resistance to a minimum. In the case of RED E, the name given to Solar Team Twente's race car, total wind resistance is the equivalent of a conventional car's wing mirror. The driver must then race as fast as possible but not so fast that the car's battery runs out of power when it is not in bright sunlight.

There are four important electrical systems in a solar race car: the array of solar panels; the battery and its management system; the inverter (motor drive), which converts the solar panels' direct current output to a three-phase alternating current supplied to the motor; and the motor itself. The team was aiming for better than 99% efficiency for the electrical power conversion circuits. To do this, it used a Precision Power Analyzer from Yokogawa.

The team uses the Yokogawa WT5000 for two crucial tasks:

- to validate the accuracy of the 'fuel gauge', the car's on-board sensor measuring the battery's state of charge. This system measures current flowing into the battery (from the solar panels) and flowing out of the battery (to the motor). By subtracting output from input, it can calculate the residual charge in the battery. This required extremely accurate continuous measurement of current flows; and
- to measure the power output of the motor system, including the inverter and the motor itself, at a range of power input values, to enable the team to refine the design and incrementally improve its efficiency. This called for extremely accurate power analysis at a high sampling frequency.

PHOTOVOLTAIC PROCESS

6.8 The photovoltaic process is the branch of technology concerned with the production of electric current at a junction of two substances. In a solar panel, photons (particles of light) knock electrons free from atoms, generating a flow of electricity. A solar panel is comprised of many smaller units called photovoltaic cells. These cells are then linked together to make a solar panel. To work, a photovoltaic cell is a sandwich made up of two slices of semiconducting material, usually silicon. The photovoltaic cells need to establish an electric field similar to that of a magnetic field which occurs because of opposite poles – an electric field where opposite charges are separated. To get this field, the manufacturers 'dope' silicon with other materials, giving each slice of the sandwich a positive or negative charge. More specifically, they see phosphorus into the top layer of silicon, which adds extra electrons with a negative charge to that layer. The bottom layer has an addition of boron, which results in fewer electrons and a positive charge. This is then an electric field which will push that electron out of the silicon junction. There are metal conductive plates on either side of the cell which collect the electrons and transfer them to wires, and then the electrons flow just like any other source of electricity.

'PV technologies' refers to a combination of an absorber material, a cell architecture in the form a wafer or a stack of thin layers, a module, and a system application. This is more specific than 'crystalline silicon' or 'thin film'.

Whereas the PV industry has been able to reduce manufacturing costs and selling prices by producing a large quantity of cells and modules that are very similar, thereby achieving economies of scale, this now also starts limiting the application possibilities of PV, as one solution no longer fits all the requirements.

PV generations

First-generation

6.9 Based on crystalline silicon technologies, both monocrystalline and polycrystalline, and on gallium arsenide (GaAs).

Second-generation

6.10 This includes amorphous silicon (a-Si) and microcrystalline silicon (m-Si) thin-film solar cells, cadmium telluride/cadmium sulphide (CdTe/CdS) and copper indium gallium selenide (CIGS) solar cells.

Third-generation

6.11 It involves technologies based on newer compounds including nanocrystalline films, active quantum dots, tandem or stacked multilayers of inorganics based on III–V materials, such as GaAs/GaInP, organic (polymer)-based solar cells, dyed-sensitised solar cells, etc.

Fourth-generation

6.12 Also known as 'inorganics-in-organics', it combines the low cost/flexibility of polymer thin films with the stability of novel inorganic nanostructures, such as metal nanoparticles and metal oxides, or organic-based nanomaterials like carbon nanotubes, graphene and its derivatives.

Looking at steps in the development of silicon PV technologies, from Generation 1 to Generation 2 and from Generation 2 to Generation 3, it is clear that the introduction of thin-film technology in various forms is important for success. High-quality passivation, heterojunction[1] technologies and efficient tandems cannot be achieved without using thin-film processes. Hence, it is the merger of Generation 1 and Generation 2 that brings both of them further and that makes them enter Generation 3 together.

Components of photovoltaic systems

6.13 Photovoltaic systems generally consist of six individual components:

- solar PV array;
- charge controller;
- battery bank;
- an inverter;
- utility meter; and
- electric grid.

However, a charge controller and battery bank are optional; although these two components help store and make better use of the generated electricity, they could also increase the total price of the photovoltaic installation.

Solar PV arrays produce power when they are exposed to sunlight; the other components are required for properly converting, distributing and storing the energy that has been produced by the solar panels.

Solar photovoltaic array

6.14 A solar photovoltaic array consists of a number of solar PV panels that are electrically connected. The solar PV array generates DC electricity from sunlight.

Charge controller

6.15 Charge controllers regulate the DC from the solar panels to make sure that the batteries do not overcharge. A charge controller can measure whether

1 Heterojunction – an interface that occurs between two layers or regions of dissimilar semiconductors. These semiconducting materials have unequal bandgaps, as opposed to a homojunction.

the batteries are fully charged and can stop the current from flowing in order to prevent the batteries from permanent damage.

Charge controllers can be divided into two types:

- Pulse Width Modulation (PWM) is a standard type and is suitable for smaller photovoltaic systems and battery banks, as they vary between 4 and 60 amperes; and
- Maximum Power Point Tracking (MPPT) charge controllers are more suitable for photovoltaic systems with a high voltage of, in most cases, up to 160 volts DC.

Inverter

6.16 A solar power inverter converts electricity from DC to AC. This is necessary, when AC power is needed for the energy supply of home appliances.

Utility meter

6.17 A PV system needs to measure the electricity consumption. The utility meter is connected to the PV system and measures how much electricity is used, and any generated from the photovoltaic panels that is not stored or used will be fed back into the electric grid.

Electric grid

6.18 Only few places in the UK are living off the grid. Although renewable technologies make living off-grid possible using solar battery solutions, most people still opt for a combination of solar- and grid-based electricity.

PHOTOVOLTAIC CELLS

6.19 There are two categories of cell:

- crystalline silicon; and
- not classified as crystalline silicon.

Crystalline silicon

6.20 Crystalline silicon (C-Si) is used in traditional, conventional, wafer-based solar cells:

- monocrystalline silicon (mono-Si);
- polycrystalline silicon (multi-Si); and
- ribbon silicon (ribbon-Si), which currently has no market.

This is the most common type of cell used in commercially available solar panels. The crystalline silicon is typically the monocrystalline form of silicon and is used for producing microchips and has much lower impurity levels that that required to produce solar cells. To produce semiconductor grade silicon involves a process of chemical purification to produce hyperpure polysilicon, followed by a process of recrystallisation to grow monocrystalline silicon. These cylindrical boules[2] are then cut into wafers for further processing.

This type of cell was developed in the 1950s and is the most common type. They are produced from thick solar wafers and are sometime called *wafer-based* solar cells.

Monocrystalline silicon (mono-Si)

6.21 Monocrystalline silicon is also used for high-performance photovoltaic (PV) devices. Since there are less stringent demands on structural imperfections compared to microelectronics applications, lower-quality solar-grade silicon (Sog-Si) is often used for solar cells. Despite this, the monocrystalline-silicon photovoltaic industry has benefited from the development of faster mono-Si production methods for the electronics industry.

Polycrystalline silicon (multi-Si)

6.22 Polycrystalline silicon is the key feedstock in the crystalline silicon-based photovoltaic industry and is used for the production of conventional solar cells. For the first time, in 2006, over half of the world's supply of polysilicon was being used by PV manufacturers. The solar industry was severely limited by a shortage in supply of polysilicon feedstock and was forced to idle about a quarter of its cell and module manufacturing capacity in 2007. Only 12 factories were known to produce solar-grade polysilicon in 2008 but, by 2013, the number increased to over 100 manufacturers. Monocrystalline silicon is higher priced and a more efficient semiconductor than polycrystalline, as it has gone through additional recrystallisation by the Czochralski method.

Ribbon silicon (ribbon-Si)

6.23 The name describes the manufacturing process, where a sheet of silicon, the ribbon, is pulled vertically from a bath of molten silicon to form multi-crystalline silicon crystals. The ribbon is then cut into lengths which are treated with traditional processes to form solar cells. The process was developed in the 1970s by Mobil-Tyco, Solar Energy Corp, Energy Materials Corp, Motorola and IBM. They made ribbons of 4–5 inches wide and less than 1/100th of an inch thick. This is similar to the dendrite process, developed by Westinghouse in the 1970s, which had the further advantage of having no ribbon (graphite or ceramic die), using only two special seed crystals, or 'dendrites', which were dipped side by side into molten silicon and pulled up slowly.

2 Boule – a single crystal ingot produced by synthetic means.

Ribbon has the capability of using less silicon, compared to other wafer production methods, as wafers are manufactured to the approximately correct specification avoiding the need for the sawing of silicon blocks. Silicon accounted for more than 50% of manufacturing costs in producing first-generation solar cells, where much of the silicon was discarded as waste at the sawing stage of manufacture. Employing the string ribbon process allows PV grade silicon wafers to be manufactured to the approximate dimensions while avoiding the waste encountered when sawing wafers from ingots. This manufacturing process uses about half the amount of input silicon required by traditional processes.

String ribbon technology, a technique where the ribbon is pulled from the silicon melt between two wires, is not capable of achieving the same electrical performance as conventional wafer technology. Typically, a cut wafer will convert 18–20% of the incoming light into electricity, whereas string ribbon solar cells are capable of converting 13–14%.

Whilst string ribbon technology has certain advantages as to the shape of the crystals, the overall thickness varies enough so that not every 'silicon strip' can be processed directly into a solar cell. Additionally, the growth process is thermally very inefficient. The radiating area per gram of crystal is extremely high, leading to very high energy expenses which offset the reduced silicon use/expense, and so it currently has no market.

Benefits of crystalline solar cells

6.24 There are a number of benefits:

- performance – a standard, industrially produced silicon cell offers higher efficiency than other mass-produced, single junction devices. This can reduce the cost of the final installation because fewer cells need to be manufactured;
- maturity – the design has been around for a while and so there is information to evaluate the reliability of the design;
- reliability – crystalline silicon cells can reach module life-time of up to 25 years, exhibiting little degradation; and
- abundance – silicon is the second most abundant element on earth (after oxygen).

Not classified as crystalline silicon

6.25 The following materials are used in thin-film and other solar cell technologies:

- amorphous silicon (a-Si);
- nanocrystalline silicon (nc-Si);
- protocrystalline silicon (pc-Si);
- other non-silicon materials, such as CdTe, CIGS;
- emerging photovoltaics;
- multi-junction (MJ) solar cells commonly used for solar panels on spacecraft for space-based solar power. They are an emerging technology

best suited for locations that receive much sunlight, and are also used in concentrator photovoltaics (CPV, HCPV).

Cadmium telluride (CdTe)

6.26 CdTe-based PV is considered a thin-film technology because the active layers are just a few microns thick, or about a tenth the diameter of a human hair. Transparent conducting oxide (TCO) layers such as SnO_2 or Cd_2SnO_4 are transparent to visible light and highly conductive to transport current efficiently. Intermediate layers such as CdS help in both the growth and electrical properties between the TCO and CdTe. The CdTe film acts as the primary photoconversion layer and absorbs most visible light within the first micron of material. In production, all these layers are deposited on incoming glass and processed into complete solar panels in just a few hours.

Benefits

6.27

- high absorption – CdTe is a direct-bandgap material with bandgap[3] energy of 1.45 defined eV;
- low-cost manufacturing – CdTe solar cells use low-cost manufacturing to produce ecells.

Production

6.28 The most common CdTe solar cells consist of a simple p-n heterojunction structure containing a p-doped CdTe layer matched with an n-doped cadmium sulphide (CdS) layer, which acts as a window layer. This structure is similar to the heterojunction in CIGS cells. As with most thin-film solar technologies, carrier collection is accomplished by drift, or field-assisted collection.

Typical CdTe thin-film deposition techniques include:

- close-spaced sublimation;
- vapour-transport deposition;
- physical-vapour deposition;
- sputter deposition;
- electrodeposition;
- metal-organic chemical-vapour deposition; and
- spray deposition and screen-print deposition.

CdTe solar cells are completed by adding a high-quality TCO (usually fluorine-doped tin oxide (SnO_2:F)) and a back electrical contact, typically a metal or carbon paste with copper (Cu). A disadvantage to using Cu in the back contact is the gradual diffusion of Cu atoms into the CdTe and CdS layers, which creates defects and promotes Cu accumulation at the CdTe/CdS junction.

3 Bandgap, or energy bandgap, is the minimum energy required by electrons in the outermost cells of a substance to be able to jump free of the parent atoms.

Copper indium gallium diselenide (CIGS)

6.29 Since its development, it is considered to be a promising way forward for solar cells because of optical and electronic properties. By substituting gallium for indium, the bandgap increased from about 1.04 electron-volts (eV) for copper indium diselenide (CIS) films to about 1.68 eV for copper gallium diselenide (CGS) films.

Benefits

6.30

- high absorption – its direct-bandgap material can absorb a significant portion of the solar spectrum, enabling it to achieve the highest efficiency of any thin-film technology;
- tandem design – having a tuneable bandgap allows the possibility of tandem CIGS devices;
- protective buffer layer – the grain boundaries form an inherent buffer layer, prevent surface recombination and allow for films with grain sizes of less than 1 micrometre to be used in device fabrication.

Production

6.31 Two of the low-cost deposition methods that produce the highest device and module efficiencies were developed in the 1980s. These methods are:

- co-evaporation, in which elements are allowed to sublimate in a high-vacuum environment and then re-deposit on a heated substrate; and
- precursor reaction processes, in which a precursor containing Cu and In/Ga is deposited at a low temperature by any of several processes, such as sputtering or electroplating. This is followed by a reactive annealing step in a Se compound, such as hydrogen selenide (H_2Se) or gaseous selenium (Se), to form CIGS films. This is also commonly known as two-stage deposition; a variant of this technique, three-stage deposition, is also commonly used.

After the CIGS deposition, the junction is formed by chemical-bath deposition of the n-type CdS layer. To finish the solar cell, a high-resistance zinc oxide (ZnO) layer and a high-conductivity n+-type ZnO layer are deposited by either sputtering or chemical-vapour deposition. Laser-scribing processes at different steps in the production process create the individual solar cells connected in series.

Alternative manufacturing techniques have been explored, such as reactive sputtering, magnetron sputtering (Cu, In and Ga are sputtered while Se is evaporated), and electrodeposition. However, co-evaporation and precursor reaction processes still remain the most popular.

Earth-abundant materials

6.32 An alternative to PV technologies that use rare elements, such as CdTe and CIGS, is copper zinc tin sulfoselenide (CZTS). There are other alternatives, such as lead sulphide and pyrite.

CZTS is similar to CIGS in its optoelectronic and crystallographic properties, and it has a laboratory efficiency of just above 10% – about half that of CIGS.

Benefits

6.33

- abundant, low-cost materials with similar thermal expansion and crystal lattice constants – CZTS can be put in a solar cell with a cadmium sulphide (CdS) window layer and molybdenum (Mo) back contact and derive about the same functionality as a CIGS cell, while using more abundant and less costly materials for the absorber layer;
- tuneable bandgap – CZTS has a tuneable bandgap that can be modified from ~1 electron-volt (eV) for copper zinc tin selenide to ~1.5 eV for copper zinc tin sulphide, by modulating the ratio of S to Se. Moreover, by doping the film with Ga, researchers have reached bandgaps as high as 2.25 eV.

Production

6.34 Neither non-silicon earth-abundant nor CZTS solar cells are currently produced in large quantities. Record CZTS cells have been produced using a CZTS solution in hydrazine, which may not be favourable for manufacturing. This solution is then deposited onto a substrate and annealed. Using this process, efficiencies of greater than 10% have been achieved. Other methods that have been used for depositing CZTS include solution processable nanocrystal inks and vacuum-based deposition systems.

Perovskite solar cells

6.35 This type of solar cell includes a perovskite[4] structured compound, usually a hybrid organic-inorganic lead or tin halide-based material and the light-harvesting active layer. Perovskite materials are cheap to produce and simple to manufacture. They have shown progress in conversion efficiency from 3% in 2006 to over 26% in 2019[5].

Advantages

6.36

- perovskite-based materials could also be used to print photovoltaic electronics directly onto glass or other materials, which would be cheaper than more complex methods for producing thin-film solar cells;
- as a hybrid material, as well as boasting good efficiencies, perovskites can take advantage of organic solar materials' capacity to be applied as a liquid solution;

4 A perovskite is a material that has the same crystal structure as the mineral calcium titanium oxide, the first discovered perovskite crystal.
5 'Best Research-Cell Efficiency Chart', National Renewable Energy Laboratory (NREL)

- spraying the perovskite as a liquid coating onto a substrate material allows solar cells to be manufactured at high volumes and at a much lower cost than the currently used silicon solar cells;
- the structure of the perovskite's cells enables them to have high charge-carrier motilities and long diffusion lengths, allowing the photo-generated electrons to travel long distances without energy loss.

Multijunction III–V

6.37 Multijunction devices use multiple bandgaps or junctions that are tuned to absorb a specific region of the solar spectrum to create solar cells having recorded efficiencies over 45%. Multijunction devices use a high-bandgap top cell to absorb high-energy photons whilst allowing the lower-energy photons to pass through. A material with a slightly lower bandgap is then placed below the high-bandgap junction to absorb photons with slightly less energy (longer wavelengths).

Benefits

6.38

- spectrum matching – high-efficiency cells (>45%) can be fabricated by matching sections of the solar spectrum with specific absorber layers having specific bandgaps;
- crystal structure – various combinations of III–V semiconductors have similar crystal structures and ideal properties for solar cells, including long exciton diffusion lengths, carrier mobility, and compatible absorption spectra.

Production

6.39 Traditional multijunction III–V cells are assembled in an epitaxial monolithic stack with sub-cells connected in series through tunnel junctions. Constructing a multijunction cell in a monolithic stack results in material constraints, and fabricating such devices is facilitated if the individual layers of the sub-cells have compatible atomic lattice positions and are lattice matched. This advantage of lattice matching is why Ge, which is lattice matched to some III–V alloys, is traditionally used as the substrate and narrow bandgap cell in MJs. Lattice-matching limitations can be overcome with additional complexity using wafer bonding or metamorphic buffer layers.

The tunnel-junction layer is constructed by the interface of highly doped p++ and n++ layers. The interaction of these layers results in a spatially narrow space-charge region, which allows current to flow between the sub-cells. High-bandgap layers, known as window layers and back-surface fields, can be added to passivate surface states at the interface between a sub-cell and the tunnel junction which, if left unpassivated, can trap carriers and accelerate recombination.

If the sub-cells are connected in series, the sub-cell that conducts the smallest current limits the maximum current that can flow through the device. Therefore, a considerable effort is placed on tuning the current of the sub-cells. Luminescent coupling between sub-cells can relax some of the current-matching design requirements.

Multijunction III–V solar cells can be fabricated using molecular-beam epitaxy (MBE) techniques, but fabrication in large metal-organic chemical-vapour deposition (MOCVD) reactors is typical for commercial-scale production of GaInP/GaInAs/Ge devices. Layers can be grown from trimethylgallium ($Ga(CH_3)_3$), trimethylindium (InC_3H_9), arsine (AsH_3), and phosphine (PH_3) in a hydrogen carrier gas and using dopants such as hydrogen selenide (H_2Se), silane (SiH_6), and diethyl zinc ($(C_2H_5)_2Zn$). Using concentrating optics allows individual cells to be quite small – at times, as small as the size of the tip of a pencil. Therefore, these techniques allow hundreds of solar cells to be grown in single batches. Research is being done to further reduce the size of cells and increase the number of cells that can be grown from a single wafer, which will help reduce the cost per cell.

Organic

6.40 An organic photovoltaic (OPV) solar cell or plastic solar cell is a type of PV which uses organic electronics – a branch of electronics that deals with conductive organic polymers or small organic molecules for light absorption and charge transport to produce electricity from sunlight by photovoltaic effect. This technology also has the theoretical potential to provide electricity at a lower cost than first- and second-generation solar technologies. Because various absorbers can be used to create coloured or transparent OPV devices, this technology is particularly appealing to the building-integrated PV market.

Unlike most inorganic solar cells, OPV cells use molecular or polymeric absorbers, which results in a localised exciton. The absorber is used in conjunction with an electron acceptor, such as a fullerene, which has molecular orbital energy states that facilitate electron transfer. Upon absorbing a photon, the resulting exciton migrates to the interface between the absorber material and the electron acceptor material. At the interface, the energetic mismatch of the molecular orbitals provides sufficient driving force to split the exciton and create free charge carriers (an electron and a hole).

Benefits

6.41

- low-cost manufacturing – soluble organic molecules enable roll-to-roll processing techniques and allow for low-cost manufacturing;
- abundant materials – the wide abundance of building-block materials may reduce supply and price constraints;
- flexible substrates – the ability to be applied to flexible substrates permits a wide variety of uses.

Production

6.42 Small-molecule OPV cells use molecules with broad absorption in the visible and near-infrared portion of the electromagnetic spectrum. Highly conjugated systems are typically used for the electron-donating system, such as phthalocyanines, polyacenes, and squarenes. Perylene dyes and fullerenes are often used as the electron-accepting systems. These devices are most commonly generated via vacuum deposition to create bilayer and tandem architectures.

Dye-sensitised solar cells are a hybrid organic-inorganic technology that uses small-molecule absorber dyes. These dyes adsorb onto a suitable electron-accepting material, such as titanium dioxide or zinc oxide, along with an electrolyte to regenerate the dye.

FLOATING SOLAR FARMS

6.43 Floating solar farms (also known as 'floatovoltaics') are photovoltaic solar power systems created for floating on reservoirs, dams and other water bodies. Floating solar farms can generate huge amounts of electricity without using valuable land. The installation costs of floating photovoltaic panels are less than land-based photovoltaic panels. Also, research has shown that the power production of floating solar panels is greater by up to 10% due to the cooling effect of water. A recent NREL publication[6] quantifies the technical potential of floating photovoltaics (FPV) on man-made bodies of water in the United States. It also quantifies the co-benefits of placing PV on water bodies.

Besides producing clean solar power, floating solar farms can help with water management. They reduce the loss of water to evaporation as they limit air circulation and block sunlight from the surface of the water. Also, floating solar farms prevent noxious algae production, thereby lowering water treatment costs. Furthermore, the water beneath keeps solar panels clean and minimises energy waste.

Co-benefits of floating photovoltaics

Land conservation

6.44 Siting a PV system on water reduces the competition for land that could be used for other purposes. In the United States, approximately 2,141,000 hectares of potential land savings have been found to be available if PV systems are placed on water instead of on land. Florida and California have relatively large amounts of water surface area available for FPV, and the cost of land is high. FPV may help land-constrained areas better deal with competing land use pressures.

Utility costs

6.45 Like land-based PV systems, FPV can generate electricity in areas with high local utility costs.

6 'Floating Photovoltaic Systems: Assessing the Technical Potential of Photovoltaic Systems on Man-Made Water Bodies in the United States' NREL: https://pubs.acs.org/doi/10.1021/acs.est.8b04735.

Evaporation losses

6.46 FPV systems can potentially mitigate evaporation losses on human-made water bodies by shading the water. The amount of mitigated evaporation depends on the technology, water body coverage, and individual water body characteristics.

Queen Elizabeth II reservoir FPV panels[7]

6.47 A solar farm the size of eight football pitches has been built in south-east England but, rather than occupying the equivalent on land, the project has been floated out onto the water. There are more than 23,000 solar panels, sitting on the Queen Elizabeth II reservoir near Walton-on-Thames in Surrey. Thames Water, which owns the QEII reservoir, has estimated that the 6.3MW of energy produced by the floating farm will assist their operations and can power the equivalent of around 1,800 homes per year. The energy will be used to power local treatment plants, ensuring that the region has clean water.

Hyde, Greater Manchester

6.48 A floating solar plant with 12,000 panels is installed at Hyde in Greater Manchester (UK) on the town's Godley reservoir. The development, which covers an area of 45,500 square metres, required an investment of £3.5 million by United Utilities to reduce energy costs. The project will provide United Utilities with 2.7GWh per year of renewable, zero-carbon power to be used directly by the site. The scheme is part of United Utilities' ongoing carbon reduction strategy.

Yamakura Plant, Japan

6.49 The world's first floating solar plant was built in Japan, in Aichi Prefecture in central Honshu. The country has many inland lakes and reservoirs that are now home to many of the world's 100 largest floating solar plants and account for half of those plants' 246MW of solar capacity. Hyogo Prefecture in southern Honshu has almost 40,000 lakes and already hosts nearly half the floating solar capacity of the world's 100 largest plants. Floating solar is particularly well suited to Asia, where land is scarce but there are many hydroelectric dams with existing transmission infrastructure. China has just connected the world's biggest floating solar plant at Anhui, which will generate almost 78,000MW in its first year, enough to power 21,000 homes.

7 https://corporate.thameswater.co.uk/media/News-releases/Thames-Water-rewarded-for-its-commitment-to-sustainability.

Yellow Tropus – submerged FPV solution

6.50 When absorbing energy, solar panels are exposed to overheating; using submerged PV modules allows the implementation of a natural cooling mechanism by generating a water layer which results in increased power output for submerged photovoltaic solar panels (SP2s). The main reasons leading to an increase in efficiency are the reduction of light reflection and the absence of thermal drift.

Indian start-up Yellow Tropus builds submerged FPV power plants with a fixed tilt to maximize cost-effectiveness and space efficiencies. This technology delivers high energy density and requires no on-site construction. The submerged FPV power plant applies aerodynamic designs with enhanced air circulation that facilitates natural evaporative cooling.

Ocean Sun – flexible FPV solution

6.51 Norwegian start-up Ocean Sun introduced an efficient, low-cost and durable solution for floating solar power generation. Its technology is based on modified silicon solar modules which are deployed on flexible floating structures. Using a proprietary non-permeable membrane, floater units are based on utility-type, dual-glass, silicon crystalline modules. Moreover, the modules are securely attached to the membrane using a unique fixation mechanism. As a result, this enables improved thermal contact with the waterbody. Additionally, the start-up offers a customised junction box, cables and attachment features.

Ciel & Terre – tracking-based FPV solution

6.52 Land-based PV plants can lead to energy waste and involve complex mechanical apparatus. Floating platforms equipped with tracking systems allow for vertical axis tracking of solar cells, enabling constant exposure to sunlight. The resultant technology allows for producing a greater amount of electricity by adding a real-time sun-tracking function to the PV module.

French company Ciel & Terre designs and builds floating solar micro-grid platforms that collect, store and redistribute renewable energy. The water-based PV concept *HYDRELIO* mixes hydro and solar power sources to save hydropower for intermittent times when energy demand is high. Also, these floating solar power generation systems are capable of tracking the movement of the sun to enhance the energy generation process and storage.

O'MEGA1, Rhone Valley, Southern France

6.53 The O'MEGA1 project is a 17MW solar plant situated in Piolenc, a commune in the Vaucluse department, near Orange and Avignon. The project is unique in several ways, and is the largest in Europe based on floating solar technology. The floating structure helps reduce conflicts over land use, because it can be installed on drinking water reservoirs, industrial pools, flood plains or quarry lakes, and the solar plant also innovates in its local community dimension, with citizens invited to take a stake in the project. Marking a first in France, the plant's capital was opened to physical people who have a home in the Vaucluse or in neighbouring départments. Akuo Energy teamed up with an independent electricity supplier, Plüm Energie, to develop a 'green electricity of controlled origin' label, which will be the first of its kind in France. Works on the O'MEGA1 project started in 2014, on the site of an old quarry that was converted into a lake. According to its promoters, the plant's annual output will be sufficient to power 4,733 homes, avoiding the emission of 1,096 tons of carbon dioxide into the atmosphere. This is very small compared to the 1,500MW of an offshore wind farm such as Hywind in Scotland, which can power up to 1 million homes. However, it is expected that similar projects could be given the green light in the coming years. In France, the potential of floating solar is estimated at 20GW, spread over a potential 1,300 sites – mainly old industrial areas, hydropower dams and water reservoirs.

HelioRec – hydropower-connected solar PV systems

6.54 Compared to traditional solar power generation, hydropower-connected floating solar systems maximise resource utilisation by combining two powerful renewable energy sources. This enables the generation of more energy, increasing economic benefits, and also solves environmental issues. Coupling photovoltaics with the hydropower system results in effective solar energy generation while the reservoir stores up water. This stored energy is released during peak demand to sustain the constant supply of renewable power.

French start-up HelioRec performs complex hydropower-connected end-to-end solar projects, and its design solutions allow it to lower the carbon footprint and produce a rapid-to-deploy and cost-effective source of power generation. The company uses recycled plastic to manufacture hybrid hydropower floating solar power plants.

Chapter 7

Geothermal Energy

INTRODUCTION

7.1 This is energy which is derived from heat within the earth. Water and/or steam carry the geothermal energy to the earth's surface, and geothermal power plants then use the energy from within the earth to generate steam to make electricity. Geothermal pumps trap heat close to the earth's surface to provide heat for buildings. The ancient Romans used hot springs to heat their homes, bathe and cook. In 1892 the first district heating system was developed in Boise, Idaho. The first geothermal energy plant was built in Italy in 1904. Geothermal energy is used in France, Turkey, New Zealand and the US and Japan. Iceland is one of the largest users of geothermal energy, with water pumped from hot springs. Almost the whole of the city of Reykjavik is heated with water pumped in from hot springs and thermal wells. In 1904, Italian scientist Piero Ginori Conti invented the first geothermal electric power plant in which steam was used to generate the power.

With the above experiment, the first geothermal plant in USA started in 1922, with a capacity of 250kW. It produced little output and, due to a technical glitch, had to be shut down. However, in 1946 the first ground-source geothermal heat pump was installed at Commonwealth Building in Portland, Oregon. During the 1960s, Pacific Gas and Electric began the operation of the first large-scale geothermal power plant in San Francisco, producing 11MW.

In 1973, when the oil crisis began, many countries started looking for renewable energy sources and. by the 1980s, geothermal heat pumps (GHPs) started gaining popularity in order to reduce heating and cooling costs.

Types of geothermal energy

Solar geothermal

7.2 Geothermal energy is stored at relatively shallow depths of around 10 metres below the surface. The ground beneath your feet is constantly absorbing latent heat from solar energy. This means that this stored warmth is right there for the taking year-round and at relatively accessible depths.

When you reach 15 metres below the surface, the ground temperature is largely unaffected by what happens in the world above, provided the ground itself remains undisturbed. Since temperature remains constant at this depth, the difference between underground and above-ground temperatures can be effectively used for heating purposes.

Water geothermal

7.3 While not present in the UK, there are bodies of water below the surface, in the vicinity of recent volcanoes in other parts of the world, that can reach temperatures of 200°C, effectively doubling water's above-ground boiling point. Also, depending on geological formations, volcanic water reservoirs can also be under pressure, which further enhances their heat-storing properties. These liquid-dominated reservoirs (LDRs) don't require pumps to circulate the water in either steam or liquid form. Deep wells can be dug and the steam can then circulate through strategically placed turbines, generating electricity, before cooling back into a liquid and repeating the cycle.

Groundwater doesn't need to be at boiling point to be useful in terms of sustainable energy generation. Water reserves with lower temperatures, ranging anywhere between 30 and 100°C, can be a source of energy. Whilst powering turbines to make electricity may not be possible at lower temperatures, warm groundwater reservoirs can still be used to power community or district heating projects.

While district heating is not very widespread in the UK, geothermal energy could provide an alternative to costly and unreliable boiler-based heating and hot water systems.

Deep geothermal and hot rocks

7.4 The UK has sizeable granite deposits that actually run hotter than surrounding earth layers due to their unique mineral properties. As a result, these rocks can act as heaters or heat exchangers. It is possible to drill into these deposits in order to pump water into them, creating a viable steam circuit in the process. The granite can heat the water at such high temperatures that it can be used to drive a turbine which, in turn, generates electricity. Cornwall is specifically suited to this type of large-scale geothermal energy project because of its significant granite deposits.

GEOTHERMAL TECHNOLOGY

Direct geothermal energy

7.5 In areas of the world where there are hot springs or geothermal reservoirs near the earth's surface, hot water can be piped directly into buildings. The geothermal water can be pumped through a heat exchanger, where the heat is transferred from the water to the building heating system and the used water can be returned down the well to be used again.

Geothermal power plants

7.6 This is where hot water and steam from deep underground can be piped up through an underground well and used to generate electricity in a power plant. There are three types of geothermal power plant.

Dry steam plants

7.7 This is where hot steam is piped directly from the geothermal reservoirs into generators in the power plant and the steam turns turbines which then generate electricity.

Flash steam turbines

7.8 This is where the water is between 148 and 371°C when it is brought up through the well. Some water will turn to steam, which drives the turbines to generate electricity and, when the steam condenses back to water, it is returned back to the ground.

Binary cycle plants

7.9 This is where hot geothermal waste is passed through a heat exchanger and the heat is transferred to a liquid (such as isobutane) that boils at a lower temperature than water. When that fluid is heated, it is returned to steam which is then used to turn turbines to generate electricity.

Geothermal heat pumps

7.10 This is where, a few feet under the ground, the soil or water remain at a constant 10–15°C each year. That warmth can be used via a series of pipes underground where fluid circulates. An electrical compressor and heat exchanger pull the heat from the pipes and send it via a duct system throughout a building. In summer the process is reversed, and the heat is then taken away from the building and carried to the ground outside where it is absorbed.

There are several different types of heat pump.

Air-source heat pumps

7.11 An air-source heat pump on a domestic house looks similar to an air conditioning unit. It takes its heat from ambient air using a fan to pass air into a heat exchanger to extract the heat and evaporate the refrigerant inside the heat pump.

Ground-source heat pumps

7.12 Ground-source heat pumps benefit from the steadier and warmer temperatures available from the ground compared to ambient air. They use boreholes or buried coils of tubing to extract the heat, and this is piped back to the heat pump.

Water-source heat pumps

7.13 Water-source and ground-source heat pumps are physically the same, but with a different heat source. Water-source heat pumps use a static or flowing water source as the heat source (for example, a river, canal or lake, or a well) and the sea can also be used. The amount of heat that can be extracted from water is much higher than from the ground and, in the case of flowing water, there is no risk of depleting the source of heat because it is being continuously replenished. There are 'open-loop' water-source heat pumps, where the water passes through an evaporator heat exchanger inside the heat pump, but there is a risk of a blockage when debris is present in the water. 'Closed-loop' water-source heat pumps overcome the risk of blocking, using a heat exchanger in the water body to transfer the heat via a 'transfer fluid' to the heat exchanger inside the heat pump.

The downside of a water-source heat pump is the added complexity of extracting heat from water and dealing with water-borne debris, plus the stricter regulatory controls that are applied to the surface waters in the UK.

Water-source heat pump site

Water source

7.14 The water to be heated should be close to, and be able to access, a running stream or river, or a canal or lake, or possibly a well or the sea. Running water is preferable, because the cooler water discharged from the heat pump is washed downstream and replaced by warmer water, whereas static water bodies tend to cool down (or heat up if the heat pump is cooling rather than heating). For industrial sites, process water can be a source of waste heat, and the relatively high temperatures will improve the heat pump efficiency.

Static water bodies can still be used, provided they are large enough. Where a well is used which is an existing borehole, there would be an abstraction borehole (the well) and a second discharge borehole would be needed, typically 10 metres away. The discharge could be a soakaway.

The sea can also be used, but a long abstraction and discharge pipe is normally needed, and this has associated pumping losses, plus the pipework must be protected against extreme storm conditions, and all of the components protected against corrosion from the salty water.

Heat load

7.15 Heat load is a calculation that identifies both the heat gain and the heat loss.

GEOTHERMAL POWER – UK

7.16 There is no deep geothermal power generation within the UK. The potential was looked at following the 1973 oil crisis. Some areas of the UK were identified but interest was lost when the petroleum prices fell. A study was carried out into deep geothermal potential by the Department for Energy & Climate Change[1]. The report covered not only a review of deep geothermal studies but also an assessment of the feasibility of geothermal power production, a review of the costs and return, the potential for technology innovation, and concluded with the possibility of next steps. Even though the UK is not actively volcanic, there is a potential for the use of shallow geothermal ground-source heat pumps.

Solar (shallow geothermal) energy

7.17 This is, technically, solar energy where the upper 10 to 15 metres of ground is heated by solar radiation. The heat can be used via ground-source heat pumps that can reduce heating bills and the associated carbon footprint.

Aquifer-based scheme

7.18 The groundwater in the UK has the potential to provide resources at depths between 1 and 3 km. Since 1979 the principle interests have been

1 Deep Geothermal Review Study Final report, DECC: https://assets.publishing.service.gov.uk/government/uploads/system/uploads/attachment_data/file/251943/Deep_Geothermal_Review_Study_Final_Report_Final.pdf.

those in East Yorkshire and Lincolnshire, Wessex, Worcester, Cheshire, West Lancashire, Carlisle and the basin of Northern Ireland.

UK schemes

Southampton District heating scheme

7.19 In the 1980s the Department of Energy looked at whether the potential of geothermal aquifers in the UK was viable. After some drilling in the Wessex basin in 1981, the project was deemed to be too small to be economically viable and the project was abandoned by the Department of Energy. Southampton City Council disagreed and took the decision to create the UK's first geothermal power scheme. The scheme was eventually developed in combination with a French-owned company, COFELY District Energy, and the Southampton Geothermal Heating Company, ENGIE, took control of Cofely BESIX Facility Management (CBFM).

Construction of the well to draw water was started in 1986 to a depth of 1,800 metres.

The scheme now heats a number of buildings, including the Southampton Civic Centre, West Quay Shopping Centre, Solent University, Carnival Office and the Royal South Hants Hospital.

As of 2011 the district heating and cooling scheme provides annually 26GWh of electricity and over 40GWh of heat. Brine from the geothermal well provided 18% of the total district heating mix, with fuel oil (10%) and natural gas (70%) making up the rest. The electricity generated from the scheme is used by Associated British Ports via a private electrical connection to the Port of Southampton, with any surplus electricity sold back to the grid.

Stoke-on-Trent

7.20 The district heat network being built in Stoke-on-Trent will offer alternative energy for businesses and residents. The district heat network is being delivered by Stoke-on-Trent City Council and will harness heat from sources including deep geothermal energy and energy from waste, which will be transferred through a system of heat exchangers into the network. Heat energy will be supplied to larger commercial and public sector premises across the city at first and, over time, the aim is to connect to a wider variety of properties including blocks of flats and clusters of houses across the city. The scheme won multi-million-pound investment through the government's City Deal that was secured by the Stoke-on-Trent and Staffordshire Local Enterprise Partnership in 2014.

North Sea

7.21 Another area with potential for geothermal energy is in the North Sea[2], on the continental shelf where the Earth's crust is thin (less than 10

2 'Geothermal power: an alternate role for redundant North Sea platforms?': www.offshore-mag.com/pipelines/article/16762144/geothermal-power-an-alternate-role-for-redundant-north-sea-platforms.

km). A 1986 work on this was undertaken by Total Energy Conservation and Management Co Ltd. An overview document was produced called 'Single Borehole Geothermal Energy Extraction System for Electrical Power Generation'. The proposal is to use the UK North Sea oil platforms, converted to run on geothermal energy, to provide power to offshore field facilities or feeding power markets in Europe via trans-North Sea interconnector grids.

Hot rock schemes

7.22 The average geothermal gradient in the UK is 26°C per km depth. The granite regions of South West England, the Lake District and Weardale and the Eastern Highlands of Scotland are considered most likely to have the best prospects for power generation. In addition to using geothermally heated aquifers, hot dry rock geothermal technology can be used to heat water pumped below ground onto geothermally heated rock. Starting in 1977, trials of the technology were undertaken at Rosemanowes Quarry, near Penryn, Cornwall.

Heat-only projects are generally considered to have the greatest potential in the UK, because the resource is more widespread and shallower. This includes the hot aquifers (ie subterranean bodies of water) in the North East, Wessex, Cheshire and Northern Ireland. The UK's only existing geothermal heat-generating station (heat only) is at Southampton, where an 1,800-metre borehole taps into the edge of the aquifer under Wessex and provides heat to the Southampton District heat network. The borehole is being refurbished.

Eden Project

7.23 The Eden Project[3] plans to drill 4.5 km into a fault line within the granites. The aim is to sink two wells: one will provide heat for the project itself, and the other will provide power. The well is drilled over 4 km deep where the rock temperature is up to 190°C. Water injected down the well will be returned to the surface at closer to 175°C.

The £16.8m investment has been secured from a mixture of public and private sources. Cornwall's final round of EU funding, the European Regional Development Fund (ERDF), has contributed £9.9m. Cornwall Council has put in £1.4m. Institutional investors have contributed the remaining £5.5m. The EU (ERDF) funding is administered by the UK Government's Ministry for Housing, Communities and Local Government. The £16.8m will pay for the first phase of the project – drilling one well, a research programme and a heat main, to prove the extent of the resource 4.5 km down in the granite that lies beneath the Eden site. This first well will initially supply a district heating system for Eden's Biomes, offices and greenhouses. It will pave the way for the second phase – another 4.5 km well and an electricity plant.

3 Eden Geothermal Energy Project: www.edenproject.com/eden-story/behind-the-scenes/eden-geothermal-energy-project.

Completing the second phase will mean that Eden will be generating sufficient renewable energy to become carbon positive by 2023, as well as aiming to be able to provide heat and power for the local area.

GEOTHERMAL RESOURCES IN THE UK

Ground-source heat pumps

7.24 In the UK, there is a resource of geothermal energy at shallow depths which can be exploited with ground-source heat pumps (GSHPs). This system uses pipes which are buried to extract heat from the ground. The upper 10–15 metres of the ground is heated by solar radiation and acts as a heat store.

This heat can then be used to heat radiators, underfloor or warm air heating systems and hot water in homes. Ground-source heat pumps are supported by the Government's Renewable Heat Incentive (RHI) scheme, which provides payments for consumers who install and use renewable heating technologies. At the end of April 2018, a total of 9,107 applications for domestic ground-source heat pumps had been accredited under either the RHI or its predecessor scheme. In addition, 887 non-domestic water- or ground-source heat pumps had been accredited to April 2018.

Deep geothermal plants

7.25 With increasing depth, the ground temperatures are no longer affected by the sun and are instead warmed by heat from the earth's core. The UK has no active volcanoes, but it does have several geological features that have potential for geothermal energy.

WHO OWNS GEOTHERMAL HEAT?

7.26 Geothermal heat has the potential to make a contribution to UK's targets set out in the Climate Change Act 2008. It is a resource that needs to be managed and regulated in a similar way to other natural resources such as oil and gas, coal and water. A key challenge to the ownership and regulation of geothermal heat is that it is regarded as a physical property, not a recoverable (raw) material such as ore or gravel. It is not a legally defined entity and so it causes difficulties when assigning legal ownership and regulating it. The rise in exploration of geothermal resources has seen countries expand national legislation with the aim of protecting against environmental damage. The regulations define rules around the development and exploration process rather than managing the resource.

This requires that technology users, companies and financiers have some safeguards for their financial commitment, and that an authority is available that can issue exploration and development licences for geothermal heat that will, in law, guarantee and protect the licensee's exclusive right to develop, exploit and profit from a geothermal resource, for a specified period, ie:

- protection and management of the geothermal resource and its long-term sustainability;
- protection of the geothermal user/licensee from other external parties depleting or damaging the geothermal resource available within their property/ licence area;
- a change to UK law is needed so that it better defines heat, and thereby allows implementation of such regulations. Currently, heat is not dealt with in UK law, except as a pollutant, ie where it has a detrimental impact on the environment. Such cases are covered by the EU Water Framework Directive and UK groundwater regulations. The detrimental impact of geothermal schemes on other users (eg neighbouring schemes) is covered by 'private nuisance', ie they are a civil issue, which cannot be regulated as described here;
- early development risks are one of the main reasons why so few geothermal energy projects have been implemented in the UK to date. According to Bader and Bauer (2017), the renaissance of geothermal in Germany is due not only to a stable regulatory framework, but also to the increasing ability to insure the associated economic risks. In Germany, insurance is offered by private insurers, but in the Netherlands and France it is funded by the state. Private insurers will only be attracted if the legal issues are resolved, and regulations and codes of practice are in place (as in Germany);
- securing long-term contracts for the supply of heat to consumers is the most important factor for a project to be economically viable. Where the prospect of a reliable, long-term customer base is damaged, or where energy prices are undercut by government subsidy, the projects quickly become economically unviable, causing investors to pull out, even at an advanced stage of project development.

CURRENT REGULATORY APPROACHES

7.27 Geothermal applications can be classified and regulated based on the depths of the sources (eg shallow or deep) and the technology used for extracting heat from the ground.

Shallow geothermal open-loop ground-source heat pump (GSHP) systems pump (abstract) groundwater and return (discharge) the water back to the ground after it has been used for heating or cooling. They fall under environmental permitting and groundwater regulations, as defined by the Water Framework Directive, in EU countries, and equivalent protection rules elsewhere. While these regulations usually include limits on the permitted return water temperatures (eg in the UK, it is (Tinlet – Toutlet) < ±8°C , Toutlet = 25°C), only a few countries require an assessment of the overall thermal impact of heat extraction on groundwater temperatures. Here, numerical modelling is required to predict changes in groundwater temperatures.

In the UK, the regulatory control of abstraction and discharges, required for open-loop GSHP systems, is solely aimed at protecting groundwater, not regulating heat (due to the legal issues mentioned earlier) or guaranteeing that the abstracted water is suitable for its intended use. The success of the design and operation of the GSHP system, and its impacts on the efficiency of other systems, is therefore the applicant's responsibility. Shallow geothermal closed-loop GSHP systems extract heat from the ground by circulating a heat exchanger fluid through buried pipes installed in trenches or boreholes. Regulations around these systems are very varied between different countries, including:

- no regulations (systems do not require any permits or registration);
- notification schemes (no permits but need to be registered/reported to authorities); and
- permitting schemes (systems require relevant permits).

In the UK, installation and operation of these systems do not require any environmental permits, consents or licences, or registration of the system, even though these systems can have considerable impact on heat availability and temperature distributions within the subsurface, specifically where groundwater flow is present, and the possibility exists that they may interfere with each other.

System interference is also a concern for open-loop systems, especially in city environments.

DEEP GEOTHERMAL

7.28 In most countries, legal procedures governing the subsurface exist and enable the development of deep geothermal resources, although they are not always tailored to geothermal energy. It usually involves a two-stage permitting process, consisting of an exploration permit to find geothermal resources, followed by a development licence or concession to exploit the geothermal resource. The extraction of heat from deep geothermal sources also involves, in most cases, the use of water, either groundwater available within the deep rocks (hydrothermal systems) or water injected from the surface (petrothermal systems or enhanced geothermal systems – EGS). Hence, in the UK, the same requirements for environmental permissions and licences from the Environment Agency apply as for the open-loop, shallow geothermal systems. However, as for shallower open-loop systems, 'an abstraction licence protects the water quantity, not heat (and) the Environment Agency is not liable for any loss of heat if a new scheme takes heat away from an existing scheme'.

REGULATION OF GEOTHERMAL HEAT IN THE UK

7.29 Heat, although not a 'substance' in the physical sense, behaves in many ways like water, but this requires a legal definition of heat, not only in the UK but EU-wide, to provide a basis for regulations. Therefore, including a definition of heat in UK law, and in the 2019 revision of the Water Framework Directive, would enable effective regulation of heat in the UK and EU-wide.

This will also require detailed resources assessments as well as the development of predictive resource management tools for geothermal heat. This would require heat being legally defined as a natural resource and would enable more integrated management of heat in the wider context, eg in the subsurface of cities where management of different heat sources may become necessary in order to avoid inefficiencies or conflict.

For shallow geothermal regulation in the UK, this could be based on a regulation model for closed-loop systems similar to that of the city of Zurich, which operates a permitting system. It considers the planned heat extraction and size of the proposed scheme, as well as the underlying geology, in its permitting procedure and imposes restrictions in areas where a high risk of interference or overexploitation has been identified.

DEEP GEOTHERMAL ENERGY REGULATION

Conventional geothermal

7.30 A conventional scheme uses the energy of deep underground sources of hot water by pumping the hot water out of a borehole. The used water can be discharged back to the ground or to surface water. To operate a conventional scheme, the following is needed from the Environment Agency:

- a groundwater investigation consent (GIC);
- an abstraction licence if more than 20 cubic metres of water a day is abstracted; and
- an environmental permit where there are discharges to ground or surface water.

An abstraction licence protects the water quantity, not heat. The Environment Agency is not liable for any loss of heat if a new scheme takes heat away from an existing scheme.

Before an application is made for an abstraction licence, a GIC will normally have to be obtained and its conditions met. This usually includes carrying out a pumping test. Any licence issued will have a time limit of up to 12 (or, in some cases, 24) years, and a 'self-destruct' condition in any abstraction licence for deep geothermal schemes – so, if no work commences within the self-destruct period, the licence ceases to have effect.

Pumping tests

7.31 Where the source of water is very deep underground (for example, more than 1 km), and there are no other deep geothermal schemes in that aquifer that may be affected, the Environment Agency may not require a pumping test. In these circumstances, it may be satisfied with a desk study and conceptual model of the system, as the abstraction is less likely to cause environmental harm. This means that an abstraction licence before drilling a borehole could be obtained, provided it can be demonstrated that there is a reasonable requirement for water, the abstraction will be sustainable, and it will not affect other legitimate water interests or features. As a condition of the abstraction licence, it is likely there will be a need to undertake a pumping test and provide the Environment Agency with a refined conceptual model, taking account of the pumping test results once drilling is completed.

Subsequent applications from the same deep aquifer

7.32 The Environment Agency is likely to require a pumping test as part of the GIC for subsequent applications before granting an abstraction licence. This is because it would need to determine that the proposed abstraction would not affect existing licensed abstractors or other protected rights.

PLANNING ADVICE: SCOTLAND[4]

7.33 Recent geothermal energy activity in the UK has been at modest depths of less than 2 km, including several schemes using mine waters (two in Scotland, at Shettleston, Glasgow and Lumphinnans, Fife) and a hot sedimentary aquifer (HSA) plant in Southampton.

Shettleston, Glasgow

7.34 This open-loop ground-source heat scheme was completed in 1999 and serves 16 new-build dwellings (two-storey houses and two-/three-storey flats). The system is heating based on mine water from flooded coal mine workings in the Glasgow Ell Seam beneath the site. The heat is abstracted via a borehole approximately 100 metres deep. Mine water at 12°C is circulated through a water-to-water heat pump, heating water to 55°C which is output to an insulated thermal storage tank of $10m^3$ volume. The hot water in the tank is supplemented by a side loop to $36m^2$ of solar collector panels which provides additional energy gain to the thermal tank, mostly in the afternoon. From the thermal store, water is distributed to hot water central heating radiators and through closed exchanger coils to domestic hot water storage cylinders (which are fitted with electric immersion heaters to further boost water temperature if necessary). Waste water from the system is discharged below the water table via a shallower re-injection borehole, at 3°C.

Lumphinnans, Fife

7.35 This open-loop ground-source heat scheme was retro-fitted to a 1950s apartment block of 18 dwellings and completed in 2000/01. Mine water is pumped from flooded coal mine workings in the Jersey / Diamond seam beneath the site via a 172-metre deep borehole. The temperature of the pumped mine water is variously reported as 12°C or 14.5°C. It is circulated through a water-to-water heat pump, heating water to 55°C which is output to a thermal storage tank. This feeds domestic hot water (which also includes supplementary immersion heaters) and central heating systems. Waste water at 3°C is returned to a permeable stratum above the flooded workings from which water is abstracted, via a shallower re-injection borehole some 100 metres away from the abstraction borehole.

4 'Deep geothermal: planning advice': www.gov.scot/publications/deep-geothermal-planning-advice/.

Suggested areas of focus for planning authorities

7.36

- Collate information on redundant mines and existing geological data, draw on available geological expertise, and work with academic institutes to help predict scope for deep geothermal within area.
- Use heat maps to identify main opportunities for developing heat networks/ providing off-gas grid heat/combating fuel poverty.
- Consider land use opportunities (including regeneration of brownfield sites) and constraints to help indicate where deep geothermal might be located.
- Detail criteria to be applied in assessing deep geothermal applications.
- Establish protocol and key consultees for involvement in spatial planning, policy making, pre-application work and applications for deep geothermal operations.
- Identify proportionate levels of information to service pre-application discussions and to assess applications on deep geothermal.
- Ensure that planning conditions and agreements for deep geothermal operations are reasonable and proportionate.

Opportunities within planning processes for planning authorities

Stage in planning process: monitoring and evidence base and main issues report (MIR)

7.37 Actions for deep geothermal:

- gather existing information on redundant mines;
- draw on available geological expertise, including academic institutes;
- build a database to provide a starting point for assessing potential for the various types of deep geothermal operations;
- consider potential economic and environmental opportunities, alongside potential impacts and constraints;
- involve key consultees for deep geothermal such as the British Geological Survey, Scottish Environment Protection Agency (SEPA) and Scottish Natural Heritage (SNH); and
- if further data becomes available, through developer assessment, determine if deep geothermal possibilities merit consideration as a main issue in the MIR.

Stage in planning process: spatial planning

7.38 Recognise that securing sufficient data to predict the potential for hot dry rock geothermal operations is likely to be outside the scope of planning authorities, but this may come forward via other sources.

Actions for deep geothermal:

- incorporate deep geothermal information in spatial planning exercises, where possible, to maximise opportunities for renewable heat;

- assess scope for using existing brownfield or industrial sites or former collieries;
- determine whether operations can be located near to facilities or areas of high heat demand or if there is a need for, or scope for, heat mains; and
- secure input from key consultees on opportunities and possible impacts.

Stage in planning process: drafting development plan policy

7.39 Actions for deep geothermal:

- ensure that policies for deep geothermal cover:
  - the potential different scales and types of deep geothermal operations; and
  - design of plant and supporting infrastructure, drilling, reservoir stimulation, pollution control, amenity issues, decommissioning; and
- engage key consultees at an early stage on the drafting of deep geothermal policies.

Stage in planning process: securing sufficient information to determine planning applications

7.40 Actions for deep geothermal:

- develop supporting guidance notes to detail typical information needs for pre-application discussion and planning applications for deep geothermal proposals;
- ensure that information needs are proportionate;
- ensure that design statements are submitted for major deep geothermal applications generating over 20MW of electricity.

Stage in planning process: pre-application stage

7.41 Actions for deep geothermal:

- ensure that key consultees are given the opportunity to be involved in pre-application meetings/site visits; and
- ensure that early advice is given on potential pre-application consultation procedures for major applications and Environmental Impact Assessment (EIA) requirements.

Stage in planning process: determining planning applications

7.42 Actions for deep geothermal:

- for major applications, ensure that developers maximise opportunities to involve communities in formal pre-application consultation procedures, where appropriate, to overcome concerns regarding noise from drilling, seismic activity and subsidence;

- ensure that key consultees are involved in meetings and site visits to help overcome constraints; and
- technical information and typical planning considerations for deep geothermal are provided below, which planning authorities should draw upon in determining applications.

Technical information for deep geothermal

Definition

7.43 For the purposes of this, deep geothermal includes any geothermal energy source below 100 metres in depth. This will include mine waters, aquifer sources (HSA) and HDR enhanced (or engineered) geothermal systems (EGS). This is distinct from ground source heat which provides low-temperature heat found at relatively shallow depths within the earth's crust, derived from solar warming.

Basic process

7.44 Deep geothermal operations involve tapping into a heat source stored naturally below the earth's surface. There are various types of geothermal resource. Works can involve recovering hot waters from mines (circa 50 to 1,000m depth, < 40°C), or from water enclosed within permeable rocks known as hot sedimentary aquifers (HSAs). In the case of EGS, water is injected to depths of around 4 to 5 km where it can be heated by suitable hot rocks to temperatures > 150°C. Water or steam is then recaptured through another borehole and returned to the surface to produce renewable heat or drive steam turbines to produce renewable electricity. This technique is being developed in several countries and on a large scale in the Cooper Basin (Innamincka) HDR project, South Australia.

Suitable locations

7.45 Former mining areas may have suitable thermal mine water resources. Elsewhere, determining suitable locations will usually involve geological, geochemical and geophysical surveys and borehole testing, as the distribution of heat sources will vary geographically. For EGS this will be governed by the availability of suitable hot rocks at accessible depth, which will invariably involve tapping into large bodies of granite 'plutons', where radiothermal processes generate useful heat. Scotland has abundant granite resources, especially in the Highlands, although further scientific testing is required to assess actual potential for EGS. There is also scope for directional (diagonal) drilling, which means that ground-level plant may be located at a significant distance away from the underground geothermal resource.

Physical works

7.46 The testing phase for the geothermal plant is likely to comprise water and diesel storage tanks, drilling rig and mast (50 metres in the recent

Cornwall case). Globally, there are several types of geothermal power plants in use and these vary in terms of physical ground works, depending on the depth, temperature and pressure of the geothermal energy source. The facilities would be expected to have connection to the grid. The greatest efficiencies are normally achieved if operations are sited close to facilities or areas of heat demand, but heat mains can transport heat over some distance.

Attributes

7.47 The waters recovered from geothermal aquifers at depths of 2 to 3 km, where temperatures are close to 100°C, are particularly suitable for district and industrial heating applications. Geothermal energy generally is well suited to producing renewable heat and has the potential advantage over other renewable energy technologies of supporting baseload power generation without being reliant on weather conditions. Geothermal power plants can also be used for cooling.

Typical planning considerations in determining planning applications for deep geothermal

Exploratory works

7.48 It is possible that several planning applications may be required to finalise the nature of deep geothermal operations. Initial boreholes are unlikely to determine the full potential of the geothermal resource, and later testing phases are normally required to clarify the full extent of the resource. This could unavoidably affect the design of the plant and supporting infrastructure. Planning authorities are therefore encouraged to work with applicants to ensure that, where possible, flexible arrangements are built into initial project designs.

Noise

7.49 Highly specialised drill rigs have been developed for drilling geothermal wells in urban areas close to dwellings, and techniques on dampening drilling noise are continually developing. In some cases, drilling operations may determine that works are not appropriate in close proximity to sensitive receptors; however, in other cases, the long-term energy benefits of drilling may outweigh short-term disturbance. A detailed noise impact assessment would be required from the applicant, to inform the planning assessment.

Subsidence

7.50 Within some volcanic regions, if extraction of geothermal fluid is too rapid, surface rocks may subside into the underlying reservoir. However, this is not likely with deep reservoirs in Scotland.

Waterway pollution

7.51 Geothermal fluid has the potential to pollute and may be toxic to aquatic life. Wastewater needs to be treated before discharge into water courses. This requirement is removed if a closed-loop system using heat exchangers is adopted, allowing fluid to be returned in a continuous system to the reservoir.

Seismic activity

7.52 EGS involves a technique known as reservoir stimulation, which is a process of fracturing rocks by injecting fluids under exceptionally high pressures. In some countries, this has been known to lead to earthquakes large enough to be felt by residents. However, this is less likely in Scotland as it is situated well away from the edge of any tectonic plate and is seismically relatively inactive. Additionally, reservoir stimulation techniques are improving.

Other planning considerations

7.53 Depending on site location, and the scale and nature of the proposal, planning authorities would be expected to consider landscape and visual impact of the temporary testing works and power plant, together with other matters relating to transport, hydrology, ecology and decommissioning.

Hot dry rock geothermal

7.54 These are schemes where water (from elsewhere) is injected into fractured hot dry rocks, allowed to heat up, and then taken out of another borehole. The steam or hot water produced can run turbines to generate electricity. If the schemes takes more than 20 cubic metres of water a day from an inland water or borehole to inject into the ground, the following are needed:

- a GIC; and
- an abstraction licence.

In some schemes, no annual charge will apply if the purpose of the scheme is to generate less than 5MW of power.

A GIC or licence is not needed to abstract heated water from a hot dry rock scheme if it is to be injected into an artificially created chamber within the underground strata.

In these cases, no natural groundwater is present or affected by the process.

Operator's role and liability

7.55 If a scheme unintentionally discharges pollutants to groundwater, the Environment Agency may serve a notice to require a permit or prevent this activity.

There is a possibility that deep geothermal abstractions could cause subsidence or have other impacts on property. It is the developer's responsibility to assess these and recognise their liabilities for loss or damage to third parties' property.

ADVANTAGES AND DISADVANTAGES OF GEOTHERMAL ENERGY

Advantages

7.56

- more environmentally friendly than many conventional fuel sources such as coal and other fossil fuels; also the carbon footprint of geothermal power is low;
- geothermal energy is a source of renewable energy and the hot reserves within the earth are naturally replenished;
- there is the potential to exploit geothermal resources. It has been estimated that geothermal power plants could provide between 0.0035 and 2TW of power;
- geothermal energy provides a reliable source of energy compared to other renewable resources such as wind and solar, as the resource is always available to be tapped into;
- to use geothermal for electricity generation requires water temperatures of over 150°C to drive turbines; also, temperature difference between the surface and a ground source can be used. Due to the ground being more resistant to seasonal heat changes than the air, it can act as a heat sink/source with a geothermal heat pump just two metres below the surface; and
- since geothermal energy is a naturally occurring resource, there is no fuel required, such as with fossil fuels that are a finite resource which needs mining or otherwise extracting from the earth.

Disadvantages

7.57

- environmental – there are greenhouse gases below the surface of the earth, some of which mitigates towards the surface and into the atmosphere. These emissions tend to be higher near geothermal power plants. Geothermal power plants are associated with sulphur dioxide and silica emissions, and the reservoirs can contain traces of toxic heavy metals including mercury, arsenic and boron;
- surface instability (earthquakes) – construction of geothermal power plants can affect the stability of land. In fact, geothermal power plants have led to subsidence (motion of the earth's surface) in both Germany and New Zealand. Earthquakes can be triggered due to hydraulic fracturing, which is a part of developing enhanced geothermal system (EGS) power plants. In January 1997, the construction of a geothermal power plant in Switzerland triggered an earthquake with a magnitude of 3.4 on the Richter scale;
- expensive – exploration and drilling of new reservoirs; upfront costs of geothermal heating and cooling systems are also steep;

- location-specific – good geothermal reservoirs are hard to come by; and
- sustainability issues – rainwater seeps through the earth's surface and into the geothermal reservoirs over thousands of years. Studies show that the reservoirs can be depleted if the fluid is removed faster than it is replaced. Efforts can be made to inject fluid back into the geothermal reservoir after the thermal energy has been utilised (ie after the turbine has generated electricity).

Geothermal power linked to earthquakes

7.58 Scientists have linked an earthquake with a magnitude of 5.5 on the Richter scale to enhanced geothermal power. This raises questions about the safety of the emerging technology when the US government and other countries are investing millions of dollars researching and deploying new systems. The findings about the disaster in Pohang, South Korea, were reported in two studies. The Pohang quake was the second-largest in the country's history since seismic records began in the late 1970s. Prior to the studies, the largest quake associated with enhanced geothermal, which was 3.4 in magnitude, occurred in Basel, Switzerland, in 2006.

The quake was the most destructive in the country's recorded history. It injured at least 60 people and caused more than $50 million in damages. Other enhanced geothermal systems were linked to smaller quakes, but those were at least 1,000 times smaller in magnitude than the quake that occurred in the South Korean city.

The event in November 2017 also indicates that injected fluid volumes much smaller than previously thought can trigger a large tremor under the right set of conditions. Enhanced geothermal, which some have called geothermal 'fracking', was considered by some to be less prone to quakes because it typically uses lower volumes of injected fluid than traditional geothermal.

Unlike traditional geothermal operations, an enhanced geothermal system (EGS) taps heat from areas of deep rock underground where there is not permeability or an easy way to pull heat up to the surface. With EGS, the water is injected underground to open existing fractures in rock so the heat can be extracted. Similar to natural gas, the idea is to broaden geothermal's use in areas that currently don't have the right geography to pull heat up from the subsurface. It has been estimated by the US Energy Department that EGS could, in theory, supply about half of US electricity.

Although studies did not conclude definitively that the $38 million Pohang geothermal plant caused the quake, they determined it was likely. The disaster and its largest aftershocks occurred within 2 km or less of the plant. Additionally, the quake activity was detected at unusually shallow depths between 3 to 7 km, suggesting the presence of an unknown fault.

GEOTHERMAL ENERGY BY COUNTRY

7.59 According to the International Renewable Energy Agency (IRENA) the top 10 countries ranked by installed capacity for geothermal energy in 2019 are:

1) USA – 2,555MW
2) Indonesia – 2,130MW
3) Philippines – 1,928MW
4) Turkey – 1,514MW
5) New Zealand – 965MW
6) Mexico – 936MW
7) Kenya – 823MW
8) Italy – 800MW
9) Iceland – 753MW
10) Japan – 525MW.

Chapter 8

Biofuels and Bioenergy

INTRODUCTION

8.1 Renewable fuel (commonly called 'biofuel') provides bioenergy. These fuels are produced directly or indirectly from organic material – biomass. This includes plant materials and animal waste.

Statistics for the use of biofuels within the UK are reported each year[1].

In 2019:

- 2,297 million litres equivalent (eq.) of renewable fuel has been supplied, which constitutes 5.1% of total road and non-road mobile machinery fuel for the year.
- 1,400 million litres eq. (61%) has been verified so far under the Renewable Transport Fuel Obligation (see para **8.21**).
- Of this 1,400 million litres eq., an aggregate greenhouse gas (GHG) saving of 82% was achieved when compared to fossil fuel use. This drops to 78% when indirect land-use change is accounted for.
- 11% of all verified renewable fuel supplied to the UK in this period was produced from UK origin feedstocks.

1 'Renewable fuel statistics 2019: Third provisional report': https://assets.publishing.service.gov.uk/government/uploads/system/uploads/attachment_data/file/863712/renewable-fuel-statistics-2019-third-provisional-report.pdf.

RENEWABLE FUELS

Biomass

8.2 Biomass is organic material that comes from plants and animals and includes crop, waste woods and trees. When biomass is burned, the chemical energy is released as heat and can generate electricity with the use of a steam turbine.

Feedstocks

8.3 The materials that renewable fuels are made from are typically a form of biomass known as feedstocks. These are either grown specifically to process into fuel or are waste products such as food waste.

These feedstocks are then processed by renewable fuel manufacturers, producing fuels which behave similarly to conventional propulsion fuel such as petrol and diesel.

These renewable fuels are then mixed with petrol, diesel and other fuels by fuel suppliers, who are required to have a set proportion of renewable fuels in their fuel stock.

These mixed fuels are then sold at pumps at petrol stations and on the market.

Renewable fuels deliver greenhouse gas savings as they are sourced from feedstocks which extract carbon dioxide from the atmosphere.

Waste feedstocks

8.4 These make up two thirds of all renewable fuel and include large quantities of used cooking oil, as well as brown grease, municipal organic waste, waste agricultural products such as corn husks, and sewerage sludge.

Types of biofuel

8.5 There are two main types of biofuels: ethanol, and biodiesel.

Biodiesel and HVO

8.6 Biodiesel is produced from vegetable oils, fats and greases. It is blended with diesel, generally at low levels (up to 7%).

Hydrated vegetable oil (HVO) differs from biodiesel in the way it is produced and the quality of the final product. It can be blended with diesel without a blending limit. HVO is usually referred to as biodiesel. It is produced through the hydroprocessing of oils and fats, such as:

- used cooking oil;
- waste pressings;

- soapstock acid oil – this is a by-product of caustic refining, which is usually acidulated to recover fatty acids whose composition is essentially the same as soybean oil;
- food waste; or
- another biodiesel.

CROPS GROWN FOR BIOENERGY IN THE UK

8.7 DEFRA produced statistics about crops grown in the UK for bioenergy in 2018.

Crops that are grown to supply the UK road transport market are reported under the Renewable Transport Fuels Obligation.

Biodiesel was produced from:

- brown grease – fat and oil removed from grease traps and sewers;
- food waste;
- soapstock acid oil;
- tallow; and
- used cooking oil.

Bioethanol was produced from:

- sugar beet; and
- wheat.

In 2018 the estimate is that 60% of the crop-derived bioethanol for road transport originated from crops grown outside of the UK. From the 39% of crops grown within the UK, this was mainly bioethanol derived from wheat.

From a total of 540.5 million litres, this was split into:

- France: 165 million litres
- UK: 99 million litres
- Ukraine: 79 million litres
- Romania: 37 million litres
- Germany: 31 million litres
- Belgium: 23 million litres

Plant biomass was produced from:

- miscanthus;
- short-rotation coppice; and
- straw.

These crops are grown primarily for use in the heat and electricity energy markets. They are burnt in power stations, combined heat and power (CHP) units or heating systems.

Unlike miscanthus, straw is not grown specifically as a bioenergy crop and is a by-product of the cereals industry. It is used for animal bedding, as animal feed and, to a small extent, as an energy crop to be burnt for heating and electricity in power stations and CHP units.

Bioethanol

8.8 Ethanol is produced by fermenting sugar or starch from products such as sugar cane, maize or wheat. It is used in blended fuels with petrol, either at low levels in regular vehicles (up to 10%) or at higher levels in cars that have been adapted to take both petrol and ethanol, known as 'flex-fuel' vehicles.

Ethanol can be produced by fermentation from:

- corn (non-EC) – this is corn imported from non-EU Member States;
- sugar cane;
- corn (EC) – corn from EU Member States;
- sugar beet;
- wheat;
- starch slurry; or
- other bioethanol.

Advanced or second-generation biofuels

8.9 A variety of waste feedstocks can be used to produce transport fuels that contribute to reducing carbon dioxide emissions when compared to traditional fossil fuels. Some of these biofuels can be blended with conventional fuels, and others are fully compatible with current vehicles and so can be used as complete replacements for conventional fuels.

Second-generation biofuels produced from feedstock are generally not food crops. The only time the food crops can act as second-generation biofuels is if they have already fulfilled their food purpose. For instance, waste vegetable oil is a second-generation biofuels because it has already been used and is no longer fit for human consumption. Virgin vegetable oil, however, would be a first-generation biofuel. Different technology is often used to extract energy from them. This does not mean that second-generation biofuels cannot be burned directly as the biomass. In fact, several second-generation biofuels, like Switchgrass, are cultivated specifically to act as direct biomass.

Second-generation extraction technology

8.10 Second-generation feedstock are processed differently than first-generation biofuels. This is particularly true of lignocellulose feedstock, which tends to require several processing steps prior to being fermented (a first-generation technology) into ethanol.

Thermochemical conversion

Gasification

8.11 The first thermochemical route is known as gasification, which is not a new technology and has been used extensively on conventional fossil fuels for a number of years. Second-generation gasification technologies have been slightly altered to accommodate the differences in biomass stock. Through gasification, carbon-based materials are converted to carbon monoxide, hydrogen and carbon dioxide. This process is different from combustion, in that oxygen is limited. The gas that results is referred to as synthesis gas or 'syngas'. Syngas is then used to produce energy or heat. Wood, black liquor, brown liquor and other feedstock are used in this process.

Pyrolysis

8.12 The second thermochemical route is known as pyrolysis. Pyrolysis also has a long history of use with fossil fuels. Pyrolysis is carried out in the absence of oxygen and often in the presence of an inert gas like halogen. The fuel is generally converted into two products: tars and char. Wood and a number of other energy crops can be used as feedstock to produce bio-oil through pyrolysis.

Torrefaction

8.13 A third thermochemical reaction, called torrefaction, is very similar to pyrolysis, but is carried out at lower temperatures. The process tends to yield better fuels for further use in gasification or combustion. Torrefaction is often used to convert biomass feedstock into a form that is more easily transported and stored.

Biochemical conversion

8.14 A number of biological and chemical processes are used for the production of biofuel from second-generation feedstock. Fermentation with unique or genetically modified bacteria is particularly popular for second-generation feedstock like landfill gas and municipal waste.

Common second-generation feedstock

8.15 To be a second-generation feedstock, the source must not be suitable for human consumption. It is not a requirement that the feedstock be grown on non-agricultural land, but a second generation feedstock should grow on what is known as marginal land. Marginal land is land that cannot be used for 'arable' crops. The second-generation feedstock should not require a great deal of water or fertilizer to grow.

Grasses

8.16 A number of grasses – such as Switchgrass, miscanthus, Indiangrass and others – have alternatively been used. The particular grass chosen depends on the location, as some are more suitable to certain climates. In the United States, Switchgrass is favoured. In Southeast Asia, miscanthus is the choice.

The advantages of grasses are:

- perennial, and so energy for planting need only be invested once;
- fast growing and can usually be harvested a few times per year;
- have relatively low fertilizer needs;

- grow on marginal land;
- work well as direct biomass; and
- have a high net energy yield of about 540%.

The disadvantages of grasses are:

- not suitable for producing biodiesel;
- require extensive processing to be made into ethanol;
- take several years for Switchgrass to reach harvest density;
- seeds are weak competitors with weeds – even though they grow on marginal land, the early investment in culture is substantial; and
- require moist soil and do not do well in arid climates.

Water demand is the biggest drawback to grasses and the factor that keeps them from becoming more popular as second-generation biofuels.

Jatropha and other seed crops

8.17 Seed crops are useful in the production of biodiesel. In the early part of the 21st century, a plant known as Jatropha became exceedingly popular among biodiesel advocates. The plant could return values as high as 40%. When compared to the 15% oil found in soybean, Jatropha looked to be preferable. It turned out that oil production drops substantially when Jatropha is grown on marginal land.

Other, similar seed crops have met with the same problems as Jatropha.

Examples include Cammelina, Oil Palm, and rapeseed. In all cases, the initial benefits of the crops were offset by the need to use crop land to achieve suitable yields.

Waste vegetable oil

8.18 Waste vegetable oil (WVO) has been used as a fuel for more than a century, as some of the earliest diesel engines ran exclusively on vegetable oil. WVO is considered a second-generation biofuel because it has already been used as a food. In fact, recycling it for fuel can help to improve its overall environmental impact.

Advantages of WVO are:

- does not threaten the food chain;
- is readily available;
- is easy to convert to biodiesel;
- can be burned directly in some diesel engines;
- is low in sulphur; and
- no associated land-use changes.

The disadvantages of WVO include:

- can decrease engine life if not properly refined.

WVO is one of the best sources of biodiesel and, as long as blending is all that is required, it can meet much of the demand for biodiesel.

Municipal solid waste

8.19 This refers to landfill gas, human waste, and grass clippings. All of these sources of energy are often allowed to go to waste. Though not as clean as solar and wind, the carbon footprint of these fuels is much less than that of traditionally derived fossil fuels. Municipal solid waste is often used in co-generation plants, where it is burned to produce both heat and electricity.

<table>
<tr><th>Waste oils, fats and algae</th><th>Municipal solid waste (MSW)</th><th>Cellulosic biomass</th></tr>
<tr><td colspan="2">Biodiesel – 5–20% blend with diesel for cars and lorries. Up to 100% for shipping</td><td></td></tr>
<tr><td colspan="3">Renewable diesel – up to 100% diesel replacement</td></tr>
<tr><td></td><td colspan="2">Biomethane – 100% with compressed gas vehicle</td></tr>
<tr><td colspan="3">Bio-jet – up to 50% blend with conventional jet fuel</td></tr>
<tr><td colspan="3">Bio-oil – up to 100% oil ship fuel replacement</td></tr>
<tr><td></td><td colspan="2">Cellulosic ethanol – 10–25% blend with petrol. Current vehicles up to 100% with flex fuel vehicles. Up to 95% with specialist engines</td></tr>
<tr><td colspan="3">Bio-gasoline – up to 100% gasoline replacement</td></tr>
</table>

Renewable Transport Fuel Certificates

8.20 Renewable Transport Fuel Certificates (RTFCs) are awarded to transport fuel suppliers whose renewable fuel meets the sustainability criteria. Provisional figures for 2019 show that 3,576 million RTFCs were issued to 2,135 million litres eq. of renewable fuel. This is out of a total 2,680 million litres eq. supplied.

Renewable Transport Fuel Obligation (RTFO)

8.21 Suppliers of fuel for road and non-road mobile machinery (eg tractors) that supply 450,000 litres or more per year have an obligation under the RTFO Order[2]. Obligated suppliers may meet their obligation by redeeming RTFCs or by paying a fixed sum for each litre of fuel for which they wish to 'buy-out' of their obligation. RTFCs are gained by supplying sustainable renewable fuels. In 2019, such suppliers must redeem RTFCs for 8.5% of their share of total fuel. This will increase to 12.4% by 2032.

One certificate may be claimed for every litre or kilogram of sustainable renewable fuel supplied. Fuel from certain wastes or residues, fuel from dedicated energy crops, and renewable fuels of non-biological origin (RFNBOs) are incentivised by awarding double the RTFCs per litre or kilogram supplied.

Companies have up to seven months after the end of the year before they must apply for RTFCs. As a result of this delay, 68% of renewable fuel so far supplied in 2019 is not yet certified. Each provisional report typically has

2 Renewable Transport Fuel Obligation (RTFO) Order: www.gov.uk/government/collections/renewable-transport-fuels-obligation-rtfo-orders.

a higher proportion of renewable fuel which has been certified, and the final report describes all renewable fuel supplied in the year.

PRIMARY AND SECONDARY BIOFUELS

Primary biofuels

8.22 Wood chips and pellets (ie organic materials) are used in an unprocessed form, primarily for heating, cooking or electricity production.

Secondary biofuels

8.23 These result from processing of biomass and include liquid biofuels such as ethanol and biodiesel that can be used in vehicles and industrial processes.

Bioenergy is mainly used in homes and, to a lesser extent, in industry, while liquid biofuels for transport still play a limited role.

Different types of liquid biofuels for transport

8.24 The most widely used liquid biofuels for transport are ethanol and biodiesel.

Ethanol

8.25 This is a type of alcohol that can be produced using any feedstock that contains a significant amount of sugar (such as sugar cane or sugar beet) or starch (such as maize and wheat). Sugar can be directly fermented to alcohol, while starch needs to be converted to sugar first.

The fermentation process is similar to that used to make wine or beer, and pure ethanol is obtained by distillation. Ethanol can be blended with petrol or burned in a nearly pure form in slightly modified spark-ignition engines. A litre of ethanol contains approximately two-thirds of the energy provided by a litre of petrol. However, when mixed with petrol, it improves the combustion performance and lowers the emissions of carbon monoxide and sulphur oxide.

Biodiesel

8.26 This is produced, mainly in the European Union, by combining vegetable oil or animal fat with an alcohol. Biodiesel can be blended with diesel fuel or burned in its pure form in compression ignition engines. Its energy content is less than that of diesel (88–95%). Biodiesel can be derived from a wide range of oils, including rapeseed, soybean, palm, coconut or Jatropha oils, and therefore the resulting fuels can display a greater variety of physical properties than ethanol.

Diesel engines can also run on vegetable oils and animal fats, such as used cooking oils from restaurants and fat from meat processing industries.

Second-generation biofuels

8.27 Currently used liquid biofuels, which include ethanol produced from crops containing sugar and starch and biodiesel from oilseeds, are referred to as 'first-generation biofuels'. These fuels only use a portion of the energy potentially available in the biomass.

Most plant matter is composed of cellulose, hemicellulose and lignin, and 'second-generation biofuel' technologies refer to processes able to convert these components to liquid fuels. Once commercially viable, these could significantly expand the volume and variety of sources that could be used for biofuel production.

Potential cellulosic sources include municipal waste and waste products from agriculture, forestry, processing industry, as well as new energy crops such as fast-growing trees and grasses. As a result, second-generation biofuel production could present major advantages in terms of environmental sustainability and reduced competition for land with food and feed production. It could also offer advantages in terms of greenhouse gas emissions.

Various techniques are currently being developed to produce second-generation biofuels. However, it is uncertain when such technologies will enter production on a significant commercial scale.

The conversion of cellulose to ethanol involves two steps. The cellulosic and hemicellulosic components of the plant material are first broken down into sugars, which are then fermented to obtain ethanol. The first step is technically difficult, although research continues on developing efficient and cost-effective ways of carrying out the process. Lignin cannot be converted to ethanol, but it can provide the necessary energy for the conversion process.

Gasification

8.28 Gasification is a technique that converts solid biomass, such as wood, into a fuel gas. Gasifiers operate by heating biomass to high temperatures in a low-oxygen environment, releasing an energy-rich gas. This gas can be burned in a boiler, used in a gas turbine, to generate electricity.

GUIDANCE AND REGULATION

Renewable Transport Fuel Obligation (RTFO): guidance 2020[3]

8.29 This provides information on complying with, reporting and verifying the RTFO process for fuel suppliers, independent verifiers and those supplying

3 www.gov.uk/government/publications/renewable-transport-fuel-obligation-rtfo-guidance-2020.

biofuels. The RFTO sets targets for the inclusion of waste-based renewable fuel within supplies, starting at 0.1% of the volume of fuel supplied and rising to 2.8% by 2032. The Government has also set a 'sustainable' target for crop biofuels, with a maximum cap of 4% of fuel in 2019 dropping to 2% by 2032. The RTFO scheme will include renewable aviation fuels and renewable fuels of non-biological origin. The changes apply to transport fuel owners supplying at least 450,000 litres a year.

Registration

8.30 Registration is compulsory if the company owns and supplies 450,000 litres or more of any road transport or non-road mobile machinery (NRMM) fuel for use in the UK during the course of an obligation year. The figure of 450,000 litres includes all fossil fuels and biofuels.

A company which supplies less than 450,000 litres a year in the UK can still register if it wants to claim Renewable Transport Fuel Certificates (RTFCs). Any company that supplies sustainable biofuel for use in road transport or NRMM in the UK can claim RTFCs, and it can trade RTFCs or sell them to companies that need them to meet their obligations under the RTFO.

Guidance is divided into three main parts:

(1) process guidance, which explains how the scheme works and what suppliers need to do to comply;
(2) carbon and sustainability guidance, which explains how suppliers should meet the sustainability criteria for biofuels; and
(3) guidance for verifiers.

Carbon calculator[4]

8.31 The carbon calculator is a stand-alone program that allows users to assess the greenhouse gas savings from a given batch of biofuels. It can be used to generate reports to upload to the RTFO reporting system.

Data on biofuel supply

8.32 Suppliers covered by the RTFO must provide data on the volumes and source of biofuel brought to market in the UK.

Voluntary sustainability schemes

8.33 Biofuels must meet certain sustainability criteria in order to qualify under the RTFO. One way of demonstrating that a biofuel meets these criteria is to use feedstocks produced under a recognised sustainability standard scheme.

The European Commission has recognised a number of voluntary schemes as offering sufficient evidence of meeting all three sustainability criteria of the

4 Biofuels carbon calculator: www.gov.uk/government/publications/biofuels-carbon-calculator-rtfo.

Renewable Energy Directive, and it is currently assessing a number of other schemes.

The RTFO administrator's approach to schemes that are not recognised by the Commission can be found in the RTFO guidance. A table outlining the schemes recognised by the Commission is published alongside the guidance.

Renewable Transport Fuel Obligation[5]

8.34 The Renewable Transport Fuel Obligation Order regulates biofuels used for transport and non-road mobile machinery.

RTFO: registered companies

8.35 'Renewable Transport Fuel Obligation: registered companies' lists all of the companies that are allowed to claim:

- RTFCs; and
- greenhouse gas credits.

ENVIRONMENTAL IMPACT OF BIOFUELS

8.36 According to the Office of National Statistics (ONS), the largest source of renewable energy consumed in the UK is from biomass, ie organic material from plants or animals[6]. Almost 40% of energy consumption comes from biomass.

About 60% of biomass energy consumption relates to the production of electricity generation. This is the result of the UK implementing policies which aim to reduce its greenhouse gas emissions and its use of coal-burning power stations. The major source within power stations was wood pellets. In 2010, 0.6 million tonnes of wood pellets were imported, compared to 7.8 million tonnes in 2018. In 2018, approximately 82% of the wood pellets were imported from the United States and Canada.

Greenhouse gas emissions

8.37 The total greenhouse gas emissions have fallen in last decade[7] and the sources of greenhouse gas emissions relating to electricity production have changed as the use of renewable sources of electricity like biomass has increased. Biomass, unlike other renewable sources of electricity, is not greenhouse gas

5 www.gov.uk/guidance/renewable-transport-fuels-obligation.

6 'A burning issue: biomass is the biggest source of renewable energy consumed in the UK': www.ons.gov.uk/economy/environmentalaccounts/articles/aburningissuebiomassisthebiggestsourceofrenewableenergyconsumedintheuk/2019-08-30.

7 'Net zero and the different official measures of the UK's greenhouse gas emissions': www.ons.gov.uk/economy/environmentalaccounts/articles/netzeroandthedifferentofficialmeasuresoftheuksgreenhousegasemissions/2019-07-24.

emission-free. A research paper from the UK Government[8], has shown that greenhouse gas emissions per unit of electricity generated from biomass can be lower or higher than those from fossil fuels like coal and gas, depending on factors such as the type of biomass that is burnt and where it comes from.

In 2017, greenhouse gas emissions from the burning of biomass for electricity production in UK power stations were around 15 million tonnes of carbon dioxide equivalent, compared to 4 million tonnes in 2010. People who have criticised the increasing use of biomass for electricity generation in the UK have argued that, by sourcing such large quantities of biomass as wood pellets from the USA and Canada, this is not sustainable in view of the emissions associated with its transport or potential impacts on land use in these countries.

WASTE-DERIVED BIODIESEL – EUROPEAN CASE LAW

8.38 The transport, storage, use and treatment processes associated with producing biodiesel from tallow (melted and clarified animal fat) and waste vegetable oil (and, in some circumstances, from virgin non-waste vegetable oils) can be subject to various controls regulated by the Environment Agency. There may be a requirement for a Pollution Prevention and Control (PPC) Permit or a Waste Management Licence (WML).

The production of biodiesel by individuals such as householders and farmers for their own use, ie for non-commercial purposes, would not be subject to the PPC Regulations. Where a PPC permit is not required and where biodiesel production involves the treatment of waste, the requirement for waste management controls still applies.

In light of European case law, the Environment Agency is obliged to consider that waste-derived biodiesel has not ceased to be waste until it has been burnt in an engine for energy recovery. The Environment Agency has set out a position that it does not consider that requiring environmental authorisations for the storage, supply and use of waste-derived biodiesel for use as a motor fuel is in the public interest. The use of waste-derived biodiesel to support combustion in industrial plant, such as a boiler, will be subject to controls under the Waste Incineration Directive[9] and regulated through PPC by local authorities or the Environment Agency.

LEGAL CHALLENGE ON BIOMASS IN THE RENEWABLE ENERGY DIRECTIVE

8.39 Six plaintiffs from Estonia, France, Ireland, Romania, Slovakia and the United States have brought a challenge to the EU's Renewable Energy

8 'Life cycle impacts of biomass electricity in 2020': www.gov.uk/government/publications/life-cycle-impacts-of-biomass-electricity-in-2020.
9 https://ec.europa.eu/environment/archives/air/stationary/wid/legislation.htm.

Directive. Each said how they have been impacted by the logging and burning of biomass to produce heat and energy in the EU. If the Court agrees to hear the case, it will set a major precedent for citizens to challenge environmental decisions by the EU. The current EU Renewable Energy Directive has given rise to expanded forest harvesting for fuel, and increased greenhouse gas emissions. The legal action states that this will create more damage to forests and the climate under the revised directive (RED II), which comes into force in 2021. The legal case, which was filed in the European General Court in Luxembourg, cites scientific evidence that wood-burning power plants pump more carbon into the atmosphere per unit of energy than coal plants. However, the EU policy does not count the carbon dioxide emissions from burning biomass fuels for heat or energy, making it appear that biomass fuels are more climate-friendly than fossil fuels. The plaintiffs are asking the Court to annul the forest biomass provisions of the RED II in order to render forest wood ineligible for meeting EU Member State renewable energy targets and subsidies.

ANAEROBIC DIGESTION

8.40 Some types of organic waste and purpose-grown crops can be used to produce bioenergy through the process of anaerobic digestion (AD). AD is a natural process in which plant and animal materials are converted into useful products by micro-organisms in the absence of air. The process releases biogas (mainly a mixture of around 60% methane and 40% carbon dioxide), which can be used directly to provide heat, power or transport fuel. Biogas can also be purified by removal of the carbon dioxide to produce biomethane, which can be fed directly into the public natural gas grid in the same way as natural gas or used as a vehicle fuel. The types of materials used for AD include food waste, slurry and manure, crops and crop residues.

Types of AD process

Hydrolysis

8.41 Large, complex polymers like carbohydrates, cellulose, proteins and fats are broken down by hydrolytic enzymes into simple sugars, amino acids and fatty acids.

Acidogenesis

8.42 Simple monomers are broken down into volatile fatty acids.

Acetogenesis

8.43 The products of acidogenesis are broken down into acetic acid, releasing hydrogen and carbon dioxide.

Methanogenesis

8.44 Bacteria called methane formers produce methane, either by cleaving two acetic acid molecules to form carbon dioxide and methane, or by reduction of carbon hydroxide with hydrogen.

Options for AD systems

Mesophilic or thermophilic

8.45

- Mesophile – an organism that grows best in moderate temperatures, neither too hot nor too cold, with an optimum growth range from 20°C to 45°C.
- Thermophile – an organism that thrives at relatively high temperatures, between 41°C and 122°C.

Mesophilic systems operate at 25–45°C and thermophilic systems operate at 50–60°C or above. Thermophilic systems have a faster throughput, with faster biogas production per unit of feedstock and cubic metre of the digester, and there is greater pathogen kill. However, the capital costs of thermophilic systems are higher, more energy is needed to heat them, and they generally require more management.

Wet or dry

8.46 The difference between what is considered a wet process and a dry process is quite small:

- Wet AD – feedstock is pumped and stirred (5–15% dry matter (DM)).
- Dry AD – feedstock can be stacked (over 15% DM).

Dry AD tends to be cheaper to run, as there is less water to heat and there is more gas production per unit of feedstock. However, wet AD has a lower set-up capital cost.

Continuous or batch flow

8.47 Most digesters are continuous flow, as opening the digester and restarting the system from cold every few weeks is a time-consuming process, and they generally give more biogas per unit of feedstock and their operating costs are lower. However, some dry systems are batch flow. To overcome peaks and troughs in gas production, there are usually multiple batch digesters with staggered changeover times.

Single, double or multiple digesters

8.48 AD occurs in several stages. Some systems have multiple digesters to ensure that each stage occurs sequentially and is as efficient as possible.

Multiple digesters can provide more biogas per unit of feedstock but at a higher capital cost, higher operating cost and greater management requirement. Most digesters in the UK are single or double digesters.

Vertical tank or horizontal plug flow

8.49 Vertical tanks simply take feedstock in a pipe on one side, whilst digestate overflows through a pipe on the other. In horizontal plug-flow systems, a more solid feedstock is used as a 'plug' that flows through a horizontal digester at the rate it is fed in. Vertical tanks are simple and cheaper to operate, but the feedstock may not reside in the digester for the optimum period of time. Horizontal tanks are more expensive to build and operate, but the feedstock will neither leave the digester too early nor stay in it for an uneconomically long period.

Feedstocks

8.50 Materials used for AD are called feedstocks. The choice of feedstock is essential, as what goes into a digester also comes out. The feedstock itself does not have to be waste; any biodegradable non-woody plant or animal matter can be a suitable feedstock for a digester. The anaerobic micro-organisms cannot break down lignin, which is the complex polymer that give plants their strength, making wood products, paper and straw slow to digest.

The yield of any particular feedstock will depend on a number of criteria:

- dry matter content;
- energy left in the feedstock – if it has been in storage for a long time, it may have already begun to breakdown;
- length of time in the digester; and
- purity of the feedstock.

Sources of feedstock

Processing residues

8.51 Examples of processing residues are bakery or brewery waste. These provide a consistent and stable supply.

Nestlé

8.52 Nestlé chose Clearfleau in 2013 to install an AD plant at its confectionery factory at Fawdon, Newcastle. The plant processes over 200,000 litres of wash-waters per day and 1,200 tonnes of residual products per year, to supply renewable energy to the site.

This resulted in:

- 8% of power requirement supplied from biogas;
- 10% reduction in site's overall carbon footprint;
- £300,000 in incentive revenue / energy savings;

- £200,000 savings on disposal and discharge costs; and
- Nestlé recognised in Dow Jones Sustainability Index as industry leader.

Agricultural residues

8.53 The UK generates millions of tonnes of manures and slurries each year. Often, these are used on the farms where they arise, recycling the nutrients that they contain.

The Nitrate Vulnerable Zone (NVZ) rules[10] mean that many organic manures cannot be spread at certain times of the year and must be stored for an extended period before being land-spread as fertilisers. This provides a potential for AD to be used to capture methane from stored slurries and manures, and also to stabilise and treat these materials.

There is guidance from the Environment Agency (EA)[11] that manures and slurries used as feedstock for AD purposes should not be treated as 'waste' if used as fertiliser. This applies to both solid and liquid digestate. There are other nutrient management regulations[12], such as the Code of Good Agricultural Practice for the protection of soil, water and air, which are still applicable.

The EA has published guidance on when crop residues are deemed a by-product or waste[13].

Crop residues may be regarded as by-products, provided that all of the following apply:

- they are not mixed with or contain any wastes;
- they are suitable for use and certain to be used as a feedstock for AD (irrespective of whether the AD plant is on a farm or not);
- they can be used directly as an AD feedstock with no additional processing apart from that which might be reasonably expected of energy crops. For example, maceration would be OK, whereas de-packaging or pasteurisation would not; and
- their use in AD will not lead to overall adverse environmental or human health impacts. NB this needs to take into account any storage and processing prior to AD, the AD process itself, as well as the subsequent storage and use of the biogas and digestate produced. The crop residues will, for example, need to be disease-free and not contaminated with pathogens.

Environmental permit

8.54 Operators do not require an environmental permit or exemption, either for the operation of the plant or for the beneficial use of the digestate produced, provided that they only take the following feedstocks:

10 Nitrate Variable Zones (NVZs): www.gov.uk/government/collections/nitrate-vulnerable-zones.

11 'Anaerobic digestion of agricultural manure and slurry', Environment Agency: https://webarchive.nationalarchives.gov.uk/20140328103528/http://www.environment-agency.gov.uk/static/documents/Research/PS_029_AD_of_agricultural_manures_and_slurry_final.pdf.

12 'Protecting our Water, Soil and Air – A Code of Good Agricultural Practice for farmers, growers and land managers', DEFRA: https://assets.publishing.service.gov.uk/government/uploads/system/uploads/attachment_data/file/268691/pb13558-cogap-131223.pdf.

13 'Crop residues used as feedstocks in anaerobic digestion plants: Briefing Note', EA: www.nfuonline.com/ea-briefing-note-crop-residues-used-as-feedstocks-in-ad-plants/.

- purpose-grown crops;
- crop residues that meet the above criteria; or
- a mixture of the above.

If any of the feedstocks consist of or contain waste (for example, an AD plant taking crops and livestock slurry), an environmental permit or exemption is required for the operation of the AD plant. An environmental permit or exemption is also required for the use of the digestate produced, except where:

- its production and use is certified under the digestate Quality Protocol; or
- it is produced only from manure or manure/non-waste feedstocks and is spread as a fertiliser on agricultural land.

Crops

8.55 Some crops are grown specifically for AD, for stabilising or supplementing other feedstocks such as low-yielding slurries or variable-quality food waste. These crops include maize, grass silage, energy beet and whole crop cereals, all of which can be incorporated into existing crop rotations or management system.

Intensive production of a single crop could cause environmental concern, whether grown for food, as an AD-specific crop biomass or for transport biofuels. The AD industry has published 'Voluntary Guidelines on Best Practice for Crop Feedstocks in Anaerobic Digestion'[14], which draws together other relevant best practice principles.

Ofgem have produced guidance on Smart Export Guarantee (SEG) sustainability criteria and reporting requirements[15]. The SEG makes sure that small-scale low-carbon generators receive payment for any electricity that they export to the grid. The scheme requires certain licensed electricity suppliers to offer export tariffs to AD, hydro, onshore wind, and solar photovoltaic (PV) exporters with a total installed capacity up to 5MW, and micro-combined heat and power (mCHP) with an electrical capacity of 50kW or less. The obligation came into force on 1 January 2020. It follows on from the Feed-in Tariff (FIT) scheme that closed on 31 March 2019 (see para **2.2**).

QV Foods

8.56 QV Foods operate a 1.4MW plant developed and operated by Tamar Energy. It uses waste from their packing and processing operations, as well as vegetable food waste from other sources. They also have a contract to supply 8,000 tonnes of maize a year for the plant, which is grown on 170 hectares of land unsuitable for potato production. In the future, however, rye and energy beet could also be considered as feedstock for the plant.

As a relatively remote farm site with relatively weak infrastructure, having an on-site power plant gives them a better platform for growth. With rising

14 'Voluntary guidelines on best practice for crop feedstocks in anaerobic digestion', ADBA: http://adbioresources.org/wp-content/uploads/2014/09/cbp-a5_Web.pdf.

15 'Guidance for Anaerobic Digestion generators: SEG sustainability criteria and reporting requirements', Ofgem: www.ofgem.gov.uk/system/files/docs/2019/12/seg_sustainability_guidance_final_0.pdf.

energy costs, the AD plant has made the site between 90–95% self-sufficient in electricity. The other factor in favour of AD is that they have out-grade produce (that is, produce which is not up to standard) and peel waste which was being used as stock feed many miles away. They now keep around 10,000 tonnes of potato out-grades and peel on site, reducing costs and transport. The supply of liquid biofertiliser (digestate) saves them around £100,000 a year before application costs. In addition, the solid soil conditioner will replace all of their current artificial sugar beet base fertiliser.

The first stage was to reduce the amount of waste generated, whilst ensuring that the right type of plant was used to maximise the value of any out-grades or waste that they did not generate. In addition, they have increased their potato rotation from 1 in 6 to 1 in 8 years as part of an effort to reduce potato cyst nematode (PCN), helping them to incorporate more energy crops into the rotation. In addition, liquid and solid digestate from the plant provides valuable fertiliser for the farm.

Food and drink waste

8.57 According to the Waste and Resources Action Plan (WRAP)[16], it is estimated that there are about 9.5 million tonnes per year of post farm-gate food and drink waste, of which 70% could be avoided. This has a value of over £19 billion a year and is associated with around 25 million tonnes of greenhouse gas (GHG) emissions. There is also waste from the manufacturing, retail and hospitality sectors, and other businesses and the public sector.

The most environmentally preferable treatment for food waste is usually AD or composting. AD is preferable because it produces both renewable energy and a biofertiliser, which do more to offset GHG emissions than producing compost. There are, however, some organic waste streams for which composting will remain the best option, such as co-collected food and garden waste, or woody garden waste that is collected on its own.

For treatment by a 'wet' AD system, food waste needs to be collected separately at source; to be treated by composting, or 'dry' AD systems, food waste can either be separately collected at source or mixed with green waste. The co-digestion of food waste in large sludge treatment plants has the potential to be an efficient way of producing energy from waste, particularly as many of the plants are conveniently located by urban centres. More information can be found at the Food Waste Resources Portal[17].

Case Study: HydroThane UK / North British Distillery Co Ltd

8.58 HydroThane UK and the North British Distillery Co Ltd (NBD) have completed the construction of the second phase of a three-phase project which introduces high-rate AD technology at the company's distillery site in central Edinburgh. It uses post-feed liquor. The project benefits are:

- it produces renewable energy (biogas – steam) which reduces natural gas imports and reduces energy costs;

16 Wrap Statistical resources: www.wrap.org.uk/content/statistical-resources.
17 Food Waste Resources Portal: www.wrap.org.uk/content/food-waste-resources-portal.

- it reduces carbon dioxide emissions by between 9,000 and 10,000 tonnes per year, significantly reducing NBD's carbon footprint;
- it reduces the load on the existing by-products evaporation process, thereby increasing the overall production capability of the distillery; and
- the water treatment plant (WTP) will reduce the company's ongoing water and effluent charges.

Sewerage sludge

8.59 AD is one of the commonest methods for treating sewage sludge, and roughly two-thirds of the country's sludge is already treated in this way. The water industry has a well-established infrastructure of AD plants and knowledge of the technology and its operation. Other organic waste can be 'co-digested' with sewage sludge, but different regulatory regimes apply.

The use of sewage sludge on agricultural land is regulated through the Sewage Sludge Directive (86/278/EEC)[18]. This is transposed through the Sludge (Use in Agriculture) Regulations 1989[19].

Advantages of AD

8.60

- net energy-producing process which produces renewable energy in the form of biogas;
- produces a liquid and a fibrous fertiliser;
- sanitises the feedstock/waste which is put through it, as long as the temperature is held above a required temperature for a pre-defined time period;
- reduces odour below unprocessed waste odou levels;
- much less likely to cause environmental pollution than spreading untreated organic waste on land; and
- effect of the fertiliser is longer lasting than for untreated organic waste.

Disadvantages of AD

8.61

- where carried out at a commercial scale on farms and at wastewater treatment works (WwTWs), requires a high level of investment in large tanks and other process vessels;
- where run inefficiently, AD can cause an odour nuisance; and
- does not convert as large a proportion of the carbon in the biomass to biogas as can be achieved using gasification.

18 Sewage Sludge Directive (86/278/EEC): https://eur-lex.europa.eu/legal-content/EN/TXT/?uri=celex%3A31986L0278.

19 Sludge (Use in Agriculture) Regulations 1989 (amended 1990): www.legislation.gov.uk/uksi/1989/1263/contents/made.

AD firm fined £19k for odour pollution

8.62 A company in Middlesbrough specialising in AD has been ordered to pay £19,670 for odour pollution. BioConstruct NewEnergy, operating in Imperial Avenue, pleaded guilty at Teesside Magistrates' Court to offences which occurred in July 2018. The plant went through some maintenance, 'causing up to four days' misery' for the local residents, most of whom decided to move out because of the smell. Environment Agency (EA) officers visited the plant and were told that overseas contractors were responsible, as the company did not know how to properly carry out the maintenance. However, the EA said BioConstruct NewEnergy had to take responsibility as it holds the environmental permit for the site, which requires the company to prevent or minimise pollution. During the same inspection, officers found around 30 large containers of pink liquid which the company was storing illegally.

Leaks from biogas plants lead to five-figure fines

8.63 Trinity Hall Biogas Ltd has been made to pay over £20,000 after poor site management led to water pollution at the site of an AD plant in Hockliffe, Bedfordshire.

Luton Magistrates' Court fined the company £10,000 and ordered it to pay £10,423 in EA costs after overflows from the plant in December 2013 and April 2014 led to the pollution of three kilometres of local watercourses. Trinity Hall Biogas leased the land of Trinity Hall Farm to run the AD plant, which was operated by Scott and Scott, a farm management company that offers AD services. Warren Scott, the controlling partner of Scott and Scott, had already accepted a caution at a previous hearing.

A company that polluted two watercourses at Emneth near Wisbech and Aldreth near Ely has been ordered to pay £45,000 in fines, costs and compensation.

Pretoria Energy Company (Arable) Limited, based in Ely, which produces feedstock for a sister company's AD plants, admitted causing the pollution incidents at Little Racy Drain (a tributary of the Forty Foot Drain) in Emneth Hungate, Norfolk, and the New Cut Drain (West) at Aldreth in Cambridgeshire. The magistrates' court was told that both pollution incidents were a result of silage liquor leaking from ag-bags and making its way into the watercourses. The ag-bags are large bags often stored on fields, filled with agricultural feeds and, once sealed, should be airtight. They vary in length, but an example of the size of ag-bag involved in this case is 77 metres long, containing 318 tonnes of silage.

Being airtight and subject to direct sunlight, there is a large amount of gas and silage liquor produced in the ag-bags which needs maintenance by the owner, typically by releasing the gas to avoid the bags bursting and removing the liquor to stop the polluting liquid escaping and getting into the environment.

In February 2017, the EA was contacted by a member of the public to advise that they believed there had been a pollution from the ag-bags located on land in Emneth. An EA officer attended the site the following day and found that the pollution was caused by silage liquor escaping from some of the eight ag-bags present on site. Some of these ag-bags had holes in the sides from where it is believed the silage liquor had leaked. Sewage fungus was found growing 300 metres downstream of the incident.

It is believed that other ag-bags had leaked silage from underneath.

A representative from the company attended the site in February 2017 to meet with the EA officer and said that he would get the ag-bags removed. The EA officer went back at the Emneth site on 29 March 2017 where he discovered that all eight of the ag-bags were still present on site. Samples showed that the pollution was continuing to have an impact on the watercourse.

Chapter 9

Energy Storage

INTRODUCTION

9.1 Electricity storage plays a crucial role in boosting solar and wind power generation. Storage based on rapidly improving batteries and other technologies will permit greater system flexibility, which is essential when considering variable renewable electricity (VRE) increases. Electricity storage makes possible a transport sector dominated by electric vehicles (EVs) and enables 24-hour off-grid solar home systems and supports 100% renewable mini-grids.

Electricity systems already require a range of ancillary services to ensure smooth and reliable operation. Supply and demand need to be balanced in real time in order to ensure supply quality (eg maintaining constant voltage and frequency), avoid damage to electrical appliances, and maintain supply to all users. All electricity systems require a degree of flexibility, which allows grid operators to react to unexpected changes in demand or to the loss of supply (eg stations going offline, loss of an interconnection). This flexibility gives operators the tools to rapidly restore systems.

Solar and wind power still have limited impact on grid operation. As the share of VRE rises, electricity systems will need to be able to respond to the capabilities of electricity storage. This needs to be part of the energy planning process. The International Renewable Energy Agency (IRENA), analysing the effects of the energy transition until 2050 in a recent study for the G20, found that over 80% of the world's electricity could derive from renewable sources by that date. Solar photovoltaic (PV) and wind power would at that point account for 52% of total electricity generation. Electricity storage will be at the heart of the energy transition, providing services throughout the electricity system value chain and into the end-use sectors.

BENEFITS OF ENERGY STORAGE

9.2 Energy storage has a number of benefits, including:

- storage technologies could decrease the need to invest in new conventional generation processes, and this could result in financial savings and reduced emissions;
- energy storage can enable the integration of more renewables (solar PV and wind) into the mixture of generation types;
- energy storage provides system stability during electricity outages, by supplying energy and reducing the financial costs of power outages;
- storage technologies improve energy security by optimising the supply and demand, thereby reducing the need to import electricity via interconnectors;
- using energy storage means that fewer and cheaper electricity transmission and distribution system upgrades are required;
- large levels of energy storage can reduce energy loss during transmission and distribution;
- energy can be stored when prices are low, and used on site when they are high, to save money for consumers and businesses, or the stored energy can be sold;
- storage can provide ancillary services to the system operator at lower cost, lower carbon intensity than traditional providers, such as conventional thermal power plants; and
- storage technologies can reduce the usage of fossil fuels, enabling a greener, lower carbon energy supply mix.

TYPES OF ENERGY STORAGE

9.3 Battery electric storage is key to transitioning to renewable energy. The battery technology is needed to support services needed to transition from providing a frequency response, reserve capacity, black start[1] capability and other grid services to storing power for electric vehicles, upgrading mini-grids and supporting 'self-consumption' of roof top solar power.

The two biggest sources of renewable energy are solar and wind power, both of which are variable in their output, depending on the weather and time of day. They are 'dispatchable', which means they cannot be turned off or on or up or down according the grid's needs. The grid needs to adjust to them.

If the grid is supplied by a lot of renewables, it needs a lot of flexibility and ways of smoothing out and balancing the fluctuations. There are many sources of grid flexibility but the one with the most potential is energy storage. Batteries, like those in a torch or mobile phone, can also be used to store energy on a large scale. Batteries can be located anywhere so they are often seen as storage for *distribution*, when a battery facility is located near consumers to provide power stability, or *end-use*, like batteries in electric vehicles.

1 Black start is the process of restoring am electric power station or part of a grid to operation without relying on the external power transmission network to recover from a partial or total shutdown.

Batteries for supplementing power generation

9.4 Many different types of batteries are available that have large-scale energy storage potential, including sodium-sulphur, metal air, lithium ion, and lead-acid batteries. There are several battery installations at wind farms.

Scottish Power hybrid power strategy

9.5 Scottish Power has a hybrid power strategy for the UK and Ireland, combining solar and battery storage with wind on both existing and new sites. This new strategy comes at the time of the energy company's first foray into solar PV and will see Scottish Power look to deploy more than one clean energy technology on the 'vast majority' of future developments in the UK and Ireland. In addition, the utility is looking to revisit existing generators and retrofit additional technologies. Planning applications have been submitted to add solar to wind farms at Carland Cross in Cornwall, Coal Clough in Lancashire and Coldham in Cambridgeshire, with further applications to add solar to wind farms in Scotland and Ireland currently under development.

Whitelee Onshore Wind Farm

9.6 Scottish Power has lined up its first battery storage project, having received Government approval to install a 50MW battery storage facility at the Whitelee Onshore Wind Farm. The planned battery storage centre will support the National Grid in maintaining the resilience and stability of the electricity grid, even at times when the wind may not be blowing. The battery storage site will be the size of half a football pitch and will comprise 50MW of lithium-ion battery technology, which is the most cost-effective storage technology for renewable electricity.

Advances in battery technologies have been made, largely due to the expanding electric vehicle (EV) industry. As more developments are made with EVs, battery cost should continue to reduce. Electric vehicles could also have an impact on energy storage through vehicle-to-grid technologies, in which their batteries can be connected to the grid and discharge power for others to use.

Electrochemical storage

Conventional batteries

Lithium-ion batteries

9.7 These were first commercially produced by Sony in the early 1990s and originally used mainly for small-scale consumer items such as mobile phones. Recently, they have been used for larger-scale battery storage and electric vehicles. They have a high energy density and low stand-by losses and tolerate recycling. They account for more than 90% of the global grid battery storage market. There have been new innovations, such as replacing graphite with silicon to increase the battery's power capacity.

Lithium-ion batteries are now used in developing countries for rural electrification. In rural communities, lithium-ion batteries are paired with solar panels to allow households and businesses to use limited amounts of electricity to charge mobile phones, run appliances, and light buildings. Previously, such communities had to rely on dirty and expensive diesel generators or did not have access to electricity.

Hornsdale Power Reserve, South Australia

9.8 At 100MW/129MWh, the Hornsdale Power Reserve is the largest lithium-ion battery in the world and provides network security services to South Australian electricity consumers in concert with the South Australian Government and the Australian Energy Market Operator (AEMO). The battery covers approximately one hectare of land, located at the Hornsdale Wind Farm 15 km north of Jamestown. The Hornsdale Wind Farm is currently South Australia's largest renewable generator.

Aliso Canyon, California, USA

9.9 The largest natural gas disaster in US history, with a carbon footprint bigger than that of the Deepwater Horizon leak in the Gulf of Mexico in 2010, left the facility with less than one-fifth of its capacity. Southern California Gas Company (SoCal Gas) is now barred from storing gas at the Aliso Canyon facility until all wells are thoroughly investigated and determined to be safe. The California Public Utilities Commission (CPUC) quickly narrowed in on energy storage as a critical solution to address reliability. It can be a fast-responding, firm and dispatchable resource, and can be constructed, interconnected and installed in a fairly short timeline. CPUC granted approval to Southern California Edison (SCE) to procure energy storage to help alleviate the outage concerns from the Aliso Canyon leak. The CPUC ruled that SCE should acquire front-of-the-meter in order to quickly start serving their purpose as a reliable alternative to natural gas. The battery storage facilities, built by Tesla, AES Energy Storage and Greensmith Energy, provide 70MW of power, enough to power 20,000 houses for four hours.

Lead-acid batteries

9.10 Lead-acid batteries were among the first battery technologies used in energy storage and have been used commercially since the 1980s. Lead-acid batteries, despite their toxicity, are very popular due to low cost/performance ratio, short life cycle, simple charging technology and low maintenance requirements. However, they are not popular for grid storage because of their low-energy density and short cycle and calendar life. They were commonly used for electric cars but have recently been largely replaced with longer-lasting lithium-ion batteries. There is a Consortium for Battery Innovation (CBI)[2] which has outlined its research goals for advanced lead-based battery concepts. The group, comprised of lead-battery industry stakeholders, says such devices can play an important role alongside lithium-ion and other storage technologies in electric vehicles, renewable energy storage and other applications.

2 Consortium for Battery Innovation – https://batteryinnovation.org

Nickel-Cadmium (NiCd)

9.11 This technology has been around since 1915 and these batteries have low round-trip efficiency, high energy density and a long life cycle. They can perform well at low temperatures ranging from –20°C to +40°C. The batteries are highly toxic, which is why they are used only for stationary purposes in Europe.

High-temperature batteries

9.12 High-temperature batteries are similar to conventional batteries but differ because their energy is based on reactions that only occur at elevated temperatures. The most frequently used are sodium sulphur (NaS) and sodium nickel chloride (NaNiCl).

Sodium Sulphur (NaS)

9.13 Deployed at grid scale in Japan, NaS batteries are used for long durations of energy storage; they have high round-trip efficiency, and relatively high energy density, but their costs continue to be high.

Sodium Nickel Chloride (NaNiCl)

9.14 The Sodium Nickel Chloride battery is a high-temperature battery which has been commercially available since 1995. These batteries can stand limited overcharge and discharge. They have been used in electric vehicles (EVs), and new research is being done to further develop these batteries and use them in alternative settings following the end of their productive life in EVs.

Copper/Zinc rechargeable battery (Cu/Zn)

9.15 Cumulus Energy Storage (CES) have recently developed a rechargeable Cu/Zn battery, combining a 200-year old battery technology with processes from the mining industry. Although still developmental, rechargeable Cu/Zn batteries provide a large-scale storage option, capable of delivering grid-scale levels of power from 1MWh to 100MWh. These batteries are stationary, with potential applications including time-shifting for commercial renewable electricity generation and security and stability of supply. Main advantages of this technology are its low cost, simplicity, scalability and sustainability. The batteries are low maintenance, with a long target lifecycle of 30 years.

Flow batteries

9.16 Flow batteries are an alternative to lithium-ion batteries. Whilst less popular than lithium-ion batteries, flow batteries make up less than 5% of the battery market. Flow batteries have been used in multiple energy storage projects that require longer energy storage durations. Flow batteries have relatively low energy densities and long life cycles, which makes them well-suited for supplying continuous power. A flow battery works by passing a solution over a membrane where ions are exchanged to charge or discharge the cell. Cell voltage is chemically determined by the Nernst equation and, in practical applications, it ranges from 1.0V to 2.2V. Storage capacity depends on the volume of solution. A flow battery is technically similar to both a fuel cell and an electrochemical accumulator cell.

Avista Utilities, Washington State

9.17 The Avista Utilities plant in Pullman, Washington State uses flow battery storage, with a 1.0MW/3.2MWh energy storage project (using a UniEnergy Technologies vanadium flow battery system); the company also has a 423kW community solar program in the Spokane Valley, Washington State.

Dalian, China

9.18 A 200MW/800MWh flow battery is currently being constructed in Dalian, China. This system will not only overtake the Hornsdale Power Reserve as the world's biggest battery, but it will also be the only large-scale battery (>100MW) that is made up of flow batteries instead of lithium-ion batteries. The battery is expected to slice off about 8% of the Liaoning Province port city's expected load once it comes online in 2020. Rongke Power has installed nearly 30 similar battery projects, including some adjacent to wind farms.

The electrochemical reactions of flow batteries are similar to conventional and high-temperature batteries, but their storing techniques differ. The electrolytes used are stored in external tanks and, during charge and discharge, they are pumped through electrochemical cells, which convert chemical energy into electricity. The most well-known types of flow batteries are redox and hybrid.

Redox flow batteries

9.19 Redox flow batteries are similar to conventional batteries except, when the battery is discharged, the fluids need to be newly loaded. The electrolyte volume and power, which are related to the electrode area in the cells, determine the energy of the batteries. These batteries have a high level of discharge but low energy density, although they have reached commercialisation. They are suitable for mobile application in theory; however, until now their energy densities have been too low for this type of application. Two common redox flow battery chemistries are zinc bromine and vanadium.

Hybrid flow batteries

9.20 Hybrid flow batteries, on the other hand, use electro-active components deposited as a solid layer. The active masses are stored separately; one is stored internally in the electrochemical cell, and the other externally in a tank. They are called hybrid because they bring properties from conventional secondary batteries and from redox batteries. A number of companies are working on commercialising Zn-Br hybrid flow batteries on utility-scale applications and in community energy storage systems.

Chemical energy storage

9.21 Chemical energy storage technology, by using hydrogen and synthetic natural gas (SNG), relies on electric energy to generate fuel that may be burned in conventional power plants. By using water electrolysis, the water is split into hydrogen and oxygen. The hydrogen can either be burned directly or it can be transformed to SNG. The efficiency of this technology is lower compared to pumped hydro storage (PHS) and lithium-ion batteries. However, it remains an important technology because it allows large amounts of energy to be stored over longer periods of time.

Hydrogen

9.22 There are many hydrogen storage techniques, but the most common is storing the gas under high temperatures, used mainly for stationary applications. Smaller amounts can be stored above ground, in tanks or bottles, and large amounts are stored underground mainly in piping systems. This technology is being examined closely for industrial applications and is not yet used commercially in a widespread way.

Utsira, Norway

9.23 Utsira is an island 20 km off the southwest coast of Norway. It is approximately 6.2 km^2 and has 235 inhabitants. It has enough wind power to be self-sufficient and excess wind power is used to produce hydrogen in an electrolyser. When the wind turbine slows or stops, electricity is provided using stored hydrogen in a hydrogen engine and a fuel cell.

Synthetic natural gas (SNG)

9.24 Synthetic gas processes are referred to as 'Power to Gas' technologies. After splitting water, another step is added to the mix and, with the help of an electrolyser, the hydrogen and carbon dioxide react to generate methane. The SNG can also be stored in over-ground pressure tanks, underground or can be directly injected into the gas grid. The advantage of synthetic methane is that it can be injected into the existing natural gas storage infrastructure without restrictions. However, it has relatively low efficiency.

Mechanical storage

Pumped-storage hydro power

9.25 Pumped-storage hydro (PSH) facilities are large-scale energy storage plants that use gravitational force to generate electricity. Water is pumped to a higher elevation for storage during low-cost energy periods and high renewable energy generation periods. When electricity is needed, water is released back to the lower pool, generating power through turbines. Recent innovations have allowed PSH facilities to have adjustable speeds, in order to be more responsive to the needs of the energy grid, and also to operate in closed-loop systems. A closed-loop PSH operates without being connected to a continuously flowing water source, unlike traditional pumped-storage hydropower, making pumped-storage hydropower an option for more locations.

In comparison to other forms of energy storage, pumped-storage hydropower can be cheaper, especially for very large capacity storage. According to the Electric Power Research Institute, the installed cost for pumped-storage hydropower varies between $1,700 and $5,100/kW, compared to $2,500/kW to $3,900/kW for lithium-ion batteries. Pumped-storage hydropower is more than 80% energy efficient through a full cycle, and PSH facilities can typically provide 10 hours of electricity, compared to about 6 hours for lithium-ion batteries. Despite these advantages, the challenge of PSH projects is that they are long-term investments: permitting and construction can take 3 to 5 years each. This can scare off investors who would prefer shorter-term investments, especially in a fast-changing market.

Pumped hydroelectric storage offers a way to store energy at the grid's *transmission* stage, by storing excess generation for later use. Many hydroelectric power plants include two reservoirs at different elevations. These plants store energy by pumping water into the upper reservoir when supply exceeds demand. When demand exceeds supply, the water is released into the lower reservoir by running downhill through turbines to generate electricity.

Dinorwig Power Station, Wales

9.26 Known locally as 'Electric Mountain' is a pumped-storage hydroelectric scheme, near Dinorwig, Llanberis in Snowdonia National Park in Gwynedd, North Wales. The scheme can supply a maximum power of 1,728MW (2,317,000hp) and has a storage capacity of around 9.1GWh (33TJ).

Bath County, Virginia, USA

9.27 In Bath County, Virginia, the largest PSH facility in the world supplies energy to about 750,000 homes. It was built in 1985 and has an output of approximately 3GW of energy. On the banks of the lower reservoir, the Bath County pumped-storage power station can be found in the foothills of the Allegheny Mountains in the US state of Virginia. Most of the complex (almost 20 storeys) is hidden beneath the surface of the water. At peak times, when around 500,000 homes and companies in Virginia require power, the spherical shut-off valves are open and more than 850 cubic metres of water per second rush down the underground pipes from the upper basin and through the six turbines located in the lower part of the building.

Compressed air energy storage

9.28 With compressed air energy storage (CAES), air is pumped underground, most likely a salt cavern, during off-peak hours when electricity is cheaper. When energy is needed, the air from the underground cave is released back up into the facility, where it is heated, and the resulting expansion turns an electricity generator. This heating process usually uses natural gas, which releases carbon; however, CAES triples the energy output of facilities using natural gas alone.

CAES also works as a *generation* storage technology, by using the elastic potential energy of compressed air to improve the efficiencies of conventional gas turbines.

One of the major issues with CAES is that, when air is compressed, it heats up. When the electricity is required, the air needs to be expanded, which requires heat. In addition, the cooler the air, the more that can be stored. Companies are therefore trying to find ways to store the heat generated during compression, so it can then be used to heat the air for the expansion which helps drive more efficiency.

There are three types of solution that can deal with heat build-up when the air is initially compressed (see paras **9.49–9.51**).

CAES systems compress air using electricity during off-peak times, and then store the air in underground caverns. During times of peak demand, the air is drawn from storage and fired with natural gas in a combustion turbine to generate electricity. This method uses only a third of the natural gas used in conventional methods. As CAES plants require some sort of underground reservoir, they are limited by their locations. Two commercial CAES plants currently operate in Huntorf, Germany, and McIntosh, Alabama, although plants have been proposed in other parts of the United States.

One of the final issues to overcome for successful CAES revolves around the pressure of the compressed air as it comes out. If the storage facility is full of compressed air, the cavern pressure is higher. If the cavern is almost empty, the cavern pressure will be low. There are two operating modes when storing compressed air in a fixed-volume cavern:

- allow the pressure to change naturally as the air is released, which will mean the turbine creates less electricity as time goes on; or
- control the flow of air out of the cavern, so it releases more of the compressed air at the end to counter the lower pressure. This will ensure constant electricity supply from the turbine / generator.

Key features of a CAES plant

9.29

- a motor/generator with clutches on both ends (to engage it to/disengage it from the compressor train, the expander train, or both);
- multi-stage air compressors with intercoolers to reduce the power requirements needed during the compression cycle, and with an aftercooler to reduce the storage volume requirements;
- an expander train consisting of high- and low-pressure turboexpanders with combustors between stages;
- control system (to regulate and control the off-peak energy storage and peak power supply, to switch from the compressed air storage mode to the electric power generation mode, or to operate the plant as a synchronous condenser to regulate volt-ampere reactive (VARs) on the grid);
- auxiliary equipment (fuel storage and handling, cooling system, mechanical systems, electrical systems, heat exchangers); and

- underground or above-ground compressed air storage, including piping and fittings. Underground storage is often performed in aquifers or mined caverns, while above-ground air storage is executed within specially designed holding tanks.

A number of CAES plants were designed and/or investigated but not built:

- During the Soviet era, a 1,050MWe CAES plant using salt cavern geology formations for the air storage was proposed for construction in the Donbas area of Russia. Underground geological development of the air storage was initiated. However, when the Soviet Union collapsed, the construction was terminated.
- Israel developed plans for several CAES facilities, including a 3 × 100MWe CAES facility using fractured hard rock aquifers.
- Luxembourg designed a 100MWe CAES plant, sharing an upper reservoir for a water compensation system with a pumped hydro plant located in a hard rock cavern at the Vianden site.
- Soyland Electric Cooperative contracted for the construction of a 220MWe hard rock based plant. Plant engineering and the cavern sample drilling/ rock analysis were completed, and all major equipment had been purchased when the project was terminated due to non-technical considerations.

McIntosh Power Plant, Alabama

9.30 The McIntosh Power Plant in Alabama is the only utility-scale CAES facility in the United States, and one of just a handful in the world. At night, the plant uses excess electricity from the grid to compress air and pump it underground into an airtight salt cavern. The caverns provide large, impermeable spaces. The compressed air stays compressed, and the oxygen in the air does not react with the salt. There the air is stored at pressures between 650 and 1058 PSI, about one-tenth of the pressure of a high-pressure oil well. When the demand for energy increases during the day, the air is released to an on-site natural gas unit, where it is heated with natural gas, combusts and produces an even hotter gas stream that turns a turbine and produces electricity.

Compressed air is the key ingredient in producing electricity at all gas plants, and it is the critical component that makes the gas combust, producing the gas stream that spins the turbine. At natural gas plants, making compressed air is the most energy-intensive part of running the plant; more than half of the energy generated by the turbine is simply fed back into the system to compress the air. The McIntosh CAES plant is able to compress the air independently of the power production process, when it is most economical to do so, because it has a place to store it, the salt mine. The plant has enough stored air to help a 110MW turbine generate power for 26 hours, powering up to 110,000 homes.

Huntorf, Germany

9.31 The plant, which is the longest in operation, since 1978, is a 290MW CAES power plant connected to the grid in order to refine base-load electricity from the Unterweser nuclear power plant. It produces peak-load electricity, functioning primarily for cyclic duty, ramping duty, and as a hot spinning reserve for industrial customers in northwest Germany. Recently, this plant has been successfully levelling the variable power from numerous wind turbine generators in Germany. This power plant has had high availability, although with relatively low overall efficiency. About 1.6kWh of gas and 0.8kWh of base-load electricity are required in order to generate 1kWh of peak-load electricity. This is essentially due to the fact that the air which is heated upon compression must be cooled down before it is stored in the cavern. Conversely, the cooling which occurs upon expansion in the turbine must be compensated for by use of natural gas.

CRYObattery, Carrington, UK

9.32 The CRYObattery facility in Carrington, UK will store spare green energy and could power up to 100,000 homes. The technology will store compressed air in huge containers which is used to generate electricity. The facility will be next to Carrington Power Station and will become one of Europe's largest battery storage systems and supply long duration energy storage. It is expected that the CRYObattery installation will begin operation in 2022.

Flywheels

9.33 Flywheels work by accelerating a rotor to high speeds using electrical energy, storing rotational energy to be converted back to electricity when required. Flywheels are not suitable for long-term energy storage but are very effective for load-levelling and load-shifting applications. Flywheels are known for their long life cycle, high energy density, low maintenance costs, and quick response speeds. Motors store energy into flywheels by accelerating their spins to very high rates (up to 50,000 rpm). The motor can later use that stored kinetic energy to generate electricity by going into reverse. Flywheels are commonly left in a vacuum so as to minimize air friction, which would slow the wheel. The Stephentown Spindle in Stephentown, New York, unveiled in 2011 with an energy capacity of 20MW, was the first commercial use of flywheel technology to regulate the grid in the United States. Several other flywheel facilities have since come online.

Flywheels can provide a variety of benefits to the grid, at either the *transmission* or *distribution* level, by storing electricity in the form of a spinning mass.

The device is shaped liked a cylinder and contains a large rotor inside a vacuum. When the flywheel draws power from the grid, the rotor accelerates to very high speeds, storing the electricity as rotational energy. To discharge the stored energy, the rotor switches to generation mode, slows down, and runs on inertial energy, thus returning electricity to the grid.

Flywheels typically have long lifetimes and require little maintenance. The devices also have high efficiencies and rapid response times. They can be placed almost anywhere; flywheels can be located close to consumers and can store electricity for distribution.

Stephentown, New York

9.34 Stephentown, New York is the site of Beacon Power's first 20MW plant (40MW overall range) and provides frequency regulation service to the

New York Independent System Operator Inc (NYISO). The facility includes 200 flywheels and is managed by Beacon Power. Initial commercial operation began in January 2011 and full output was reached in June 2011. In this market, Beacon flywheels perform between 3,000 and 5,000 full depth-of-discharge cycles a year. Although the plant provides only 10% of the NYISO market regulation market capacity, this amounts to over 30% of the Area Control Error correction, doing so with over 95% accuracy.

AdD HyStor Project, University of Sheffield, UK

9.35 The grid-connected research facility is one of the largest and fastest battery storage systems in the UK. Flywheel and battery energy storage systems are well suited to provide CO_2-neutral dynamic grid stabilisation. However, when each is used in isolation, they may not be able to mitigate all types of destabilisation event – for example, flywheels are often used for short-term energy storage and can respond quickly (in the order of milliseconds) to dynamic frequency destabilisation, whereas battery systems may be of better use during longer destabilisation periods. Additionally, there are technical limitations to each technology – for example, existing flywheels have a fixed ratio of power (kW) to capacity (kWh), which for most applications leads to an oversized installation, resulting in poor economics for the installation and long payback terms. Utilisation of both technologies in a combined system will provide an advanced grid stabilisation solution which can effectively deal with a range a stability events.

High-temperature and thermal energy storage

9.36 There are a number of thermodynamic energy storage technologies in development and operational – notably, thermal energy storage, high-temperature thermal energy storage, pumped heat electrical storage and liquid air energy storage. Thermal storage is used for electricity *generation* by using power from the sun, even when the sun is not shining. Concentrating solar plants can capture heat from the sun and store the energy in water, molten salts or other fluids. This stored energy is later used to generate electricity, enabling the use of solar energy even after sunset.

Plants like these are currently operating or proposed in California, Arizona and Nevada. For example, the proposed Rice Solar Energy Project in Blythe, California will use a molten salt storage system with a concentrating solar tower to provide power for approximately 68,000 homes each year.

Thermal storage technologies also exist for *end-use* energy storage. One method is freezing water at night using off-peak electricity, then releasing the stored cold energy from the ice to help with air conditioning during the day.

Ice Energy's Ice Bear Energy Project

9.37 Ice Energy's Ice Bear system creates a block of ice at night, and then uses the ice during the day to condense the air conditioning system's refrigerant. In this way, the Ice Bear system shifts the building's electricity consumption from the daytime peak to off-peak times when the electricity is less expensive.

Thermal energy storage (TES)

9.38 There are three main types of TES: sensible heat storage; latent heat storage; and thermo-chemical storage.

Sensible heat storage

9.39 These technologies store heat in a solid or liquid, without any change of state. These are widely used for domestic systems, district heating and industrial needs through electric storage heaters and hot water tanks. Common materials used include water, sand, molten salt and rocks, with water the most cost-effective. While this is the cheapest of the three TES technologies, capacity is subject to space restrictions and materials can have low energy density. Thermal energy storage facilities use temperature to store energy. When energy needs to be stored, rocks, salts, water or other materials are heated and kept in insulated environments. When energy needs to be generated, the thermal energy is released by pumping cold water onto the hot rocks, salts or hot water in order to produce steam, which spins turbines. Thermal energy storage can also be used to heat and cool buildings instead of generating electricity. For example, thermal storage can be used to make ice overnight to cool a building during the day. Thermal efficiency can range from 50% to 90%, depending on the type of thermal energy used.

Drake Landing Solar Community, Alberta, Canada

9.40 The Drake Landing Solar Community (DLSC) is a planned neighbourhood in the town of Okotoks, Alberta, Canada that has successfully integrated Canadian energy-efficient technologies with a renewable, unlimited energy source, the sun. The first of its kind in North America, DLSC is heated by a district system designed to store solar energy underground during the summer months and distribute the energy to each home for space heating needs during winter months. The scheme fulfils more than 90% of each home's space heating requirements from solar energy, resulting in less dependency on limited fossil fuels.

Project status

9.41

- after nearly 12 years of continuous monitoring, performance analysis and improvements, a significant body of knowledge and experience has been learned about the solar borehole thermal energy storage (BTES) system for Canadian applications. Natural Resources Canada (NRCan) is currently looking into expanding the focus of the research to other areas of applied low-carbon community energy systems, such as technology integration, complementary renewable energy production technologies, cost reduction and emerging large-scale solar PV-thermal technologies;
- 100% solar fraction in the 2015–2016 heating season, meaning that all of the heat required by the houses for space heating was supplied by solar energy;

- consistent solar fractions above 90% over the last 5 years, with an average of 96% for the period 2012–2016;
- high solar fraction of 92% even during the very cold winter of 2013–2014,
- very low electricity usage, with coefficient of performance (COP) above 30. This means that, for every kWh of electricity, the system delivers more than 30kWh of heat;
- throughout the years, the electricity used for pumps was reduced by energy efficiency measures, and on-site solar PV generation was increased with the addition of 18kW in 2011. The operation is now net-zero electricity for pumping power, which includes pumping through the solar collectors, district heating loop and BTES; and
- strong educational component, with frequent site visits by professionals and students. The technology is currently being considered by several communities in Canada as well as internationally by China, United States and several European countries.

Latent heat storage

9.42 Latent heat storage stores energy using materials with high latent heat, known as 'phase change materials' (PCMs). PCMs store energy as they change state, usually from solid to liquid. This technology has higher storage capacities and target-oriented discharging temperatures.

Thermo-chemical storage

9.43 This storage technology uses chemical reactions, such as absorption, to store and release thermal energy, as well as to control humidity. Thermo-chemical storage systems are highly efficient, with high energy density.

High-temperature thermal energy storage

9.44 This technology is used to store heat above 250°C from concentrating solar facilities. Adding this technology to existing or future solar thermal power plants may present flexibility options in order to be able to feed the power into the grid at times of no sunshine. However, for widespread deployment control technology, containment mediums and material stability need to be improved for high temperatures; such plants do not exist in the UK at scale, and they are not expected to in the future.

Pumped heat electrical storage

9.45 One technique is pumped heat electrical storage, which transfers heat loads between a 'cold' store and a 'hot' store, acting like a fridge. A heat pump is used to transfer the heat between stores, recovering the energy as it pumps between the two; chemicals with particular qualities are used to enable the process.

Pumped Heat Energy Storage, Fareham, UK

9.46 The world's first grid-scale pumped heat energy storage (PHES) system has been commissioned and entered into operation as part of Newcastle University's National Facility for Pumped Heat Energy Storage. The system has been developed as part of the work of the Energy Technologies Institute (ETI) and places the UK as a leader in the research and development of low-cost and grid-scalable electrical and thermal energy storage. It consists of two containers, a cold store and a hot store, filled with gravel and an inert gas. The two containers are connected via a reversible 150kW heat pump. When surplus energy needs to be stored, the inert gas is withdrawn from the cold store and compressed using an electrically powered pump, thereby raising its temperature. This gas is then injected into the hot store where the heat transfers to the gravel. The gas is then withdrawn from the hot store and returned to the cold store once it has sufficiently cooled. To release the energy that is stored in the gravel, the process is reversed. Gas from the cold store is compressed and injected back into the hot store, where it is reheated by the gravel. This newly heated gas is then used to drive the engine.

Liquid air energy storage

9.47 Liquid air energy storage (LAES), also known as cryogenic energy storage (CES), uses electricity to cool purified air until liquefied and then stores the liquid air at low pressures in a large insulated tank. When the stored energy is required, the liquid air is pumped to high pressure and vaporised before being heated and expanded to drive a turbine. LAES consequently provides large-scale, long-duration energy storage with no geographical constraints. Although requiring electrical energy to cool and heat the air, waste heat/cold from other industrial processes can be used to increase efficiency.

LAES has also been compared to pumped hydro, where excess electricity is used to pump water up to a reservoir above a hydroelectric turbine. Pumped hydro and LAES can both be designed to provide power for hundreds of thousands of homes. But, unlike pumped hydro, LAES does not require a water system or elevation differences to operate.

LAES Plant, Bury, Manchester

9.48 The world's first grid-scale LAES plant is located at Bury, near Manchester, UK. This new LAES system was built by Highview Power and is connected to the Pilsworth Landfill gas site, a power plant that burns methane from the landfill to create electricity. The plant was built in partnership with Viridor, a recycling and renewable energy company, and it received £8 million from the UK government (about US$10.7 million).

The power stored at Pilsworth will be aggregated by a company called Kiwi Power, which will manage when the LAES system will charge and discharge.

Adiabatic storage

9.49 This process retains the heat from compression and re-uses this when the air is expanded to produce the power; expected efficiency around 70% (although theoretically 100%).

Diabatic storage

9.50 This process takes the heat and dissipates it into the atmosphere via heat intercoolers. When the air is released to go through the turbines, it needs to be heated; expected efficiency around 70%.

Isothermal storage

9.51 This process involves using heat exchangers to try to keep the internal and external temperatures the same so that, as the air is compressed, heat dissipates into the atmosphere. Once the air is released to drive the turbine and produce the electricity, heat is brought in from the external environment.

Electrical methods

Capacitor

9.52 A capacitor (originally known as a 'condenser') is a passive two-terminal electrical component used to store energy electrostatically. Capacitors vary widely in their construction, but all contain at least two electrical conductors (plates) separated by an insulator. A capacitor can store electric energy when disconnected from its charging circuit, so it can be used like a temporary battery, or like other types of rechargeable energy storage system. Capacitors are commonly used in electronic devices to maintain power supply while batteries change.

Superconducting magnets

9.53 Superconducting magnetic energy storage (SMES) systems store energy in a magnetic field created by the flow of direct current in a superconducting coil that has been cooled to a temperature below its superconducting critical temperature. A typical SMES system includes a superconducting coil, power conditioning system and refrigerator. Once the superconducting coil is charged, the current does not decay, and the magnetic energy can be stored indefinitely. The stored energy can be released to the network by discharging the coil. Due to the energy requirements of refrigeration and the cost of superconducting wire, SMES is used for short-duration storage such as improving power quality. It also has applications in grid balancing. SMES is very efficient for rapid exchange of electrical power with the grid during small and large disturbances to address those instabilities. In addition, SMES plays an important role in integrating renewable sources such as wind generators to the power grid by controlling output power of wind plant and improving the stability of the power system. Efficient application of SMES in various power system operations depends on the proper location in the power system, exact energy and power ratings, and appropriate controllers.

STORAGE AND ELECTRIC VEHICLES

9.54 Energy storage is especially important for electric vehicles (EVs). As EVs become more widespread, they will increase electricity demand at peak times, as professionals come home from work and plug in their cars for a nightly recharge. To prevent the need for new power plants to meet this extra demand, electricity will need to be stored during off-peak times. Storage is also important for households that generate their own renewable electricity. It isn't possible for a car to be charged overnight by solar energy without a storage system. Electric vehicles can be used as back-up storage during periods of grid failure or spikes in demand. Although most EVs today are not designed to supply energy back into the grid, vehicle-to-grid (V2G) cars can store electricity in car batteries and then transfer that energy back into the grid later. EV batteries can still be used in grid storage even after they are taken off the road: utilities are using the batteries from retired EVs as second-hand energy storage. These batteries can be used to store electricity for up to a decade for grid applications.

Battery Storage, Elverlingsen, Germany

9.55 An example of this can be found in Elverlingsen, Germany, where almost 2,000 batteries from Mercedes-Benz EVs were collected to create a stationary grid-sized battery that can hold almost 9MW of energy.

UK PLANNING LAW CHANGES COULD HELP MEGA-PROJECTS CLEAR 'SIGNIFICANT HURDLE'

9.56 The UK Government is set to remove a significant barrier to utility-scale storage sites, proposing changes to planning regulations to allow projects over 50MW to proceed without Government approval. The new proposals from the Department for Business, Energy and Industrial Strategy (BEIS) follow a previous consultation in January 2019 on planning policy for storage sites.

Currently, projects over 50MW in England and 350MW in Wales must secure approval via the Nationally Significant Infrastructure Project (NSIP) process. The previous consultation proposed keeping the 50MW threshold but creating a new capacity threshold for storage co-located with generation to bypass the requirement for NSIP approval. Under the new proposals, larger storage projects could receive consent from local planning authorities under the Town and Country Planning Act 1990.

Requiring storage projects to go through the NSIP has been said to be a major problem for large storage projects to overcome, in particular by the Electricity Storage Network (ESN), for the additional time and cost that it requires. According to ESN members, NSIP adds an estimated 18 months to three years to project lead times, and costs can reach hundreds of thousands, compared to tens of thousands.

The consultation stated that, although energy storage is considered to be a subset of generation for planning and licensing purposes, it is 'not always suitable' to treat storage in the same way as other generation, as it may fail to account for the 'distinctive characteristics' and benefits of storage. It follows industry feedback that the original proposals would not alleviate the additional costs and time associated with the NSIP.

Responses also indicated the potential loophole of co-locating a large storage project with a small turbine, as well as examples of projects which had been either deliberately capped at 49.9MW or split into multiple 49.9MW projects to avoid the NSIP. Clustering of projects just under the 50MW threshold were also cited as a reason for the need for either a higher threshold or complete removal.

The consultation document said that, as lithium-ion storage projects typically have a smaller footprint compared to other forms of generation such as wind and solar with equal capacity, as well as a relatively quick construction time, NSIP approval is not required. Whilst the proposals apply to lithium-ion batteries, as well as several forms of storage including flow batteries and liquid air that could be deployed at scale as the technology matures, pumped hydro is excluded due to the larger planning impacts, as well as the projects often requiring other consents.

Chapter 10

Integration into the Energy System

INTRODUCTION

10.1 In order for renewable energy systems to be installed and used, many countries have established renewable energy targets for electricity supply. As solar and wind tend to be more variable and uncertain than conventional sources of electricity, changes have to be made to the power system planning and operations, to be able to meet these targets. The UK has set such policies and targets. In moving to renewable energy and away from fossil fuel production, the energy generated by the variable renewable electricity (VRE) processes need to be integrated into the grid system. This raises a number of challenges.

Grid integration is the practice of developing efficient ways to deliver VRE to the grid. In order for integration to work, it has to maximise the cost-effectiveness of incorporating VRE into the power system and, at the same time, maintain or increase system stability and reliability. Looking at grid integration requires policymakers, regulators and system operators to consider a number of issues.

New renewable energy generation

10.2 The new VRE generation needs targets that are aligned and incentives which consider grid integration. Long-term renewable energy targets can drive innovation in the policies and system operations that support clean energy. Also, some 'grid-aware' incentives (ie rewarding wind and solar generators that incorporate technologies that contribute to grid stability) can motivate investment in renewable energy and mitigate negative impacts of integrating this type of resource into the grid.

Many of these incentives are in place and they are already driving a move towards VRE and away from non-renewable energy resources.

When considering whether to scale up VRE generation, the variability of wind and solar resources complicates evaluations of whether a system with significant VRE has an adequate supply to meet long-term electricity demand.

Integrating distributed photovoltaic (PV) solar power results in benefits and challenges compared to the integration of utility-scale wind and solar power. Localised growth in PV can raise problems such as voltage violations and reverse power flow in low-voltage distribution systems. However, studies have shown that positive impacts can also result from distributed PV. Updating interconnection standards, procedures and distribution planning methodologies, to better reflect the characteristics of distributed PV, can help realise these benefits and delay or even prevent the need for grid reinforcement.

Scaling up renewable energy generation whilst aligning targets and incentives with grid integration

10.3 As can be seen in Chapter 14, countries have established ambitious targets for increasing the contribution of renewable energy towards meeting their national energy demand. As the proportion of VRE connected to the grid increases, power system planners will need to evaluate and manage the impact of increased variability and uncertainty on system operations. They will also need to ensure that the policy and regulatory environment offers sufficient certainty and revenue streams to encourage investment in new VRE generation.

Establish renewable energy targets

10.4 Long-term renewable energy targets can drive innovation in the policies and system operations that support clean energy. Renewable energy targets take a variety of forms:

- focus on the contribution of renewables towards primary energy supply;
- electricity production; and/or
- installed capacity.

Mexico has adopted a generation target of obtaining 35% of its electricity from renewable sources by 2024. India, on the other hand, has announced a capacity target of establishing 175GW of renewable energy capacity (comprising 100GW solar, 60GW wind, 10GW biomass and 5GW small hydro) by 2022.

Grid integration study

10.5 A grid integration study is an analysis of a set of scenarios that looks at the ability of a power system to accommodate significant amounts of VRE.

A pathway for meeting targets

10.6 Grid integration studies can identify specific needs for a power system to meet its renewable energy targets. This can also help planners to identify milestones for meeting the targets.

Create smart renewable energy incentives

10.7 To meet renewable energy targets, these may include changes to the policy and regulatory environment to encourage the uptake of renewable energy options. Grid-aware incentives include:

- grid support capabilities;
- planning processes to address congestion;
- aligning generation with demand;
- the provision of forecasting data;
- integration with dispatch optimisation; and
- dispatchable renewable resources.

Using wind and solar to reliably meet electricity demand

Capacity value

10.8 The determination of the capacity value of VRE is more complicated than with conventional generation methods, as VRE is inherently variable. The simplest way to calculate capacity value of a renewable generator is to look at how VRE generation will align with regional demand patterns. This considers the output of a generator over a number of periods during which the system faces a high risk of an outage, such as 10 to 100 hours.

Operational flexibility

10.9 Accessing operational flexibility becomes important in systems with significant grid-connected solar and wind energy. Operational coordination between balancing authority areas enables sharing of resources through reserve sharing, coordinated scheduling and/or consolidated operation. Other sources of flexibility include conventional generation and transmission networks.

Distributed solar

10.10 Using distributed PV can reduce transmission and distribution line losses, increase grid resilience, lower generation costs, and reduce requirements to invest in new utility generation capacity. Distributed PV systems can also mitigate reliability issues experienced in developing areas by providing standby capacity capable of offering stable power during times of poor power quality.

There are a number of challenges

Operation

10.11 In most utility systems, power flows in one direction, from centralised generators to sub-stations, and then to consumers. With distributed generation (DG), power can flow in both directions. Most electric distribution systems were not designed to accommodate DG and the two-way flow of power. Fluctuating power generation from distributed PV can impact the operation of any voltage regulation and complicate the task of maintaining the voltage levels within regulated limits. Occasional cloud variability affecting solar energy production may accelerate cycling of voltage regulation equipment, especially critical for longer, rural feeders.

Planning

10.12 Traditional distribution and transmission planning does not address the benefits and challenges of DG systems. Quantifying the ability of distributed PV to help meet electricity demand can be a challenge.

Interconnection standards and codes

10.13 Interconnection standards and codes define the requirements for distributed generators to interconnect with the grid and ensure that the behaviour of these generators supports reliable distribution system operations. These standards have previously required inverters to disconnect from the grid and interrupt energy production when certain grid disturbances (eg over-/under-voltage or frequency) are detected. Germany has updated its interconnection requirements instead to require PV inverters to support appropriate frequency levels (eg by implementing fault ride-through capabilities) that prevent large-scale simultaneous PV disconnection in over-frequency situations. This requires distributed PV to use equipment to remotely and selectively stop system output when generation significantly exceeds demand at the sub-station level.

Interconnection procedures

10.14 Interconnection procedures balance the deployment of distributed PV and ensure reliable operation of the distribution system. As the amount of distributed PV increases, it may become important to replace 'first-come, first-served' interconnection processes.

EUROPEAN ENERGY INTEGRATION PLANS

10.15 The energy integration plans of the EU are likely to give rise to new regulation that will affect energy companies, vehicle makers, refiners, heavy industries and more. This policy is not just the integration of VRE into the existing network, but it goes much further and looks at integration of all energy systems. The UK, having now left the EU, still needs to be cognisant of the plans as it will still be trading with the EU and has companies that trade with, and have offices in, the EU.

In its 'Strategy for Energy System Integration' (dated 8 July 2020), the European Commission has shown what can be expected and is ready to use all of the legislation that it can to make this happen. There are a number of policies which are incentives to increase the share of renewable energy, taxes on some energy products, some state aid, and targeted funding for technologies that are still a way from being in the marketplace, which include carbon capture and storage.

The plans still lack detail but they offer a vision of how energy-producing and energy-using sectors will meet the goal of cutting emissions to net zero by 2050.

What is energy integration?

More 'circular' energy system, with energy efficiency at its core

10.16 Here, the least energy-intensive choices are prioritised, unavoidable waste streams are reused for energy purposes, and synergies are exploited across sectors. This already happens in combined heat and power plants and also through the use of some waste and residues. There is further potential, in reusing waste heat from industrial processes, data centres, or energy produced from bio-waste or in wastewater treatment plants.

Greater direct electrification of end-use sectors

10.17 Rapid growth and cost competitiveness in renewable electricity production can also service a growing share of energy demand – for example, the use of heat pumps for space heating or low-temperature industrial processes, electric vehicles for transport, or electric furnaces in certain industries.

Use of renewable and low-carbon fuels

10.18 This includes hydrogen, where direct heating or electrification is not feasible, is not efficient or has higher costs. Renewable gases and liquids produced from biomass, or renewable and low-carbon hydrogen, can offer solutions allowing storage of the energy produced from variable renewable sources. Examples include using renewable hydrogen in industrial processes and heavy-duty road and rail transport, synthetic fuels produced from renewable electricity in aviation and maritime transport, or biomass in the sectors where it has the biggest added value.

More integrated system will also be 'multi-directional'

10.19 Here, consumers will play an active role in energy supply:

- 'vertically', decentralised production units and customers contribute to the overall balance and flexibility of the system; and
- 'horizontally', exchanges of energy take place between consumers.

Benefits of energy integration

10.20 Energy system integration can help to reduce greenhouse gas emissions in sectors that are more difficult to decarbonise – for example, by using renewable electricity in buildings and road transport, or renewable and low-carbon fuels in maritime, aviation or certain industrial processes.

EUROPEAN GREEN DEAL[1]

10.21 To overcome the challenges of climate change and environmental degradation, Europe has a strategy whereby:

- there are no net emissions of greenhouse gases by 2050;
- economic growth is decoupled from resource use; and
- no person and no place is left behind.

Timeline

10.22

- 11 December 2019: presentation of the European Green Deal

1 'A European Green Deal – Striving to be the first climate-neutral continent': https://ec.europa.eu/info/strategy/priorities-2019-2024/european-green-deal_en.

- 14 January 2020: presentation of the European Green Deal Investment Plan[2] and the Just Transition Mechanism[3]
- 4 March 2020: proposal for a European climate law[4] to ensure a climate-neutral European Union by 2050; public consultation (open until 17 June 2020) on the European Climate Pact[5] bringing together regions, local communities, civil society, businesses and schools
- 10 March 2020: adoption of the European Industrial Strategy[6], a plan for a future-ready economy
- 11 March 2020: proposal of a Circular Economy Action Plan[7] focusing on sustainable resource use
- 20 May 2020: presentation of the 'Farm to fork strategy'[8] to make food systems more sustainable
- 20 May 2020: presentation of the EU Biodiversity Strategy for 2030[9] to protect the fragile natural resources of our planet
- 8 July 2020: adoption of the EU strategies for energy system integration and hydrogen[10] to pave the way towards a fully decarbonised, more efficient and interconnected energy sector.

EU energy policies have focused on diversifying the EU's imports of gas away from Russia, and therefore creating a competitive internal market based on unbundled operators, and pushing the rise of renewables in power generation. There have been three driving principles:

(1) security of supply;
(2) competitiveness; and
(3) sustainability.

Hydrogen

10.23 The EU plans development of hydrogen production and use across the industrial and long-haul transport sectors. Hydrogen can be used as a feedstock, a fuel or an energy carrier and storage.

2 'Green Deal Investment Plan': https://ec.europa.eu/regional_policy/en/newsroom/news/2020/01/14-01-2020-financing-the-green-transition-the-european-green-deal-investment-plan-and-just-transition-mechanism.

3 'Just Transition Mechanism': https://ec.europa.eu/info/strategy/priorities-2019-2024/european-green-deal/actions-being-taken-eu/just-transition-mechanism_en.

4 European climate law: https://eur-lex.europa.eu/legal-content/EN/TXT/?qid=1588581905912&uri=CELEX:52020PC0080.

5 European Climate Pact: https://ec.europa.eu/clima/policies/eu-climate-action/pact_en.

6 European Industrial Strategy: https://ec.europa.eu/info/strategy/priorities-2019-2024/europe-fit-digital-age/european-industrial-strategy_en.

7 'Circular Economy Action Plan': https://ec.europa.eu/commission/presscorner/detail/en/fs_20_437.

8 'From Farm to fork': https://ec.europa.eu/info/strategy/priorities-2019-2024/european-green-deal/actions-being-taken-eu/farm-fork_en.

9 EU Biodiversity Strategy for 2030: https://ec.europa.eu/info/strategy/priorities-2019-2024/european-green-deal/actions-being-taken-eu/eu-biodiversity-strategy-2030_en.

10 EU Hydrogen strategy: https://ec.europa.eu/commission/presscorner/detail/en/fs_20_1296.

Path towards European hydrogen eco-system

10.24

- 2020–2014: the installation of at least 6GW of renewable hydrogen electrolysers in the EU, and the production of up to 1 million tonnes of renewable hydrogen
- 2025–2030: hydrogen needs to become an intrinsic part of our integrated energy system, with at least 40GW of renewable hydrogen electrolysers and the production of up to 10 million tonnes of renewable hydrogen in the EU
- 2030 onwards: renewable hydrogen will be deployed on a large scale across all hard-to-decarbonise sectors.

EUROPEAN ENERGY SYSTEM INTEGRATION

10.25 Energy system integration is the planning and operating of the whole energy system across many different carriers, infrastructures and consumer sectors. This should create a link which provides objective low-carbon, reliable and resource-efficient energy services. The EU's energy integration plans are likely to require new regulation that will affect energy companies, vehicle makers, refiners, heavy industries and more. In its 'Strategy for Energy System Integration' (dated 8 July 2020), the European Commission has shown EU companies what to expect in the coming years, and is ready to make full use of legislation. The policies which are proposed include:

- incentives to boost the share of renewable energy;
- taxes on some energy products;
- state aid measures; and
- targeted funding for technologies that are not yet in the market.

The plans have the ultimate goal of cutting emissions to net zero by 2050.

The main aspect of the strategy is the intention to deal with the energy value chain as a whole, rather than regulating each segment individually.

The strategy sets out 38 actions to implement the necessary reforms[11] as follows, with explanatory footnotes added by the author:

> '*To better apply the energy-efficiency-first principle:*
>
> - Issue guidance to Member States on how to make the energy-efficiency-first principle operational across the energy system when implementing EU and national legislation (by 2021).
> - Further promote the energy-efficiency-first principle in all upcoming relevant methodologies (e.g. in the context of the European resource adequacy assessment) and legislative revisions (e.g. of the TEN-E Regulation[12]).

11 'Powering a climate-neutral economy: An EU Strategy for Energy System Integration': https://ec.europa.eu/energy/sites/ener/files/energy_system_integration_strategy_.pdf.

12 Regulation (EU) No 347/2013 on guidelines for trans-European energy infrastructure: https://eur-lex.europa.eu/legal-content/en/TXT/?uri=celex%3A32013R0347.

- Review the Primary Energy Factor, in order to fully recognise energy efficiency savings via renewable electricity and heat, as part of the Energy Efficiency Directive[13] (June 2021).

To build a more circular energy system:

- Facilitate the reuse of waste heat from industrial sites and data centres, through strengthened requirements for connection to district heating networks, energy performance accounting and contractual frameworks, as part of the revision of the Renewable Energy Directive and of the Energy Efficiency Directive (June 2021).
- Incentivise the mobilisation of biological waste and residues from agriculture, food and forestry sectors and support capacity-building for rural circular energy communities through the new Common Agriculture Policy, Structural Funds and the new LIFE programme[14] (from 2021 onwards).

To ensure continued growth in the supply of renewable electricity:

- Through the Offshore Renewable Strategy[15] and follow-up regulatory and financing actions, ensure the cost-effective planning and deployment of offshore renewable electricity, taking into account the potential for on-site or nearby hydrogen production, and strengthen EU's industrial leadership in offshore technologies (2020).
- Explore establishing minimum mandatory Green Public Procurement[16] (GPP) criteria and targets in relation to renewable electricity, possibly as part of the revision of the Renewable Energy Directive (June 2021), supported by capacity building financing under the LIFE programme.
- Tackle remaining barriers to a high level of renewable electricity supply that matches the expected growth in demand in end-use sectors, including through the review of the Renewable Energy Directive (June 2021).

To further accelerate the electrification of energy consumption:

- As part of the Renovation Wave[17] initiative, promote the further electrification of buildings' heating (in particular through heat pumps), the deployment of on-buildings renewable energy, and the roll-out of electric vehicle charging points (from 2020 onwards), using all available EU funding, including the Cohesion Fund and InvestEU[18].
- Develop more specific measures for the use of renewable electricity in transport, as well as for heating and cooling in buildings and industry, in particular through the revision of the Renewable Energy Directive, and building on its sectoral targets (June 2021).
- Finance pilot projects for the electrification of low-temperature process heat in industrial sectors through Horizon Europe[19] and the Innovation Fund[20] (by 2021).

13 Energy Efficiency Directive: https://eur-lex.europa.eu/legal-content/EN/TXT/?qid=1399375464230&uri=CELEX:32012L0027.
14 LIFE Programme – the EU's funding instrument for the environment and climate action created in 1992: https://ec.europa.eu/easme/en/life.
15 'Preparing an EU strategy for offshore renewables': https://ec.europa.eu/info/news/preparing-eu-strategy-offshore-renewables-have-your-say-2020-jul-16_en.
16 Green Public Procurement: https://ec.europa.eu/environment/gpp/index_en.htm.
17 Renovation Wave initiative: https://ec.europa.eu/energy/topics/energy-efficiency/energy-efficient-buildings/renovation-wave_en.
18 InvestEU: https://europa.eu/investeu/home_en.
19 Horizon Europe: https://ec.europa.eu/info/horizon-europe-next-research-and-innovation-framework-programme_en.
20 Innovation Fund: https://ec.europa.eu/clima/policies/innovation-fund_en.

- Assess options to support the further decarbonisation of industrial processes, including through electrification and energy efficiency, in the revision of the Industrial Emissions Directive[21] (2021).
- Propose to revise CO_2 emission standards for cars and vans to ensure a clear pathway from 2025 onwards towards zero-emission mobility (June 2021).

To accelerate the roll-out of electric vehicle infrastructure and ensure the integration of new loads:

- Support the roll-out of 1 million charging points by 2025, using available EU funding, including the Cohesion Fund[22], InvestEU and Connecting Europe Facility[23] funding, and communicate regularly on the funding opportunities and regulatory environment to roll out a charging infrastructure network (from 2020 onwards).
- Use the upcoming revision of the Alternative Fuels Infrastructure Directive[24] to accelerate the roll-out of the alternative fuels infrastructure, including for electric vehicles, strengthen interoperability requirements, ensure adequate customer information, cross- border usability of charging infrastructure, and the efficient integration of electric vehicles in the electricity system (by 2021).
- Take up corresponding requirements for charging and refuelling infrastructure in the revision of the Regulation for the Trans-European Transport network[25] (TEN-T) (by 2021) and explore greater synergies through the revision of the TEN-E Regulation in view of possible energy network related support for cross border high capacity recharging as well as possibly hydrogen refuelling infrastructure (by 2020).
- Develop a Network Code on Demand Side Flexibility[26] to unlock the potential of electric vehicles, heat pumps and other electricity consumption to contribute to the flexibility of the energy system (starting end-2021).

Promote renewable and low-carbon fuels, including hydrogen, for hard-to-decarbonise sectors:

- Propose a comprehensive terminology for all renewable and low-carbon fuels and a European system of certification of such fuels, based notably on full life cycle greenhouse gas emission savings and sustainability criteria, building on existing provisions including in the Renewable Energy Directive (June 2021).
- Consider additional measures to support renewable and low-carbon fuels, possibly through minimum shares or quotas in specific end-use sectors (including aviation and maritime), through the revision of the Renewable Energy Directive and building on its sectoral targets (June 2021), complemented, where appropriate, by additional measures assessed under the REFUEL Aviation[27] and FUEL Maritime[28] initiatives (2020). The support

21 Industrial Emissions Directive 2010/75/EU: https://ec.europa.eu/environment/industry/stationary/ied/legislation.htm.

22 Cohesion Fund: https://ec.europa.eu/regional_policy/en/funding/cohesion-fund/.

23 Connecting Europe Facility: https://ec.europa.eu/inea/en/connecting-europe-facility.

24 Alternative Fuels Infrastructure Directive 2014/94/EU: https://eur-lex.europa.eu/legal-content/en/TXT/?uri=CELEX%3A32014L0094.

25 Trans-European Transport Network (TEN-T): https://ec.europa.eu/transport/themes/infrastructure/ten-t_en.

26 Under Regulation (EU) No 2019/943 on the internal market for electricity: https://eur-lex.europa.eu/legal-content/EN/TXT/?uri=CELEX%3A32019R0943.

27 ReFuelEU Aviation: https://ec.europa.eu/info/law/better-regulation/have-your-say/initiatives/12303-ReFuelEU-Aviation-Sustainable-Aviation-Fuels.

28 FUEL EU Maritime: https://www.europarl.europa.eu/legislative-train/theme-a-european-green-deal/file-fuel-eu-maritime.

regime for hydrogen will be more targeted, allowing shares or quota only for renewable hydrogen.

- Promote the financing of flagship projects of integrated, carbon-neutral industrial clusters producing and consuming renewable and low-carbon fuels, through Horizon Europe, InvestEU and LIFE programmes and the European Regional Development Fund[29] (from 2021).
- Stimulate first-of-a-kind production of fertilisers from renewable hydrogen through Horizon Europe (from 2021).
- Demonstrate and scale-up the capture of carbon for its use in the production of synthetic fuels, possibly through the Innovation Fund (from 2021).
- Develop a regulatory framework for the certification of carbon removals based on robust and transparent carbon accounting to monitor and verify the authenticity of carbon removals (by 2023).

To promote a level-playing field across all energy carriers:

- Issue guidance to Member States to address the high charges and levies borne by electricity and to ensure the consistency of non-energy price components across energy carriers (by 2021).
- Align the taxation of energy products and electricity with EU environment and climate policies, and ensure a harmonised taxation of both storage and hydrogen production, avoiding double taxation, through the revision of the Energy Taxation Directive[30].
- Provide more consistent carbon price signals across energy sectors and Member States, including through a possible proposal for the extension of the ETS, (Emissions Trading System), to new sectors (by June 2021).
- Further work towards the phasing out of direct fossil fuel subsidies, including in the context of review of the State aid framework and the revision of the Energy Taxation Directive (from 2021 onwards).
- Ensure that the revision of the State aid framework supports cost-effective decarbonisation of the economy where public support remains necessary (by 2021).

To adapt the gas regulatory framework:

- Review the legislative framework to design a competitive decarbonised gas market, fit for renewable gases, including to empower gas customers with enhanced information and rights (by 2021).

To improve customer information:

- In the context of the Climate Pact, launch a consumer information campaign on energy customer rights (by 2021).
- Improve information to customers on the sustainability of industrial products (in particular steel, cement and chemicals) as part of the sustainable product policy initiative, and, as appropriate, through complementary legislative proposals (by 2022).

A more integrated energy infrastructure:

- Ensure that the revisions of the TEN-E and TEN-T regulations (in 2020 and 2021, respectively) fully support a more integrated energy system, including through greater synergies between the energy and transport infrastructure, as well as the need to achieve the 15% electricity interconnection target for 2030.

29 European Regional Development Fund: https://ec.europa.eu/regional_policy/en/funding/erdf/.

30 Energy Taxation Directive 2003/96/EU: https://eur-lex.europa.eu/LexUriServ/LexUriServ.do?uri=CELEX:32003L0096:en:HTML.

- Review the scope and governance of the TYNDP[31] to ensure full consistency with the EU's decarbonisation objectives and cross-sectoral infrastructure planning as part of the revision of the TEN-E Regulation (2020) and other relevant legislation (2021).
- Accelerate investment in smart, highly-efficient, renewables-based district heating and cooling networks, if appropriate by proposing stronger obligations through the revision of the Renewable Energy Directive and the Energy Efficiency Directive (June 2021), and the financing of flagship projects.

A digitalised energy system and a supportive innovation framework:

- Adopt a Digitalisation of Energy Action plan[32] to develop a competitive market for digital energy services that ensures data privacy and sovereignty and supports investment in digital energy infrastructure (2021).
- Develop a Network Code on cybersecurity in electricity with sector-specific rules to increase the resilience and cybersecurity aspects of cross-border electricity flows, common minimum requirements, planning, monitoring, reporting and crisis management (by end 2021).
- Adopt the implementing acts on interoperability requirements and transparent procedures for access to data within the EU (first one in 2021).
- Publish a new impact-oriented clean energy research and innovation outlook for the EU to ensure research and innovation supports energy system integration (by end 2020).'

31 Ten-Year Network Development Plan.
32 Digitalisation of the Energy sector: https://setis.ec.europa.eu/publications/setis-magazine/digitalisation-of-energy-sector.

Chapter 11

Environmental Impact of Renewable Energy

INTRODUCTION

11.1 Just because renewable energy uses a source of energy which is renewable and not extracted from the earth – types such as solar and wind do not emit carbon dioxide and other gases that contribute to global warming – does not mean that it has no, or only a green, impact.

Part of the growing demand for renewable energy resources is that it makes the energy sector more resilient, expands energy access to growing countries and can help to lower energy bills. As greenhouse gases trap heat in the atmosphere that would otherwise escape into space, average temperatures on the surface of the earth are rising. Global warming is one symptom of climate change, due to the complex shifts affecting the planet's weather and climate systems. Climate change encompasses not only rising average temperatures but also extreme weather events, shifting wildlife populations and habitats, rising seas, and a range of other impacts. Renewables, like any source of energy, have trade-offs. 'Renewable' does not necessarily mean 'sustainable', as those opposed to corn-based ethanol or large hydropower dams may often argue.

SOLAR POWER

11.2 From the rooftops of domestic dwellings to large-scale solar farms, solar power is reshaping energy markets around the world. Solar photovoltaic capacity has grown from around 5GW in 2005 to approximately 509.3GW in 2018[1].

Solar energy and solar power plants do not produce any air pollution, water pollution or greenhouse gases, and the use of solar energy also reduces the need to use other energy resources which have a larger impact on the environment.

However, as with any type of power plant, they can affect the environment in which they are situated. The clearing of the land for construction and

1 Statista, 'Solar PV – Statistics and Facts': www.statista.com/topics/993/solar-pv.

placement of the solar panels can have a long-term effect on the habitats of native plants and animals.

Land use and ecological impacts

11.3 When generating electricity using a solar farm, these solar facilities require large areas for collection of energy. Because of this, the facilities may interfere with existing land uses and can impact the use of areas such as wilderness or recreational management areas.

The system may also have an impact on land through materials exploration, extraction, manufacturing and disposal, hence the energy footprint can become very high. Thus, returning the land to a pre-disturbed state may involve a significant amount of energy input or time, or both. In some cases, it may not be possible to do so, and the incurred changes are irreversible.

Natural England looked at the evidence of the impact of solar farms on birds, bats and ecology. The review looked at scientific and grey literature[2] to provide a comprehensive report on current thinking towards potential ecological impacts of solar developments. It found that no experimental studies specifically designed to investigate the in-situ ecological impacts of solar PV developments existed in the peer-reviewed literature. It found also that there was incidental and informal evidence suggesting that the collision risk presented by solar panels to birds is low but not impossible, and that it is likely that the infrastructure associated with transporting electricity (e.g. powerlines) presents more of a collision risk for birds than the solar arrays themselves. There was no evidence of collision risk to bats. The Building Research Establishment (BRE) published biodiversity guidance to support developers in the siting and maintenance of solar farms[3].

Impacts on soil, water and air resources

11.4 The construction of solar facilities on large areas of land means clearing and grading the land, which results in soil compaction, changes to drainage channels and increased erosion.

Rabbit Hills, Oregon State campus

11.5 A paper[4] which studies the Rabbit Hills agrivoltaic array, two years after the solar array was installed, found that significant differences in mean air

2 'Grey literature' is used to describe a wide range of different information that is produced outside of the traditional publishing and distribution channels, and which is often not well-represented in indexing databases.

3 BRE National Solar Centre Biodiversity Guidance for Solar Developments: www.bre.co.uk/filelibrary/nsc/Documents%20Library/NSC%20Publications/National-Solar-Centre---Biodiversity-Guidance-for-Solar-Developments--2014-.pdf.

4 'Remarkable agrivoltaic influence on soil moisture micrometeorology and water-use efficiency': https://journals.plos.org/plosone/article?id=10.1371/journal.pone.0203256.

temperature, relative humidity, wind speed, wind direction, and soil moisture were observed. Areas under PV solar panels maintained higher soil moisture throughout the period of observation. A significant increase in late season biomass was also observed for areas under the PV panels (90% more biomass), and areas under PV panels were significantly more water efficient (328% more efficient).

Other impacts

11.6 Solar energy facilities can also influence the socio-economics of an area. Construction and operation of utility-scale solar energy facilities in an area can produce direct and indirect economic impacts:

- direct impacts occur as a result of expenditure on wages and salaries, as well as the acquisition of goods and services which are required for project construction and operation; and
- indirect impacts occur in the form of project wages, salaries and procurement expenditures, which create additional employment, income and tax revenues. Facility construction and operation would require in-migration of workers, affecting housing, public services, and local government employment.

Solar power tower

11.7 In some cases, the solar power plant may require water to clean the solar collectors and concentrators or for cooling turbine generators. In arid regions, the use of water can also affect the ecosystems that depend on that water resource. In California, a solar power plant that concentrates sunlight is accidentally killing 6,000 birds every year, as the birds keep flying into its concentrated solar beam. This has been happening since 2014. The plant's design and location at the Ivanpah Solar Plant in the Mojave Desert uses large-scale photovoltaic panels and is built on a different principle to many other solar plants. Here, in order to catch the sunlight, the plant uses 5 square miles (12.9 square kilometres) of giant mirrors that focus beams of concentrated sunlight at three 40-storey-tall towers. Once the beams are focused on the towers, their energy can be used to power turbines inside, which generates energy for the power grid.

The concentrated light around the towers makes them a good location for insects to be, and this attracts the birds. When the birds cross in front of the concentrated light to get at the insects, they burn up in seconds. The situation is made worse by the fact that the plant sits along the Pacific Flyway, which is a popular migratory route for many different types of birds, including protected species like varied thrushes and northern goshawks. Federal biologists estimate that upwards of 6,000 birds perish at the plant every year, and even though officials at the facility say that they are trying to find a solution, little has changed since its launch in 2014.

The plant installed a large fence to keep out endangered desert tortoises, but this has made it easier for coyotes to kill roadrunners. However, there are plans to add 'roadrunner doors' to the fences so they can easily hop through, instead of getting trapped. With no easy solution in sight, the US Fish and Wildlife Service and other federal agencies are stepping in to collaborate on potential solutions.

What makes this problem stand out (besides the large number of deaths) is that it shows that even solar power plants, which are supposed to be beneficial for the environment, can still have unforeseen impacts on local ecosystems. This problem with the birds, however, is related only to this design of solar plant and is not an issue with the more common design used on solar farms or as panels on domestic dwellings.

Heavy metals

11.8 Solar panels which use thin-film technology are manufactured using heavy metals, such as cadmium telluride (CdTe).

Recycling solar panels

11.9 It was estimated in 2016 that there were 250,000 metric tonnes of solar panel waste in the world. The International Renewable Energy Agency (IRENA) also projected that this could reach 78 million metric tonnes by 2050[5]. Solar panels often contain lead, cadmium and other toxic materials that can only be removed by breaking apart the entire solar panel. Currently, the recycling of solar panels is a big problem – specifically, there are not enough locations to recycle old solar panels, and there are not enough non-operational solar panels to make recycling them economically viable. The materials used to make the panels are rare or precious metals, all of them being composed of silver, tellurium or indium. Due to the limited ability of recycling the panels, those recoverable metals may be going to waste, which may result in resource scarcity issues in the future.

Silicon is one resource that is needed to make the majority of present-day photovoltaic cells and of which there is currently an abundance; however, a silicon-based solar cell requires a lot of energy input in its manufacturing process, and the source of that energy, which is often coal, determines how large the cell's carbon footprint is.

Veolia and PV CYCLE

11.10 In 2018, Veolia and PV CYCLE opened the first recycling plant in Europe for end-of-life solar panels. In France, 190,000 metric tonnes of solar panels were sold in 2016/2017. By 2020, it is likely to represent 35,000 metric tons of waste every year, which world-wide will be tens of millions of metric tons of end-of-life solar panels by 2050 (notably in China, the US, Japan, India

5 End-of-life management – Solar Photovoltaic Panels (June 2016), IRENA: www.irena.org/publications/2016/Jun/End-of-life-management-Solar-Photovoltaic-Panels.

and Germany). Since 2014, solar panel importers and manufacturers have been required to collect and treat them when they reach the stage of being waste. Many panels ended up in landfill. The plant opened in July 2018 in Rousset, a small town in the Bouches-du-Rhône region. Before redirecting them into various sectors, the site separates and recycles the panels' components, from the glass to the aluminium frame, junction boxes and connection cables. The scrap glass is used as a raw material in the glass industry, the frame goes back to aluminium refineries, and the silicon goes back into precious metal channels. The cables and connectors are crushed and sold in the form of copper shot, a mixture of granules that can be used to manufacture new cables and electronic components.

HYDROPOWER

11.11 People have harnessed the energy of river currents, using dams to control water flow, for centuries. Whilst hydropower is theoretically a clean energy source replenished by rain and snow, it also has several drawbacks.

Large dams

11.12

- Large dams can disrupt river ecosystems and surrounding communities, causing harm to wildlife and displacing residents.
- Hydropower generation is vulnerable to silt build-up, which can compromise capacity and harm equipment.
- Drought can also cause problems. In the western US, carbon dioxide emissions over a 15-year period were 100 megatons higher than they normally would have been, according to a 2018 study, as utilities turned to coal and gas to replace hydropower lost to drought. Even hydropower at full capacity has its own emissions problems, as decaying organic material in reservoirs releases methane.

Environmental consequences of big dams

11.13 Although the impacts of large dams have been well documented, new ones are being proposed. A 1989 paper[6] looked at the environmental factors associated with large-storage dam projects and the economic analysis of environmental effects. It looked at the effects that occur upstream, on-site and downstream, and techniques of economic analysis that can be used to value environmental effects in monetary terms.

Samples of actual and proposed dam projects were examined to see what could be learned from completed projects and what are the environmental issues associated with several proposed dams.

6 Dams and Environment – Considerations in World Bank projects: http://documents1.worldbank.org/curated/en/300561468782146320/pdf/multi-page.pdf.

Aswan Dam, Egypt

11.14 One of the projects considered was the Aswan Dam. Construction began in 1960 and the dam was completed in 1967. By 1970, all major power facilities were in place.

The 1989 paper found that the main downstream effects were:

- channel degradation from the release of relatively silt-free waters resulted in degradation in bed level of between 25 and 70 Ms. Measures were being taken to strengthen certain downstream structures, and a pilot project to cover the first 22 km of the channel had begun;
- navigation benefited from the regulation of Nile River flow, and maximum fluctuation in water level decreased from 9 to 3 metres. Navigation also developed in the reservoir behind the dam;
- water quality changed in various ways: turbidity dropped with the reduction in the silt load, but the amount of dissolved solids increased by about 30%. Shalaby[7] estimates that the loss of nitrogen fertilizer from silt that is no longer deposited on the downstream fields amounts to about 1,800 tons of nitrogen a year, with an annual monetary value of about $150,000. This does not include the value of other nutrients and trace elements;
- irrigation benefits resulted from increased reliability of supply to existing irrigated fields, conversion of some areas from basin irrigation to perennial irrigation, and horizontal expansion of agriculture into new areas. At the same time, some agricultural lands were lost due to waterlogging and salinity and alkalinisation. The loss of agricultural lands to industrial and urban uses also continued. On balance, both net irrigated and cropped areas increased, with a resulting increase in production;
- drainage has been a major problem. Due to rapid expansion of perennial irrigation, overuse of water, poor land levelling and intensification of agricultural production, groundwater levels have risen in many areas. Drainage problems are being addressed by greater use of tile drains, remodelling and deepening of main drains, and improved water management practices;
- fisheries, both in the downstream part of the Nile and in the eastern Mediterranean, declined. The number of species caught also declined;
- aquatic weeds have become a common problem in many downstream areas as a result of clearer water and improved year-round water availability. Weeds are being controlled by manual chemical and biological means;
- agricultural production grew due to an increase in the cropping intensity, a direct result of the enhanced availability of irrigation water. Yields, on average, increased, with the use of irrigation, new seeds and chemical fertilizer. The large-scale drainage program has helped to counteract the negative effects (waterlogging, salinity) of perennial irrigation; and
- endemic diseases. Schistosomiasis and malaria are endemic diseases in Egypt wherever perennial irrigation is practised. Available evidence indicates that, on average, urinary schistosomiasis has declined (in part due to a major village water supply programme) but intestinal schistosomiasis has spread somewhat in the delta and was transmitted to parts of Upper Egypt. So far, there has been no evidence of malaria along the reservoir.

7 Gilbert White and A. M. Shalaby (1988) assess the environmental effects of the High Dam 18 years after its completion.

There have been benefits of the Aswan High Dam. It has resulted in protection from floods and droughts and an increase in agricultural production and employment, electricity production and improved irrigation. The dam traps sediment, which has led to increased coastline erosion in the Nile Delta estimated at 125–175 metres per year[8]. With no annual floods and heavy year-round irrigation, groundwater levels remained high with little fluctuation, which leads to waterlogging. The soil's salinity has also increased because the distance between the surface and the groundwater table was small enough (1–2 metres, depending on soil conditions and temperature) to allow water to be pulled up by evaporation, so that the relatively small concentrations of salt in the groundwater accumulated on the soil surface over the years.

However, against the predictions that prevalence of schistosomiasis (bilharzia) would increase, it did not. The assumption did not take into account the extent of perennial irrigation that was already present throughout Egypt decades before the High Dam closure. Large-scale treatment programmes in the 1990s, using single dose oral medication, contributed greatly to reducing the prevalence and severity of Schistosoma mansoni in the delta.

Great Ethiopian Renaissance Dam

11.15 Ethiopia is currently building a dam, the Grand Ethiopian Renaissance Dam, which has caused a great deal of concern. Egypt gets 90% of its fresh water from the Nile which runs south to north from Ethiopia's highlands, with the main source being the Blue Nile, one of two tributaries. This new dam, when it fills up, will allow Ethiopia to control the flow of the Nile. The longer it take to fill, the less the impact will be on the river, but Ethiopia wants to achieve this in six years. One of Egypt's concerns is that, if the water flow drops, it could affect Lake Nasser, the reservoir further downriver behind Egypt's Aswan Dam, even though it only accounts for a small share of Egypt's electricity and it could impede transport on the river. So far, the assessment of impact on water below the dam has not been made.

Effects on river systems

11.16 Reducing the flow of water from a river changes the landscape it flows through, which in turn can affect the ecosystem's flora and fauna. A dam holds back sediments, especially the heavy gravel and cobbles. If a river is deprived of its sediment load, it will seek to recapture it by eroding the downstream channel and banks, which can undermine bridges and other riverbank structures. Riverbeds are typically eroded by several metres within a decade of first closing a dam, and the damage can extend for tens or even hundreds of kilometres below a dam.

Hoover Dam

11.17 The Hoover Dam was opened in 1935. In 1928, President Calvin Coolidge signed a bill which authorised the dam's construction and earmarked

8 M Schwartz (ed) *Encyclopaedia of Coastal Science* (Springer Science and Media).

$128 million dollars for the project. It was built at the time of the Great Depression and was a way of dealing with unemployment. It is a concrete arch-gravity dam which is 279 metres high and 221 metres tall and 201 metres wide at its base, and it uses Lake Mead as its reservoir.

Riverbed lowering

11.18 After closing the Hoover Dam, within nine years the riverbed below the dam had lowered by more than 4 metres. The water in Lake Mead kept digging at the riverbed, this threatens many of the plants in the flood plain as they could not reach the new depth of the ground water table. This riverbed deepening also lowers the groundwater table along a river, which threatens vegetation and local wells in the floodplain and requires crop irrigation in places where there was previously no need. When the riverbed gravels are reduced then this reduces the habitat for many fish that spawn in the gravelly river bottom, and for invertebrates such as insects, molluscs and crustaceans.

Greenhouse gases

11.19 People think that using hydropower instead of fossil fuels means that there will be fewer greenhouse gases. However, dams themselves are a source of greenhouse gases such as carbon dioxide and methane.

Ecosystem destruction

11.20 Closing the Hoover Dam led to changes in native species such as Bighorn sheep, coyotes, ground squirrels, ring-tailed cats, desert tortoise and golden eagles. Their survival relies on specialised plants and, when these plants are destroyed, this affects the animals that rely on them. Also, human activity, such as increased traffic, resulted in water pollution.

Fish species are also affected by aspects of the dam (for instance, the change in water temperature). The Hoover Dam turbines lowered the water temperature, which resulted in the extinction of warm water fish after the dam's completion. Rainbow trout were introduced for recreational fishing and this created competition for native species. There is also significant yearly erosion of the bank as a result of the poured concrete which prevents natural silt deposits, and this also affects the feeding and reproductive environment of native fish species, such as the bonytail chub, Colorado pike minnow, humpback chub and razorback sucker.

Water problems

11.21 The temperature of the water below the dam is not as high as that before the dam, and it often remains unchanged and unaffected by seasonal variations. The free-flowing water usually has a higher oxygen level and lower dissolved salt than the water in Lake Mead.

Other dams

11.22 The Akosombo Dam in Ghana has cut off the supply of sediment to the Volta Estuary, affecting also neighbouring Togo and Benin, whose coasts are now being eaten away at a rate of 10–15 metres per year. A project to strengthen the Togo coast has cost US$3.5 million for each kilometre protected.

Hydrological effects

11.23 Dams also change the pattern of the flow of a river, both reducing its overall volume and changing its seasonal variations. The nature of the impacts depends on the design, purpose and operation of the dam, among other things. All parts of a river's ecology can be impacted by changes to its flow. Where a river's fresh water meets the sea, there is a particularly rich ecosystem. The alteration of the flows reaching estuaries because of dams and diversions causes a decline of sea fisheries in the Gulf of Mexico, the Black and Caspian Seas, California's San Francisco Bay, the Eastern Mediterranean and others. The regulation of the Volta River in Ghana by the Akosombo and Kpong Dams has led to the disappearance of the once-thriving clam industry at the river's estuary, as well as the serious decline of barracuda and other sport fish.

Changes to flooding

11.24 The storage of water in dams delays and reduces floods downstream. River and floodplain ecosystems are closely adapted to a river's flooding cycle where native plants and animals depend on these variations for reproduction, hatching, migration and other important lifecycle stages. The annual floods deposit nutrients on the land, flush out backwater channels, and replenish wetlands. The floodplain itself is also affected by dams.

Pongola and Tana Rivers

11.25 The floodplain of the Pongola River in South Africa has shown a reduction in diversity of forest species after it was dammed; and forests along Kenya's Tana River appear to be slowly dying out because of the reduction in high floods due to a series of dams.

Tidal and wave energy

11.26 Many projects have the aim to capture the ocean's natural rhythms. Programmes like Scotland's Saltire Prize have encouraged innovation in this area.

Hydro schemes can have a potentially adverse impact on the environment, so it is important to take care at the planning stage. The Environment Agency will not grant permission to a scheme that does not comply with environmental legislation and has the potential for doing harm to the surrounding area. This applies to small-scale installations as well as larger operations.

Coastal erosion

11.27 Both onshore and nearshore schemes may have an effect on coastal erosion due to alteration of currents and waves. Tidal velocities, wave amplitude and water flow may be altered in proportion to the scale of the array. A computer model was developed by Dr Simon Neill and Professor Alan Davies from the School of Ocean Sciences, Bangor University, along with colleagues from Edinburgh University and Plymouth Marine Laboratory. They looked at the environmental impact of extracting energy from the Bristol Channel, which is a proposed site for a tidal dam. They found that a large tidal stream turbine farm would have a significant and wide-spread influence on the natural transport of sands in the Bristol Channel.

Device construction

11.28 There are possible impacts during installation from anchoring systems of the devices. Many wave energy devices are secured or tethered to the ocean floor using pilings, concrete blocks, anchors and chains. The preparation of the site may involve dredging and scouring of the seabed to install electrical cables, and the amount of seabed disturbance would depend on the number of devices installed and the mooring systems employed.

Tidal energy systems come at a high cost. The Sihwa Lake Tidal Power Station in South Korea cost $560m, and the La Rance Tidal Power Station cost 620 million francs back in 1966. By comparison, the Tengger Desert Solar Park in China cost around $530m for a total installed capacity of 850MW, making it more cost-efficient than Sihwa Lake, at 254MW total capacity.

Environmental

11.29 Whilst wave energy produces no greenhouse gases or other atmospheric pollutants when generating electricity, emissions can arise from other stages of construction, transportation and life cycle. There are also the potential impacts that are associated with the release and leakage of hydraulic fluids for hydraulic rams, power trains, lubricating oils and fluids, anti-corrosion and biofouling paints and coatings into the surrounding seas.

EMF emissions

11.30 Emissions from electromagnetic fields (EMF) might also disrupt sensitive marine life; a European Commission Study[9] found that EMF could have an impact on migratory routes of sea life in the area. In particular, the species susceptible to EMF are sharks, rays, crustaceans, whales, dolphins, bony fish and marine turtles. One study found that EMF caused eels to divert from their instinctual migratory route, but 'the individuals were not diverted too long and resumed their original trajectory'.

9 'Environmental impacts of noise vibrations and electromagnetic emissions from marine renewable energy: final study report': https://op.europa.eu/en/publication-detail/-/publication/01443de6-effa-11e5-8529-01aa75ed71a1/language-en.

Fishing industry

11.31 Where there are exclusion zones around offshore devices, this could impact on local fishing areas. Anchor lines, tethers and power cables may restrict the use of nets, while floating devices can create sheltered conditions, providing benefits to some marine species and habitats by limiting access and fishing at the site. However, as with marine reserves, fishing activity may increase directly outside the boundary of the installation.

Marine ecosystem

11.32 Marine mammals may be vulnerable to floating structures, or the structures may act as barriers to marine movement and migration, affecting the fauna and flora on the seabed. Most offshore wave energy devices are moored directly to the sea floor, and mooring lines could pose a threat of entanglement for some animals, especially larger whales. Floating wave energy devices could entice sea birds to use the structures as temporary roosts.

Navigational hazards

11.33 Installations could pose navigational hazards to shipping, as their low profile could result in them being difficult to detect visually or by a ship's radar. There is a potential impact on shipping if wave energy devices are not illuminated at night or if their moorings break away during storms. Also, water quality may be affected due to potential oil spills from increased boat traffic in the area for maintenance and repair.

Noise pollution

11.34 The constant noise from wave capture devices, especially in rough conditions, may have an impact on whales and dolphins that use echolocation to hunt. For shoreline and nearshore devices, the levels of operational noise may constitute a noise nuisance locally on the beach or shoreline.

Recreational activities

11.35 Offshore and nearshore devices could have an effect on some forms of recreational swimming and of water sports around the floating devices. Sub-aqua diving and water skiing might benefit from the shelter provided by these devices, but sailing and wind surfing may suffer.

Sedimentary flow

11.36 The placement of onshore and nearshore wave energy installations, such as device platforms, anchors and cables, could change the flow of the water and sands immediately around the structures. Changes in water velocities will impact on sediment transport, coastal erosion and the deposition of coarse sediments such as pebbles or rocks. Slower or restricted water currents will increase the depositing of sediment.

La Rance, France

11.37 The barrage has caused progressive silting of the Rance ecosystem. Here, sand-eels and plaice have disappeared, although sea bass and cuttlefish have returned to the river. Tides still flow in the estuary, and the operator, EDF, endeavours to adjust their level to minimise the biological impact.

Land use and hydroelectric power

11.38 For large-scale plants that involve the building of a dam, the impact on the use of the surrounding land can be significant. A full assessment of the value of this has to be done in order for planning permission to succeed and construction to begin.

Although smaller plants that use run-of-the-river systems may have a lesser impact, there still needs to be an assessment as to how that will affect the course of the river and what impact it may have on river life. There is also the issue of silt and sediment build-up as a result of the process, that could have a detrimental impact over a long period of time.

WIND POWER

11.39 Harnessing the wind as a source of energy started more than 7,000 years ago. Now, electricity-generating wind turbines are to be found in most countries. There have been objections to how the wind farms look and sound, but wind energy is proving a valuable resource. Wind power comes from both onshore turbines and offshore projects.

Assessing and mitigating environmental impacts

11.40 Wind energy can have adverse environmental impacts, including the potential to reduce, fragment or degrade habitat for wildlife, fish and plants. The spinning turbine blades can pose a threat to flying wildlife like birds and bats.

The Royal Society for the Protection of Birds (RSPB) has looked at where wind turbines have affected bird populations[10]. It has found three ways in which wind farms may harm birds: disturbance, habitat loss and collision.

10 RSPB – Wind Farms: www.rspb.org.uk/our-work/our-positions-and-casework/our-positions/climate-change/action-to-tackle-climate-change/uk-energy-policy/wind-farms/.

Some poorly sited wind farms have caused major bird casualties, particularly at Tarifa and Navarra in Spain and the Altamont Pass in California. At these sites, the planners did not consider adequately the likely impact of putting hundreds, or even thousands, of turbines in areas which are important for birds of prey. Thorough environmental assessment is vital to ensure that all ecological impacts are fully identified prior to consent of any development. If wind farms are located away from major migration routes and important feeding, breeding and roosting areas of those bird species known or suspected to be at risk, it is likely that they will have minimal impacts.

BIOMASS

11.41 Biomass energy includes biofuels such as ethanol and biodiesel, wood and wood waste, biogas from landfills, and municipal solid waste. Like solar power, biomass is a flexible energy source, able to fuel vehicles, heat buildings and produce electricity. But biomass can raise thorny issues.

There are critics of corn-based ethanol who say that it competes with the food market for corn and supports the same harmful agricultural practices that have led to toxic algae blooms and other environmental hazards. There have also been issues around whether it is a good idea to ship wood pellets from US forests over to Europe so that they can be burned for electricity (see para **8.36**). Scientists and companies are working on ways to more efficiently convert corn stover, wastewater sludge and other biomass sources into energy, aiming to extract value from material that would otherwise go to waste.

Using biomass for energy has positive and negative effects

11.42 Biomass and biofuels made from biomass are alternative energy sources to fossil fuels – coal, petroleum and natural gas. Burning either fossil fuels or biomass releases carbon dioxide, a greenhouse gas. However, the plants that are the source of biomass for energy capture almost the same amount of carbon dioxide through photosynthesis while growing as is released when biomass is burned, which can make biomass a carbon-neutral energy source.

Burning wood

11.43 Using wood, wood pellets and charcoal for heating and cooking can replace fossil fuels and may result in lower carbon dioxide emissions overall. Wood can be harvested from forests, from coppices that have to be thinned, or from urban trees that fall down or have to be cut down.

Wood smoke contains harmful pollutants such as carbon monoxide and particulate matter. Modern wood-burning stoves, pellet stoves and fireplace inserts can reduce the amount of particulates from burning wood. Wood and charcoal are major cooking and heating fuels in poor countries; but, if people harvest the wood faster than trees can grow, it causes deforestation. Planting fast-growing trees for fuel and using fuel-efficient cooking stoves can help slow deforestation and improve the environment.

Burning municipal solid waste or wood waste

11.44 Burning municipal solid waste (MSW), or *garbage*, in waste-to-energy plants could result in less waste buried in landfill sites. On the other hand, burning garbage produces air pollution and releases the chemicals and substances in the waste into the air. Some of these chemicals can be hazardous to people and the environment if they are not properly controlled.

The US Environmental Protection Agency (EPA) applies strict environmental rules to waste-to-energy plants, which require waste-to-energy plants to use air pollution control devices such as scrubbers, fabric filters and electrostatic precipitators to capture air pollutants.

Scrubbers clean emissions from waste-to-energy facilities by spraying a liquid into the combustion gases to neutralise the acids present in the stream of emissions. Fabric filters and electrostatic precipitators also remove particles from the combustion gases. The particles (called fly ash) are then mixed with the ash that is removed from the bottom of the waste-to-energy furnace.

A waste-to-energy furnace burns at high temperatures (1,800°F to 2,000°F), which break down the chemicals in MSW into simpler, less harmful compounds.

Disposing of ash from waste-to-energy plants

11.45 Ash from waste-to-energy plants can contain high concentrations of various metals that were present in the original waste. Textile dyes, printing inks and ceramics, for example, may contain lead and cadmium.

Separating waste before burning can solve part of the problem. Because batteries are the largest source of lead and cadmium in municipal waste, they should not be included in regular trash. Fluorescent light bulbs should also not be put in regular trash, because they contain small amounts of mercury.

The EPA tests ash from waste-to-energy plants to make sure that it is not hazardous. The test looks for chemicals and metals that could contaminate ground water. Some MSW landfills use ash that is considered safe as a cover layer for their landfills, and some MSW ash is used to make concrete blocks and bricks.

Collecting landfill gas or biogas

11.46 Biogas forms as a result of biological processes in sewage treatment plants, waste landfills and livestock manure management systems. Biogas is composed mainly of methane (a greenhouse gas) and carbon dioxide. Many facilities that produce biogas capture it and burn the methane for heat or to generate electricity. This electricity is considered renewable and, in many US states, contributes to meeting renewable portfolio standards (RPS). This electricity may replace electricity generation from fossil fuels and can result in a net reduction in carbon dioxide emissions. Burning methane produces carbon dioxide but, because methane is a stronger greenhouse gas than carbon dioxide, the overall greenhouse effect is lower.

Liquid biofuels: ethanol and biodiesel

11.47 Biofuels are transportation fuels such as ethanol and biodiesel. The US federal government promotes biofuels as transportation fuels to help reduce oil imports and carbon dioxide emissions. In 2007, the US government set a target to use 36 billion gallons of biofuels by 2022. As a result, nearly all gasoline now sold in the United States contains some ethanol.

Biofuels may be carbon-neutral, because the plants that are used to make biofuels (such as corn and sugar cane for ethanol, and soy beans and oil palm trees for biodiesel) absorb carbon dioxide as they grow and may offset the carbon dioxide emissions when biofuels are produced and burned.

Growing plants for biofuels is controversial because the land, fertilisers, and energy for growing biofuel crops could be used to grow food crops instead. In some parts of the world, large areas of natural vegetation and forests have been cut down to grow sugar cane for ethanol and soy beans and oil palm trees for biodiesel. The US government supports efforts to develop alternative sources of biomass that do not compete with food crops and that use less fertiliser and pesticides than corn and sugar cane. The US government also supports methods to produce ethanol that require less energy than conventional fermentation. Ethanol can also be made from waste paper, and biodiesel can be made from waste grease and oils and even algae.

Ethanol and gasoline-ethanol blends burn cleaner and have higher octane ratings than pure gasoline, but they have higher *evaporative emissions* from fuel tanks and dispensing equipment. These evaporative emissions contribute to the formation of harmful, ground-level ozone and smog. Gasoline requires extra processing to reduce evaporative emissions before it is blended with ethanol. Biodiesel combustion produces fewer sulphur oxides, less particulate matter, less carbon monoxide, and fewer unburned and other hydrocarbons, but it does produce more nitrogen oxide than petroleum diesel.

GEOTHERMAL ENERGY

11.48 Used for thousands of years in some countries for cooking and heating, geothermal energy is derived from the Earth's internal heat. Underground reservoirs of steam and hot water can be tapped through wells that can go a mile deep or more to generate electricity. On a smaller scale, some buildings have geothermal heat pumps that use temperature differences several feet below ground for heating and cooling. Unlike solar and wind energy, geothermal energy is always available, but it has side effects that need to be managed, such as the 'rotten egg' smell that can accompany released hydrogen sulphide.

Cities, states and federal governments around the world are instituting policies aimed at increasing renewable energy. At least 29 US states have set renewable portfolio standards – policies that mandate a certain percentage of energy from renewable sources; more than 100 cities worldwide now boast at least 70% renewable energy, and still others are making commitments to reach 100%. Other policies that could encourage renewable energy growth include carbon pricing, fuel economy standards and building efficiency standards.

Corporations are making a difference, too, purchasing record amounts of renewable power in 2018.

11.49 The environmental effects of geothermal energy depend on how geothermal energy is used or how it is converted to useful energy. Direct-use applications and geothermal heat pumps have almost no negative effects on the environment. They can have a positive effect by reducing the use of energy sources that may have negative effects on the environment.

Geothermal power plants have low emission levels

11.50 Geothermal power plants do not burn fuel to generate electricity, so the levels of air pollutants that they emit are low. Geothermal power plants use scrubbers to remove the hydrogen sulphide naturally found in geothermal reservoirs, and most geothermal power plants inject the geothermal steam and water that they use back into the earth. This recycling helps to renew the geothermal resources.

Many geothermal features are national treasures

11.51 Geothermal features in national parks, such as geysers and fumaroles in Yellowstone National Park, are protected by law.

Geothermal power plants can have impacts on both water quality and consumption. Hot water pumped from underground reservoirs often contains high levels of sulphur, salt and other minerals. Most geothermal facilities have closed-loop water systems, in which extracted water is pumped directly back into the geothermal reservoir after it has been used for heat or electricity production. In these systems, the water is contained within steel well casings cemented to the surrounding rock.

Most geothermal plants re-inject water into the reservoir after it has been used, to prevent contamination and land subsidence (see para **11.53** below). In most cases, however, not all water removed from the reservoir is re-injected, because some is lost as steam. In order to maintain a constant volume of water in the reservoir, outside water must be used. The amount of water needed depends on the size of the plant and the technology used; however, because reservoir water is 'dirty', it is often not necessary to use clean water for this purpose. For example, the Geysers geothermal site in California injects non-potable treated wastewater into its geothermal reservoir.

Air emissions

11.52 The distinction between open- and closed-loop systems is important. In a closed-loop system, gases removed from the well are not exposed to the atmosphere and are injected back into the ground after giving up their heat, so air emissions are minimal. In contrast, open-loop systems emit hydrogen sulphide, carbon dioxide, ammonia, methane and boron. Hydrogen sulphide, which has a distinctive 'rotten egg' smell, is the most common emission.

Land use

11.53 The amount of land required by a geothermal plant varies, depending on the properties of the resource reservoir, the amount of power capacity, the type of energy conversion system, the type of cooling system, the arrangement of wells and piping systems, and the substation and auxiliary building needs. The Geysers have a capacity of approximately 1,517MW and the area of the plant is approximately 78 square kilometres, which translates to approximately 13 acres per megawatt. Like the Geysers, many geothermal sites are located in remote and sensitive ecological areas, so project developers must take this into account in their planning processes.

Land subsidence, a phenomenon in which the land surface sinks, is sometimes caused by the removal of water from geothermal reservoirs. Most geothermal facilities address this risk by re-injecting wastewater back into geothermal reservoirs after the water's heat has been captured.

ENERGY STORAGE

Environmental impacts of electricity storage

11.54 Storing electricity can provide indirect environmental benefits. For example, electricity storage can be used to help integrate more renewable energy into the electricity grid. Electricity storage can also help generation facilities operate at optimal levels and reduce the use of less-efficient generating units that would otherwise run only at peak times. Further, the added capacity provided by electricity storage can delay or avoid the need to build additional power plants or transmission and distribution infrastructure.

Potential negative impacts of electricity storage will depend on the type and efficiency of the storage technology. For example, batteries use raw materials such as lithium and lead, and they can present environmental hazards if they are not disposed of or recycled properly. In addition, some electricity is wasted during the storage process.

Energy can be stored in a variety of ways, as set out below.

Pumped hydroelectric

11.55 Electricity is used to pump water up to a reservoir. When water is released from the reservoir, it flows down through a turbine to generate electricity.

Compressed air

11.56 Electricity is used to compress air at up to 1,000 pounds per square inch and store it, often in underground caverns. When electricity demand is high, the pressurised air is released to generate electricity through an expansion turbine generator.

Flywheels

11.57 Electricity is used to accelerate a flywheel (a type of rotor), through which the energy is conserved as kinetic rotational energy. When the energy is needed, the spinning force of the flywheel is used to turn a generator. Some flywheels use magnetic bearings, operate in a vacuum to reduce drag, and can attain rotational speeds of up to 60,000 revolutions per minute.

Flywheels can assist in the penetration of wind and solar energy in power systems by improving system stability. The fast response characteristics of flywheels make them suitable in applications involving renewable energy sources (RES) for grid frequency balancing.

Batteries

11.58 Similar to common rechargeable batteries, very large batteries can store electricity until it is needed. These systems can use lithium-ion, lead-acid, lithium-iron or other battery technologies.

Unfortunately, less than 5% of lithium-ion batteries are currently recycled. Experts predict that, between 2017 and 2030, around 11 million tons of lithium-ion batteries will be disposed of, which presents both a major need and opportunity for recycling programmes. Some companies, like the Belgian mining company Umicore, are already recycling lithium-ion batteries and are looking to expand their recycling capacity. However, it would take major investment for the worldwide capacity to sufficiently meet the large-scale influx of discarded batteries that will occur around 2025.

In the past, mining new lithium has been more economic than recycling discarded batteries. The recycling process has traditionally been expensive and time-consuming, but recent breakthroughs may change that.

Chapter 12

Renewable Energy in Developing Countries

INTRODUCTION

12.1 The industrialisation of the Western world over the past 200 years has benefited from fossil fuels. The rest of the world is confronted with difficulties when wanting to industrialise using fossil fuels. Some countries, however, have found other ways forward, such as China and India.

In the last 10 years or so, there has been a significant cost reduction for renewable energy systems. Renewable energy is now dominating many countries' energy systems, combined with policies to reduce greenhouse gas emissions. Many developing countries with limited energy infrastructure can now make use of these technologies for harnessing their wind, solar and hydro power which is readily available. They are faced with increasing demands for energy supply and often have dispersed rural populations. Renewables are clean and can enhance energy security.

As discussed in other chapters, variable renewable energy (VRE) has challenges; for example, solar and wind energy only produce when the sun shines, and therefore the supply may not always meet the demand.

An article for the Annual Review of Resource Economics[1] looked at the trends in energy from 2007 to 2017. Between 2010 and 2017, the levelised cost of electricity (LCOE) from solar PV and wind decreased by 81% and 62%, respectively, while coal and gas costs decreased by 15% and 37%, respectively, based on data from the US Energy Information Administration (EIA)[2]. Costs were overestimated in the past, along with underestimated renewable energy resource potential, which resulted in projected electricity production that did not include a significant role for VRE technologies. The current cost of other electricity fuel sources differs from that expected in 2007. In particular, natural gas prices were forecast to remain relatively flat, in line with prices expected for 2008, but the application of hydraulic fracturing in the United States led to a 41% expansion of US natural gas production, despite a 70% decline in prices. Nuclear power production worldwide has decreased since 2007 due to safety concerns, ongoing high costs, and long lead times, and construction costs for nuclear power plants have not been reduced with increased experience.

1 Channing Arndt, Doug Arent, Faaiqa Hartley, Bruno Merven, Alam Hossain Mondal, 'Faster than you think: Renewable Energy and Developing Countries': www.annualreviews.org/doi/full/10.1146/annurev-resource-100518-093759.

2 Annual Energy Outlook 2020: 'Levelized Cost and Levelized Avoided Cost of New Generation Resources in the Annual Energy Outlook 2020': www.eia.gov/outlooks/aeo/electricity_generation.php.

CONSIDERATIONS FOR A REGION LOOKING AT VRE

12.2 Within the region being considered (eg a country), these questions need to be answered:

- When and where is it windy and sunny?
- How far in advance can wind and sun be predicted?
- How does the wind vary over time, and do the winter and summer hold significant differences?
- How should the wind and solar assets be distributed to provide a stable power environment?
- Does the best wind and solar generation match with the current power distribution network?
- How does the distribution of VRE system output, driven by weather conditions, match demand patterns?
- what resources (hydropower, thermal generation, storage) can be used to complement the VRE, to match supply and demand?

Hydropower

12.3 Hydropower offers a low marginal cost source of power. Unless the cost of releasing water by running turbines is high, the electricity supply for a hydropower plant is preferable to thermal generation, which requires the purchase of fuel. The turning on and off of the turbines means that the power can be generated when needed.

Wind and solar

12.4 This is even lower marginal cost that hydropower. The hydropower can be used when it isn't windy or sunny, and so the types of VRE can be linked. There are, however, the impacts of hydropower to be considered (see para **4.27**).

Biofuels

12.5 Bioethanol and biodiesel are good biofuel options, followed in some cases by vegetable oils. The Brazilian sugar cane ethanol programme produces fuel that is cost-effective and has a positive energy balance of up to ten outputs to one unit of input. An increase in ethanol consumption, and the implementation in 2020 of the RenovaBio federal programme in Brazil to cut carbon emissions, is expected to benefit Brazil's sugar cane industry. The RenovaBio programme aims to cut carbon emissions by 10% in 2028, in line with the Paris Agreement on climate change, and is due to enter into force in the country next year. Under RenovaBio, tradeable carbon credits (known as 'CBios') will be granted to certified producers generating an extra revenue source, and fuel distributors will meet their annual carbon emission reduction targets through the purchase of CBios. A CBio is a tradeable certificate – one CBio corresponds to a reduction of one tonne of carbon dioxide equivalent, when compared to fossil fuel emissions. Brazil's low production cost helps local ethanol production to remain competitive even under stressed oil prices.

Second-generation biofuels, especially cellulosic ethanol (produced from wood, grasses or the non-edible parts of plants), could promote a real clean energy revolution when achieving competitive costs.

PROSPECTS FOR VRE

12.6 The potential for renewable energy to contribute substantially to GHG reductions, while providing reliable and reasonably priced power, has increased significantly over the past decades as costs have been reduced, performance has increased, and resource potentials have increased with changes in technologies (eg taller wind turbines access higher wind speed at higher altitudes).

Systems integration

12.7 Although there have been concerns about the integration of systems, this has been shown to be a problem that can be managed:

- Denmark, Portugal, Ireland and multiple additional locations regularly provide 50–100% of total power from VRE sources; and
- whilst penetration rates are high in some energy markets, in many energy markets, penetration of VRE remains relatively low, which means that systems integration is relatively straightforward.

GLOBAL ENERGY TRANSFORMATION

12.8 An IRENA report from 2019[3] looks at the way in which countries are using renewable energy as a way of increasing their energy security by decreasing their reliance on fossil fuels.

China

12.9 China is currently the world's largest producer, exporter and installer of solar panels, wind turbines, batteries and electric vehicles. Being able to reduce its reliance on fuel imports means that the risk to energy disruption is reduced. The official target of the Chinese government is for non-fossil fuels to grow to 20% of total energy consumption by 2030, rising from the current level of 11%, and coal consumption is to be capped at 4.2bn tons by 2020.

3 A New World – The Geopolitics of the Energy Transformation: http://geopoliticsofrenewables.org/assets/geopolitics/Reports/wp-content/uploads/2019/01/Global_commission_renewable_energy_2019.pdf.

China is also committed to a significant increase of the electricity-generating capacity based on renewable sources, doubling wind and quadrupling solar by 2020. There are divergent views in China over the future for renewables beyond 2030. A recent study by the Energy Research Institute[4] within China's central planning body has made a strong case for renewables to account for 60% of the total energy consumption and 85% of electricity by 2050. It is both technically and economically feasible for China to phase out fossil fuels, replacing them with cleaner energy sources such as solar and wind.

Belt and Road Initiative

12.10 China's Belt and Road Initiative (BRI) is also referred to as the New Silk Road. It was launched in 2013 by President Xi Jinping and is a large collection of investment and development initiatives from Asia to Europe. This BRI consists of two parts: the Overland Silk Road Economic Belt, and the Maritime Silk Road. The two were referred to as the One Belt, One Road initiative but have come to be known as the Belt and Road Initiative. This consists of creating a network of railways, energy, pipes, highways and streamlined border crossings, westwards through the former Soviet republics and southwards to Pakistan, India and the rest of Southeast Asia. There are nearly 80 projects. As part of this, State Grid, China's largest state-owned company, wants to create a supergrid called the Global Energy Interconnection (GEI) that aims to link every continent with undersea transmission cables to power the world with green energy. The BRI and the GEI have strategic objectives to reduce China's dependence on energy and commodity imports that pass through points such as the Straits of Malacca and the South China Sea.

Switching to renewable energy has the potential to create jobs in the sector; however, fossil fuel extraction is labour intensive, and more than half of the global workforce of 9 million people are employed in China. The switch to renewable energy is also a threat to jobs. The protests against air pollution have encouraged the government to move towards renewable energy.

India

12.11 India is one of the fastest-growing economies in the world in the last few years and has an estimated 20% of the population without access to electricity. In 2018, India's primary energy consumption was 809.2 million tons of oil equivalent[5]. India has set some targets for renewable energy: 175GW of renewable energy by 2022; and 450GW by 2030. India's installed capacity, for all energy sources, was just under 369GW at the end of January 2020. The renewable elements – small hydro, wind, solar and bio-power – were 86.3GW of this. Amongst the renewable resources, wind generated the highest amount of power, followed by solar.

4 'China High Renewable Energy Penetration Scenario and Roadmap Study 2015', Energy Foundation: www.efchina.org/Reports-en/china-2050-high-renewable-energy-penetration-scenario-and-roadmap-study-en.

5 BP's Statistical Review of World Energy.

Afghanistan

12.12 Approximately 70% of Afghanistan's total power capacity of 1,450MW is imported from neighbouring countries, and only 34% of the population have access to electricity and thus mostly in urban areas. Some of the country's most challenging characteristics support the growth of renewable energy. The fragmented nature of the country, both geographically and politically, means that it will always be difficult to build and maintain a large-scale electricity grid powered by coal or gas. Decentralised power generation, owned and controlled by local people, which can harness local sources of energy, is a better option.

Afghanistan has renewable energy sources in abundance. Much of the country enjoys high levels of sunshine and its upland areas have good wind potential. Its rivers can be harvested by small-scale hydro plants. These don't involve large, damaging dams, but small diversions of enough water to drive turbines producing electricity for a few villages.

Afghanistan has a Renewable Energy Roadmap RER2032[6]. The target for 2032 is to achieve around 5,000MW of renewable energy capacity:

- Solar power park. De-risking the deployment of utility-scale wind and solar projects by identifying suitable sites, providing infrastructure for evacuation and security, and streamlining regulatory clearance.
- Mini-grids with Renewable Energy Service Company (RESCO) model. A cluster of mini-grid projects to be developed and bid, either individually or collectively, following the RESCO business model.
- Solar hot water systems for institutions. As an effective demand-side-management strategy to reduce electricity generation requirements, whilst offering potential for economic development through local manufacture, solar hot water systems (SHWS) to be promoted in a programmatic mode.
- Kabul roof-top solar. Following the maturity and proven viability of this market globally, Kabul roof-top solar pilot project will seed this market for Afghanistan.
- Renewable energy (RE) atlas. A national-level initiative that could build upon the RE database and provide both a national strategic overview of RE deployment and link to project-level monitoring, providing insights on new development opportunities and overall RE roadmap progress.
- Pilot-scale geothermal. In line with the 55MW Roadmap target, and recognising the need for impetus in this sector, geothermal resource assessment linked, where viable, to pilot geothermal projects (either direct heat or electricity) to catalyse activity.
- Pilot-scale Renewable Energy and Energy Efficiency Partnership (REEEP) project. Although not directly identified in the Roadmap, this pilot-scale project to integrate RE with energy efficiency measures in the commercial and industrial sector will improve the viability and acceptance of Renewable Energy Technologies (RETs).

6 Renewable Energy Roadmap for Afghanistan RER2032: https://policy.asiapacificenergy.org/sites/default/files/Renewable%20Energy%20Roadmap%20for%20Afghanistan%20RER2032.pdf.

- Daikundi Mini-grid. Mini-grids being strategically important for Afghanistan, this project will help in standardising mini-grid designs and business models.
- Hisar-e-Shahi industrial park solar project. Strategically important project for industrial development that forms the backbone of the Afghan economy.

Badakhstan and Takhar

12.13 In the northern provinces of Badakhshan and Takhar, 11,500 homes, schools, markets, local businesses and hospitals are currently being supplied with power by a mix of hydro and solar plants. These were installed by the German development agency, GiZ, in collaboration with both the government and local people, who are trained to operate and run them as semi-independent enterprises. The scheme won an Ashden Award for sustainable energy[7].

Albania

12.14 Water is Albania's most important natural resource. At least eight large rivers run through the country, fed by hundreds of smaller streams, and total hydropower resources are estimated at 4500MW. In addition, solar energy potential (for both photovoltaics and solar hot-water heaters) is excellent, as the country has among the highest number of sunshine hours per year in Europe (an average of 2,400). Wind energy potential for Albania is also very good along the Adriatic coast.

Free and Open Indo-Pacific Strategies

12.15 Japan, the United States and India have advanced their own 'Free and Open Indo-Pacific Strategies', and the US will invest $113.5 million in infrastructure and connectivity projects. The vision for the Asia-Pacific Economic Cooperation (APEC) summit, which was held in Hanoi in 2017, was set out by US President Donald Trump, and is based on values that have underpinned peace and prosperity in the Indo-Pacific. Free, fair and reciprocal trade, open investment environments, good governance, and freedom of the seas are goals shared by all who wish to prosper in a free and open future. In November 2019, The US Government issued a progress report[8] which details two years of diplomatic, economic, governance and security initiatives to show that the United States has a continuing commitment to the Indo-Pacific and it will have strengthened people-to-people and bilateral ties.

7 'GIZ and INTEGRATION – Brighter prospects in rural Afghanistan': www.ashden.org/winners/giz-and-integration.

8 'A Free and Open Indo-Pacific: Advancing a Shared Vision': www.state.gov/wp-content/uploads/2019/11/Free-and-Open-Indo-Pacific-4Nov2019.pdf.

Connectivity 2025

12.16 The countries of the Association of Southeast Asian Nations (ASEAN) have developed a strategy called 'Connectivity 2025'[9]. The member states are Thailand, Malaysia, Singapore, Philippines, Vietnam, Brunei, Cambodia, Myanmar (Burma) and Laos.

The vision for the ASEAN Connectivity 2025 is to 'achieve a seamlessly and comprehensively connected and integrated ASEAN that will promote competitiveness, inclusiveness, and a greater sense of Community'.

There are five strategic areas:

(1) *Sustainable infrastructure* – To coordinate existing resources to deliver support across the full life cycle of infrastructure projects in ASEAN, including project preparation, improving infrastructure productivity, and capability building. This strategy also includes exchanging lessons on 'smart urbanisation' models across ASEAN Member States that can simultaneously deliver economic growth and a good quality of life.

(2) *Digital innovation* – Digital technologies in ASEAN could potentially be worth up to US$625 billion by 2030 (8% of ASEAN's GDP in that year), which may be derived from increased efficiency, new products and services, etc. Capturing this opportunity requires the establishment of regulatory frameworks for the delivery of new digital services (including data management and digital financial services), support for the sharing of best practices on open data, and equipping micro, small and medium enterprises (MSMEs) with the capabilities to access these new technologies.

(3) *Seamless logistics* – Enhancing ASEAN Connectivity presupposes excellent logistics. However, logistics efficiency has not improved at the pace originally envisaged by the Masterplan on ASEAN Connectivity 2010 (MPAC 2010), as measured by the length of time taken and cost of transportation in the region. One of the underlying challenges is coordination issues between government departments and a lack of sharing of best practices. There is the opportunity to create mechanisms to support greater collaboration between logistics firms, academic institutions and ASEAN Member States: this would help to identify bottlenecks across key areas of the region's supply chains, to collect and share best practices about how to tackle those issues across the region, and to identify critical policy areas requiring attention.

(4) *Regulatory excellence* – A need to embed good regulatory practice (GRP) in the preparation, adoption and implementation of rules, regulations and procedures in the region. The aim of this strategy is to support implementation of key policies critical for the ASEAN Connectivity agenda, particularly focusing on standards harmonisation, mutual recognition and technical regulations, as well as addressing trade-distorting non-tariff measures.

(5) *People mobility* – Restrictions on travel for ASEAN nationals within the region are largely a thing of the past. However, there are still opportunities to improve mobility in ASEAN. Opportunities include facilitating travel

9 Masterplan on ASEAN Connectivity 2015: https://asean.org/storage/2016/09/Master-Plan-on-ASEAN-Connectivity-20251.pdf.

for tourists by addressing the lack of information on travel options and providing simpler mechanisms to apply for necessary visas. Additionally, there is an opportunity to strengthen skills mobility in the region and, where appropriate, by establishing high-quality qualification frameworks in critical vocational occupations, and to encourage greater mobility of intra-ASEAN university students.

It aims to prioritise processes to resolve issues within the ASEAN energy infrastructure projects and facilitate regional energy connectivity. ASEAN Member States need to rethink approaches to natural resource efficiency and resource supply in order to meet imminent challenges. ASEAN is exposed to the risks of climate change and to the environmental pressures of groundwater depletion, air pollution and unsustainable management of fisheries, while also facing fiscal pressure from the mounting cost of resource subsidies and challenges with ensuring access to basic resources such as energy and water. There are prospects across ASEAN to capture natural resource productivity energy, water, land, and materials, as well as to develop additional energy resources, such as biofuels, geothermal, biomass, solar and hydropower. As an example, ASEAN has hydropower. Myanmar alone has potential hydropower production capacity of 108,000MW, and Laos already receives over 13% of its energy needs from hydropower.

Small Island Developing States

12.17 Developing countries that lack domestic fuel reserves will benefit the most from exploiting renewable energy resources – notably, Small Island Developing States (SIDS), of which there are 38 UN members:

Atlantic, Indian Ocean and South China Sea

Bahrain	Guinea-Bissau	Sao Tomé and Principe
Cabo Verde	Maldives	Seychelles
Comoros	Mauritius	Singapore

Caribbean

Antigua and Barbuda	Dominican Republic	Saint Kitts and Nevis
Bahamas	Grenada	Saint Lucia
Barbados	Guyana	Saint Vincent and the Grenadines
Belize	Haiti	Suriname
Cuba	Jamaica	Trinidad and Tobago
Dominica		

Pacific

Fiji	Palau	Timor-Leste
Kiribati	Papua New Guinea	Tonga
Marshall Islands	Samoa	Tuvalu
Micronesia (Federated States of)	Solomon Islands	Vanuatu
Nauru		

In addition, there are 20 non-UN Members/Associate Members of Regional Commissions:

American Samoa	Curacao	Niue
Anguilla	French Polynesia	Puerto Rico
Aruba	Guadeloupe	Sint Maarten
Bermuda	Guam	Turks and Caicos Islands
British Virgin Islands	Martinique	US Virgin Islands
Cayman Islands	Montserrat	
Commonwealth of Northern Marianas	New Caledonia	
Cook Islands		

Many rely on imported fuels for their electricity needs. SIDS also sit on the frontline of climate change, having done the least to cause it. To increase their resilience in the face of extreme weather events, as well as bolster their energy security and reduce prohibitive import bills, 13 SIDS – including Cabo Verde, the Cook Islands, Fiji, Saint Vincent and the Grenadines, Samoa and Vanuatu – have announced plans to increase the contribution of renewable energy to between 60% and 100% of the power they consume.

Strategy on Connecting Europe and Asia

12.18 In 2019, the EU unveiled a 'Strategy on Connecting Europe and Asia[10]'. It has four main themes:

- **Transport** – Diversified trade and travel routes linking existing and future transport networks, shorter transit times and simplified customs procedures.
- **Energy** – More interconnected regional energy platforms, modern energy systems and environmentally friendly solutions.
- **Digital** – Increased access to digital services while maintaining a high level of protection of consumer and personal data.
- **Human dimension** – Advanced cooperation in education, research, innovation, culture and tourism.

Connectivity partnerships

12.19 The Partnership on Sustainable Connectivity and Quality Infrastructure between the EU and Japan sets out the principles, thematic areas and methods for strengthening cooperation with Japan within the four pillars of connectivity (digital, transport, energy, people-to-people), bilaterally and with third countries.

10 Connecting Europe and Asia – The EU Strategy: https://eeas.europa.eu/sites/eeas/files/eu-asian_connectivity_factsheet_september_2019.pdf_final.pdf.

Electricity transmission systems

12.20 Within the framework of the 'CASA 1000' project, the European Investment Bank (EIB) is contributing €70 million to enable Central Asian countries to sell their electricity surplus during summer months to deficient countries in South Asia, improving the electricity access, and expand markets in a sustainable way.

IRENA/ADFD PROJECTS

12.21 The IRENA/ADFD project facility is a partnership between the two organisations to promote renewable energy in developing countries. The report[11] by the International Renewable Energy Agency (IRENA) and the Abu Dhabi Fund for Development (ADFD) reviews the progress over the first five years of their joint enterprise to finance these types of project.

IEA

12.22 The International Energy Agency (IEA) is made up of 30 member countries[12] and 8 association countries[13]. For a country to be a member, it must be a member country of the OECD and also demonstrate certain requirements. The IEA produces a review of its member countries' energy policies[14].

Funding and projects

12.23 As part of the United Arab Emirates (UAE) bid to host the International Renewable Energy Agency (IRENA), the ADFD committed to provide US$350 million in concessional co-financing for the implementation of government-supported renewable energy projects in developing countries. This is spread over seven annual selection cycles.

Since January 2014, a total of 21 projects have been selected through the IRENA/ADFD initiative to receive concessional loans in five annual cycles. Those loans, allocated by ADFD, are based on IRENA recommendations and amount to US$214 million. Seven projects from early cycles reached the construction or installation stage, with renewable power generation set to start in 2019.

11 'Advancing Renewables in Developing Countries': www.irena.org/publications/2019/Jan/Advancing-Renewables-in-Developing-Countries.

12 IEA member countries (as of 2019): Australia, Austria, Belgium, Canada, Czech Republic, Denmark, Estonia, Finland, France, Germany, Greece, Hungary, Ireland, Italy, Japan, Korea, Luxembourg, Mexico, New Zealand, Norway, Poland, Portugal, Slovakia, Spain, Sweden, Switzerland, The Netherlands, Turkey, United Kingdom and United States.

13 IEA association countries (as of 2019): Brazil, China, India, Indonesia, Morocco, Singapore, South Africa and Thailand.

14 IEA (2019), 'Energy Policies of IEA Countries: United Kingdom 2019 Review', Executive summary.

First cycle

12.24 Solar PV projects in Mali and Sierra Leone, a wind power project in Mauritania, and a waste-to-energy project in the Maldives have all reached the construction/installation stage.

Maldives

12.25 Small-scale waste-to-energy, 4MW. The Ministry of Environment and Energy, in partnership with the Waste Management Corporation Limited (WAMCO) have undertaken this project to address waste management, access to fresh water and sustainable energy solutions. The construction of two small demonstration waste-to-energy facilities to provide renewable electricity for the population through the combustion of municipal waste, and also powering an integrated desalination plant through a heat recovery system.

Key points:

- provision of clean energy for 122,000 people;
- 55,000 tonnes of waste incinerated annually, enabling reductions in local marine pollution that threaten coral reef health;
- 551,000 litres of desalinated water annually, to reduce national water stress;
- 3.5 million litres of diesel fuel saved annually; and
- 9,200tCO_2e per year avoided.

Mali

12.26 Hybrid systems for rural electrification, 32 villages. Solar PV, 4MW. This installation of decentralised solar PV mini-grid systems aims to provide clean energy to 32 villages in six regions of Mali. The project uses a public–private partnership model for co-operation between Agence Malienne pour le Développement de l'Energie Domestique et de l'Electrification Rurale (AMADER), Mali-Folkecenter Nyetaa and ACCESS, a local rural energy service company. Existing diesel mini-grids will be converted to solar hybrid systems and 154 km of grid extension infrastructure will be installed to increase access to power for communities.

Key points:

- increasing energy in rural communities, from 10% to 25% of people, for a population of 123,000 in 32 villages;
- creating 2,000 direct and indirect jobs; and
- 5,000tCO_2e emissions avoided annually.

Mauritania

12.27 Wind electrification for coastal communities. Wind, 1MW. This will provide four off-grid coastal fishing villages with decentralised renewable power for domestic use, desalination plants and ice production facilities. A total of 18 wind turbines of 15kW capacity will be installed, providing 270kW capacity for each of the localities of Lemcid, Lemhaijratt, Bellewakh and Loubeir.

Key points:

- providing energy access for 8,000 people in off-grid locations;
- providing electricity for ice-making facilities for fishing communities, and boosting productivity; and
- energy for schools and health centres.

Sierra Leone

12.28 A solar park for the capital, Freetown. Solar PV, 6MW. This project, put forward by the Ministry of Energy and Water Resources, involves the construction of a grid-connected solar PV park near the capital city of Freetown. It represents one of the first large-scale PV installations in Western Africa and aims to have a multiplier effect in the region, whilst setting standards for additional renewable energy developments.

Key points:

- bringing renewable energy benefits to 15,000 people;
- improving the national power reliability; and
- mitigating 8,000tCO_2e emissions annually.

Second cycle

Argentina

12.29 Nahueve hydropower project, 7MW. The Nahueve hydropower project is a government-driven multi-purpose project located in Neuquen province. The project involves the development of a 7MW mini-hydropower plant and will also provide both potable and irrigation water for the population of Villa de Nahueve. The project will be used as a model for future small-scale hydro development in Argentina.

Key points:

- improving electricity reliability;
- providing energy for 54,000 people;
- increasing land productivity by irrigating 120 hectares;
- creating employment for 130 people;
- reducing GHG emissions by 22,800tCO_2e annually; and
- saving 7.3 million litres of fossil fuels annually.

Cuba

12.30 Grid connect solar, 10MW. Four grid-connected solar PV power plants will be installed in various locations in Cuba, with a total generation capacity of 10MW. The solar PV power plants will directly contribute to the government's national objectives to reduce the use of fossil fuels for electricity generation in Cuba and consequently reduce greenhouse gas emissions.

Key points:

- increasing Cuba's renewable energy mix by adding 10MW of generation;

- benefiting 6,500 people with reliable energy and enabling electricity stability; and
- mitigating 10,800tCO_2e annually.

Saint Vincent and the Grenadines

12.31 La Soufriere geothermal energy project, 10–15 MW. This project, providing a sustainable and reliable source of renewable power, is being developed as a public–private partnership between the Government of Saint Vincent and the Grenadines, Light & Power Holdings and Reykjavik Geothermal. The project will contribute to achieving the country's Energy Action Plan target to increase the amount of renewable energy to 60% of the energy mix by 2020. Once operational, the plant will bring the share of renewable energy sources to approximately 73% of total national power generation, well in excess of the country's Energy Action Plan target.

Key points:

- increasing renewable energy to 75% of the country's generation capacity;
- electricity more affordable through a lower tariff structure and cheaper generation;
- mitigating 53,000tCO_2e emission annually; and
- reducing reliance on fossil fuel imports by 17 million litres and reducing national foreign exchange expenditure.

Third cycle

Antigua and Barbuda

12.32 Hybrid wind and solar, 4MW. This project was implemented by the Government of Antigua and Barbuda's Department of Environment as part of a wider scheme to transform the water sector and provide low-emission and climate-resilient energy for critical services in the small island state. The project involves the installation of foldable wind turbines and solar PV panels, with battery backup for electricity storage in the event of extreme weather events. Beneficiary facilities include reverse osmosis desalination plants for clean water provision, as well as providing electricity to hospitals, community clinics and emergency response public service buildings. This project directly contributes to the Government's objective to obtain 20% of electricity from renewable sources by 2018, and to make its critical services resilient to the impacts of climate change.

Key points:

- providing access to clean water for 90,000 inhabitants of Antigua;
- mitigating 8,725tCO_2e emissions annually;
- reducing dependence on imported fuels and thereby improving national energy security; and
- making electricity more affordable for 33,000 customers.

Burkina Faso

12.33 Rural electrification, solar PV/diesel and power distribution mini-grids. This project, for the rural electrification of 42 localities in Burkina

Faso with mini-grids, grid extensions and solar home system technologies, is being implemented by Agence Burkinabé de l'Electrification Rurale (formerly Fonds de Développement de l'Electrification), the Burkina Faso Government agency for electrification. The project utilises a holistic approach by matching the most suitable and cost-effective technology with each end user. In rural trading localities where populations are sufficiently dense, mini-grids will provide technical and economic competitive advantages over grid connections or individual solar kits. In sparsely populated areas, however, households will be most cost-effectively served by individual solar kits – which will be provided by the project.

Key points:

- 73,400 people benefiting from electricity generation, 70 schools, 25 health centres and 16 water supply locations;
- 10,714 new electricity connections;
- 2,500tCO_2e emissions avoided annually; and
- cost savings from displacing 1.1 million litres of fossil fuel use.

Senegal

12.34 Renewable energy rural electrification, solar PV, 2MW. This project was developed by the Senegalese Rural Electrification Agency (ASER) to electrify 100 villages located in isolated regions of Senegal. It is part of a broader government emergency rural electrification strategy that aims to achieve 60% rural electrification by 2025. The project will power medium-sized, remote villages using solar PV plants that feed into mini-grids. The mini-grids will include solar battery storage devices to provide power during the evenings. This project supports the government's national electrification programme, which aims to provide universal access to energy by 2025–2030.

Key points:

- enhanced energy access for 80,000 people in rural communities;
- providing electricity to 150 health centres and 200 schools;
- improving productivity for 450 small businesses; and
- mitigating 3,200tCO_2e emission annually.

Fourth cycle

Marshall Islands

12.35 Solar micro-grid hybrid project for four islands, solar PV, 4.6MW. The Government, together with Solar City, developed this project to contribute to the policy objective by deploying hybrid micro-grids on the four islands of Ebeye, Jabor, Rongrong and Wotje. Solar PV will be combined with advanced lithium-ion battery storage and control systems (specially designed for the harsh near-ocean environment) and integrated with existing diesel generation as the primary electricity generation source. The energy will be used for domestic and productive uses, including powering freshwater supply.

Key points:

- access to affordable electricity for 16,000 customers;
- reducing diesel-based power generation by 36% for the island of Ebeye and 90% for Jabor, Rongrong and Wotje;
- provision of 18.5 million litres of water annually; and
- foreign exchange saving equal to 1.7 million litres of diesel imports annually.

Niger

12.36 Solar rural electrification for 100 villages, solar PV, 2.1MW. This project will provide electricity through solar PV systems to 100 villages in order to offer sustainable and clean electricity services to the beneficiaries. Given Niger's national electricity access rate of around 10% (49% in urban areas and 0.4% in rural areas), the Nigerian Agency for the Promotion of Rural Electrification (ANPER) was created to accelerate rural electrification and has since embarked on work to electrify 100 localities.

Key points:

- 21,000 new connections in 100 villages;
- benefits for 150,000 people;
- improved access to basic services powered by renewable energy, including schools, health centres, provision of water for drinking and agriculture, and food processing and preservation; and
- reducing pollution from diesel generators and kerosene lamps.

Seychelles

12.37 Ile de Romainville solar park, solar PV, 5MW. The construction of a 5MW solar PV plant will be integrated into an existing offshore wind farm, located 500 metres from the largest island of Mahé. The Public Utilities Corporation (PUC) is wholly owned by the government and comes under the authority of the Ministry of Environment, Energy and Climate Change. The solar park will be located on the same site as existing wind turbines on Ile de Romainville, resulting in a highly space-efficient concentration of renewable energy plants.

The electricity generated will be injected into the national grid using the existing transmission network and will benefit the entire population of Mahé island.

The project will contribute to achieving the long-term objective of the Government of Seychelles to achieve a 15% renewable energy contribution to the power generation mix by 2030.

Key points:

- supply of clean water to 5,000 people;
- foreign exchange savings equivalent to 1.6 million litres of diesel imports each year; and
- mitigating 5,000tCO_2e emissions annually.

Solomon Islands

12.38 Tina River hydropower project, 20MW. The Tina River hydropower project is a national priority energy project initiated by the Solomon Islands Government to introduce renewable energy to the country's energy mix and reduce dependence on diesel fuels. The project aims to convert the Solomon Islands power sector, which is presently 100% dependent on imported diesel fuel. Currently, the retail cost of electricity is very high and greenhouse gas emissions are significant.

Key points:

- 183,000 people to benefit from renewable energy access;
- reducing tariffs to make electricity affordable;
- reducing GHG emissions by 2.5 million tCO_2e annually; and
- reducing annual expenditure on diesel by 75%, saving US$28 million.

Fifth cycle

Mauritius

12.39 10,000 solar PV systems for households. Grid-connected rooftop solar PV, 10MW. This project involves the installation of 10,000 solar PV kits of 1kWp each on the rooftops of low-income households. The kits are grid-connected and offer net-metering benefits to participating households in the form of 50kWh of free electricity each month. The project will contribute to achieving the government's target of generating 35% of its electricity from renewable sources by 2025. By lowering energy expenditures for low-income households, the project will also contribute to poverty alleviation, which is a strategic priority for the government.

Key points:

- making electricity more affordable for low-income households, benefiting 30,000 people;
- increasing the share of renewables in the grid by 10MW;
- reducing dependence on fossil fuels by saving US$400,000 annually; and
- 15,000 tCO_2e emissions avoided annually.

Rwanda

12.40 Ignite Rwanda. Solar PV home systems, 7.5MW. This project is a joint venture between Ignite Power, a private limited liability company, and the Government of Rwanda to distribute and install 500,000 solar home systems to households through an affordable payment scheme. The systems are distributed through agents in districts across the country, creating employment for young people (50% women) along the value chain. An affordable pay-as-you-go (PAYGO) model enables off-grid, low-income households to make small payments daily or weekly. The project will install solar PV kits to power lights and FM radios, as well as to charge phones, providing increased information access to rural communities. Installation work is on-going, with funding from the equity partner having enabled 60,000 installations so far.

Key points:

- giving 5,000 households access to affordable electricity;
- creating 2,000 jobs (50% women);
- replacing kerosene lamps with solar PV, saving US$200 per household;
- adding 7.5MW of renewable energy to Rwanda's electricity supply; and
- reducing dependence on fossil fuels, saving US$100 million annually.

SMART GRID TECHNOLOGY

12.41 A smart grid uses technology to match supply and demand and to keep the system operating at optimal efficiency.

There are several types of smart grid technology available.

Advanced metering infrastructure

12.42 Advanced metering infrastructure (AMI) enables two-way communication meters, reading electrical consumption at a higher frequency. This information can be processed in real-time and signals can be sent to manage demand. Demand-side management requires a lot of data processing to understand the load patterns and to design proper signals that enable optimal use of the distribution grid and manage reserve and frequency response.

Advanced electricity pricing

12.43 This has higher tariffs during peak demand and lower tariffs during lower demand; this type of pricing structure can help smooth out the periods of high demand.

South Korea

12.44 South Korea's wholesale electricity market operates on a cost-based pool, where the price of electricity has two components:

- the marginal price, representing the variable cost of generating electricity; and
- the capacity price, representing the fixed cost of generating electricity.

In the South Korean electricity market, the market price is set by actual variable costs, as opposed to the common method of using the bidding price. The nation's only utility, KEPCO, majority-owned by the government, has used this system to keep prices low and reduce black-out times.

Distribution automation

12.45 Distribution automation (DA) is a family of technologies, including sensors, processors, information and communication networks and switches, through which a utility can collect, automate, analyse and optimise data to improve the operational efficiency of its distribution power system.

Chapter 13

Emerging Technologies

INTRODUCTION

13.1 Between 2004 and 2014, the change from the acknowledgement that renewable energy was a way forward to the large-scale deployment made the need and drive for advances in technology very important. Since then, there has been a steady demand globally for renewable energy and a move away from fossil fuels. This has driven research into improving the existing forms of renewable energy and thinking of innovative ways of improving them and looking for new ones. Not all of them will prove a commercial way forward, but the increased investment and research into renewable energy makes some of the innovations exciting in a fast-growing energy market.

ARTIFICIAL PHOTOSYNTHESIS

13.2 Photosynthesis is the process whereby green plants use sunlight to photosynthesise foods from carbon dioxide and water. This process combines six molecules of carbon dioxide and six molecules of water to produce one molecule of glucose and six molecules of hydrogen. The glucose is stored in the plant as starch and cellulose which are long chain glucose molecules (known as polysaccharides) as a source of food for the plant to survive and grow. The oxygen that is produced as a by-product of photosynthesis is what most animals rely on to breathe.

Solar photovoltaic cells already use light from the sun to produce electricity. There is, however, a problem with storing the electricity produced (see Chapter 9). Photosynthesis locks energy from the sun within the chemical bonds in the glucose molecule. Therefore, plants are not only producing energy, but they also have the ability to store it.

Artificial photosynthesis uses techniques including nanotechnology[1] to store solar electromagnetic energy in chemical bonds by splitting water to produce hydrogen and then using carbon dioxide to make methanol. However, it often relies on catalysts which can be expensive.

There are several challenges to artificial photosynthesis.

Light capture and moving the electrons to the reaction centres

13.3 In plants, the light is handled by the leaves which contain the green pigment chlorophyll, which absorbs photons with a wavelength of ~430–700nm; using a complex process, it splits the water into its constituent parts, and then combines the hydrogen and carbon dioxide to make sugars. The proposal is that, in artificial photosynthesis, this would be carried out by nanoparticles.

Using light-capturing titanium dioxide nanoparticles on any surface dramatically increases the surface area and therefore the light-capturing potential of the surface. If titanium dioxide is coupled with a dye and then immersed in an electrolyte solution with a platinum cathode, electrons are excited to the extent that they are displaced and produce a current.

Splitting water into hydrogen and oxygen

13.4 The current that is produced (see above) can then be used to split the water into its molecular components, thereby storing the solar energy in chemical bonds, particularly in the reduced form of hydrogen, again in the presence of nanoparticles (more specifically, iridium oxide nanoparticles).

Reducing carbon dioxide

13.5 In the final part of natural photosynthesis (known to biologists as the 'dark reactions'), carbon dioxide is captured by the chemical ribulose biphosphate, before undergoing the Calvin Cycle, eventually producing one molecule of glucose.

1 Nanotechnology: the design, production and application of structures, devices and systems by manipulation of size and shape at the nanometre scale.

Transforming carbon dioxide into liquefiable fuels

13.6 Chemists successfully produced fuels using water, carbon dioxide and visible light through artificial photosynthesis[2]. The study uses metal catalysts to absorb green light and transfer electrons and protons needed for chemical reactions between carbon dioxide and water, performing the role of the pigment chlorophyll in natural photosynthesis. Gold nanoparticles work as a catalyst, because their surfaces interact favourably with the carbon dioxide molecules, and are efficient at absorbing light and do not break down or degrade like other metals that can tarnish easily.

ARTIFICIAL LEAF

13.7 Traditional silicon-based photovoltaic cells rely on the photoelectric effect, absorbing light to trigger the release of electrons which generates current that can power or charge a battery. In 2011, Daniel Nocera and colleagues at the Massachusetts Institute of Technology (MIT) developed a cell composed of a silicon sandwich, with a cobalt catalyst on top and a new nickel-molybdenum-zinc alloy on the bottom. This is able to split water into its component parts, hydrogen and oxygen. Although hydrogen can be a difficult fuel to handle, Nocera then worked with Harvard colleague Pamela Silver and they combined hydrogen with ambient carbon dioxide into liquid fuel using what is effectively a 'bionic leaf'. The nickel alloy in the cell poisoned the bacteria by damaging its DNA; however, in 2017, Nocera came up with a replacement cobalt-based catalyst.

DIRECT AIR CAPTURE PLANT

13.8 The Climeworks[3] facility in Zurich takes waste energy from a nearby refuse plant and uses that, plus carbon dioxide from the air, to boost plants' photosynthesis in a commercial greenhouse operation. This process is aiming to take 900 tonnes of carbon dioxide from the air each year. It's not just for improving the tomato crop, but also to sell concentrated carbon dioxide to companies that are producing carbon-neutral hydrocarbons.

HYDROGEN FUELS

13.9 Hydrogen is a fuel that, when consumed, produces only water, and the hydrogen itself can be produced from a number of sources.

2 'Artificial photosynthesis transforms carbon dioxide into liquefiable fuels', Yoksoulian, University of Illinois at Urbana-Champaign: https://phys.org/news/2019-05-artificial-photosynthesis-carbon-dioxide-liquefiable.html.

3 www.climeworks.com.

Thermal processes

13.10 This type of process for hydrogen production typically involves steam reforming, a high-temperature process in which steam reacts with a hydrocarbon fuel to produce hydrogen. Many hydrocarbon fuels can be reformed to produce hydrogen and include natural gas, diesel, renewable liquid fuels, gasified coal and gasified biomass.

Natural gas reforming

Steam methane reforming

13.11 High-temperature steam (700°C–1,000°C) is used to produce hydrogen from a methane source, such as natural gas. In steam methane reforming, methane reacts with steam under 14.5psi in the presence of a catalyst to produce hydrogen, carbon monoxide and a relatively small amount of carbon dioxide. The reaction is endothermic, and so heat must be supplied to the process for the reaction to proceed.

There is the 'water-gas shift reaction', where the carbon monoxide and steam are reacted using a catalyst to produce carbon dioxide and more hydrogen. The final process step is called a 'pressure-swing adsorption', where carbon dioxide and other impurities are removed from the gas stream, leaving essentially pure hydrogen. Steam reforming can also be used to produce hydrogen from other fuels, such as ethanol, propane or even gasoline.

Partial oxidation

13.12 In this case the methane and other hydrocarbons in natural gas react with a limited amount of oxygen (typically from air) that is insufficient to completely oxidise the hydrocarbons to carbon dioxide and water. The reaction products contain primarily hydrogen and carbon monoxide (and nitrogen, if the reaction is carried out with air rather than pure oxygen), and a relatively small amount of carbon dioxide and other compounds. Subsequently, in a 'water-gas shift reaction', the carbon monoxide reacts with water to form carbon dioxide and more hydrogen.

This is an exothermic process, meaning that it gives off heat.

Coal gasification

13.13 Coal is a complex and highly variable substance that can be converted into a variety of products. The gasification of coal is one method that can produce power, liquid fuels, chemicals and hydrogen. Hydrogen can be produced by first reacting coal with oxygen and steam under high pressures and temperatures to form synthesis gas, a mixture consisting primarily of carbon monoxide and hydrogen. After the impurities are removed, the carbon monoxide in the gas mixture is reacted with steam, through the water-gas shift reaction, to produce additional hydrogen and carbon dioxide. Hydrogen is removed by a separation system, and the highly concentrated carbon dioxide stream can subsequently be captured and stored.

Biomass gasification

13.14 The gasification process converts organic or fossil-based carbonaceous materials at high temperatures (>700°C), without combustion, with a controlled amount of oxygen and/or steam into carbon monoxide, hydrogen and carbon dioxide. The carbon monoxide then reacts with water to form carbon dioxide and more hydrogen via a water-gas shift reaction. Adsorbers or special membranes can separate the hydrogen from this gas stream.

Biomass derived from liquid reforming

13.15 Biomass resources can be converted to cellulosic ethanol, bio-oils or other liquid biofuels. Some of these liquids may be transported at relatively low cost to a refuelling station or other point of use and reformed to produce hydrogen. Others (for example, bio-oils) may be reformed on-site.

The process of natural gas reforming includes the following steps:

- the liquid fuel is reacted with steam at high temperatures in the presence of a catalyst, to produce a reformate gas composed mostly of hydrogen, carbon monoxide and some carbon dioxide;
- additional hydrogen and carbon dioxide are produced by reacting the carbon monoxide (created in the first step) with high-temperature steam in the water-gas shift reaction; and
- finally, the hydrogen is separated out and purified.

Electrolytic processes

13.16 Water can be separated into oxygen and hydrogen through the process of electrolysis. Electrolytic processes take place in an electrolyser, which functions in a similar way to a fuel cell in reverse; instead of using the energy of a hydrogen molecule, like a fuel cell does, an electrolyser creates hydrogen from water molecules.

Mohamed Bin Rashid Al Maktoum Solar Park, Dubai

13.17 A solar park is under construction and will spread over a total area of 77 km^2 in Seih Al Dahal about 50 km south of Dubai. The plant is being built by the Dubai Electricity and Water Authority and the first phase was commissioned in October 2013.

- Phase 1 – construction of a 13MW solar PV project; completed October 2013;
- Phase 2 – construction of a 200MW CSP/PV plant (revised from the earlier 100MW capacity);

- Phase 3 – construction of an 800MW solar power plant on 1,600 hectares of land; construction work was completed in 2018; and
- Phase 4 – construction of a parabolic trough and solar tower.

The fourth phase also includes a solar-driven hydrogen electrolysis testing facility at the park, and the construction activities for the entire project are scheduled for completion by 2030. The hydrogen testing facility will test and demonstrate an integrated megawatt-scale plant to produce hydrogen using solar PV, store the gas, and then deploy it for re-electrification, mobility or other industrial uses. If the Dubai plant only uses daylight solar power from PV at the solar park, each unit can produce up to 240 kilograms of hydrogen per day; an average fuel cell electric vehicle requires about one kilogram of hydrogen per 100 kilometres of range, depending on the model, environmental conditions and other factors.

Solar-driven processes

13.18 Solar-driven processes use light for hydrogen production, and include photobiological, photoelectrochemical and solar thermochemical.

Photobiological

13.19 Photobiological processes use the natural photosynthetic activity of bacteria and green algae to produce hydrogen. In photolytic biological systems, microorganisms (such as green microalgae or cyanobacteria) use sunlight to split water into oxygen and hydrogen ions. The hydrogen ions can be combined through direct or indirect routes and released as hydrogen gas. Issues with this pathway include low rates of hydrogen production and the fact that splitting water also produces oxygen, which quickly inhibits the hydrogen production reaction and can be a safety issue when mixed with hydrogen in certain concentrations. Researchers are looking at developing methods to allow the microbes to produce hydrogen for longer periods of time and to increase the rate of hydrogen production. Some photosynthetic microbes use sunlight as the driver to break down organic matter, releasing hydrogen – known as 'photofermentative hydrogen production'. The issues with this pathway include a very low hydrogen production rate and low solar-to-hydrogen efficiency, making it a commercially unviable pathway for hydrogen production at this time.

Photoelectrochemical water splitting

13.20 Photoelectrochemical (PEC) processes use specialised semiconductors to separate water into hydrogen and oxygen. The PEC water-splitting process uses semiconductor materials to convert solar energy directly to chemical energy in the form of hydrogen. The semiconductor materials used in this process are similar to those used in photovoltaic solar electricity generation but, for PEC applications, the semiconductor is immersed in a water-based electrolyte, where sunlight energises the water-splitting process. PEC reactors can be constructed in panel form (similar to photovoltaic panels) as electrode systems or as slurry-based particle systems, with each approach having its own advantages and challenges. To date, panel systems have been the most widely studied, owing to the similarities with established photovoltaic panel technologies.

Solar thermochemical water splitting

13.21 Solar thermochemical hydrogen production uses concentrated solar power to drive water-splitting reactions, often along with other substances such as metal oxides. This process uses high-temperature heat (500°C–2,000°C) to drive a series of chemical reactions that produce hydrogen. The chemicals used in the process are reused within each cycle, creating a closed loop that consumes only water and produces hydrogen and oxygen. The necessary high temperatures can be generated in the following ways:

- concentrating sunlight onto a reactor tower using a field of mirror 'heliostats'; or
- using waste heat from advanced nuclear reactors.

Biological processes

13.22 Biological processes use microbes such as bacteria and microalgae to produce hydrogen through biological reactions. In microbial biomass conversion, the microbes break down organic matter like biomass or wastewater to produce hydrogen; while, in photobiological processes, the microbes use sunlight as the energy source.

Microbial biomass conversion

13.23 In fermentation-based systems, microorganisms, such as bacteria, break down organic matter to produce hydrogen. This organic matter can be refined sugars, raw biomass sources such as corn stover[4], and even wastewater. As no light is required, these methods are sometimes called 'dark fermentation' methods. In direct hydrogen fermentation, the microbes produce the hydrogen themselves and can break down complex molecules through many different pathways, and the by-products of some of the pathways can be combined by enzymes to produce hydrogen. Research is looking at how to make fermentation systems produce hydrogen faster and produce more hydrogen from the same amount of organic matter. Microbial electrolysis cells (MECs) are devices that harness the energy and protons produced by microbes breaking down organic matter, combined with an additional small electric current, to produce hydrogen. This technology is very new, and researchers are working on improving many aspects of the system, from finding lower-cost materials to identifying the most effective type of microbes to use.

4 Corn stover consists of the leaves, stalks and cobs of maize plants left in the field after harvest.

Photobiological

13.24 In photolytic biological systems, microorganisms, such as green microalgae or cyanobacteria, use sunlight to split water into oxygen and hydrogen ions. The hydrogen ions can be combined through direct or indirect routes and released as hydrogen gas. Challenges for this pathway include low rates of hydrogen production and the fact that splitting water also produces oxygen, which quickly inhibits the hydrogen production reaction and can be a safety issue when mixed with hydrogen in certain concentrations. Researchers are working to develop methods to allow the microbes to produce hydrogen for longer periods of time and to increase the rate of hydrogen production.

Some photosynthetic microbes use sunlight as the driver to break down organic matter, releasing hydrogen – known as 'photofermentative hydrogen production'. Some of the major challenges of this pathway include a very low hydrogen production rate and low solar-to-hydrogen efficiency, making it a commercially unviable pathway for hydrogen production at this time.

Researchers are looking at ways to make the microbes better at collecting and using energy to make more available for hydrogen production, and to change their normal biological pathways to increase the rate of hydrogen production.

ALGAE FUELS

13.25 Producing liquid fuels from oil-rich varieties of algae is an ongoing research topic. Various microalgae grown in open or closed systems are being tried, including some systems that can be set up in brownfield and desert lands. Many years ago, this type of fuel was dubbed the 'third-generation biofuel'. It had several advantages over plant crops such as sugar cane and corn ('first-generation') and waste streams ('second-generation').

The advantages included:

- higher biofuel yields;
- a diverse list of possible fuel types, including biodiesel, butanol, ethanol and even jet fuel;
- that large-scale algae cultivation, whether in open ponds or more advanced closed-loop systems, can be done on land unsuitable for food crops, removing a key concern that biofuel feedstock crops would compete with food producers.

Around 2005 there were a number of algal-based fuel companies that raised a great deal of money in private investment with the prospect that chemically engineering algae could scale up production to millions of gallons of fuel. Despite the large investment spent on developing the conversion process, it is yet to be realised. The major oil price declines in 2008 and 2014 did not help biofuel competitiveness, and technical challenges have also been an issue, such as:

- the energy balance of lipid extraction;
- maintaining suitable growing conditions in open ponds and large volumes of water; and

- the requirement for carbon dioxide and fertiliser to allow the algae to photosynthesise fast enough on a large scale.

One of the problems is the lipid extraction from the algal biofuel production and the need to remove all moisture from the algae in advance, leaving a dry powder from which the lipids can be separated. This often requires more energy to power the process than the resulting fuel provided.

Researchers at the University of Utah have developed a new jet mixer technology that has no need for the energy-intensive drying processes. The new mixing reactor shoots jets of solvent into jets of algae in liquid suspension, creating the turbulence needed to prompt the lipids to transfer into the solvent stream. Not only does this process require much less energy, but the researchers say it is also faster, with lipids extracted in mere seconds.

Fuel types

Biodiesel

13.26 Biodiesel is a diesel fuel derived from animal or plant lipids (oils and fats). Studies have shown that some species of algae can produce 60% or more of their dry weight in the form of oil. Because the cells grow in aqueous suspension, where they have more efficient access to water, carbon monoxide and dissolved nutrients, microalgae are capable of producing large amounts of biomass and usable oil in either high-rate algal ponds or photobioreactors. This oil can then be turned into biodiesel which could be sold for use in vehicles. Regional production of microalgae and processing into biofuels will provide economic benefits to rural communities.

Much of the biodiesel produced in the UK is from waste vegetable oil sourced from restaurants, chip shops and industrial food producers.

Macdonald's

13.27 Macdonald's restaurant chain has been sending its grease from its fryers for reprocessing into biofuel for over 10 years. It installed grease recovery units (GRU) to do this in all of its UK locations, and it has been using closed-loop biodiesel made from its own grease to power its fleet of vehicles since 2007. Across Europe, around 80% of the company's waste grease by volume is reprocessed into biofuel.

Biobutanol

13.28 Butanol can be made from algae or diatoms[5] using only a solar-powered biorefinery. In most gasoline engines, butanol can be used in place of gasoline with no modifications and, in several tests, butanol consumption was similar to that of gasoline; and, when blended with gasoline, butanol provides better performance and corrosion resistance than that of ethanol. The green

5 Diatoms: photosynthesising algae, that have a siliceous skeleton.

waste left over from the algae oil extraction can be used to produce butanol. It has also been shown that macroalgae (seaweeds) can be fermented by bacteria to butanol and other solvents.

Biogasoline

13.29 Biogasoline is gasoline produced from biomass and, like conventionally produced gasoline, contains between 6 and 12 carbon atoms per molecule and can be used in internal-combustion engines.

Rainforest Energy

13.30 Rainforest Energy signed a Memorandum of Understanding (MoU) with Infinity Biofuels for the licensing of patented technology to produce biogasoline from biomass across the Americas. The MoU is for a technology framework for North America, South America and the Caribbean Islands, under which Rainforest Energy has the right to license the proprietary technology and know-how of Infinity Biofuels for the production of gasoline from biomass and other feedstocks. Rainforest Energy will also develop refineries that have a technology licence with Infinity Biofuels, which includes the basic terms and conditions of the MoU. The Infinity Biofuels process is one of the very few renewable energy technologies that can produce high-octane, premium biogasoline.

Methane

13.31 Methane, the main constituent of natural gas, can be produced from algae by various methods, including gasification, pyrolysis and anaerobic digestion. In gasification and pyrolysis, methane is extracted under high temperature and pressure. Anaerobic digestion is involved in decomposition of algae into simple components, then transforming it into fatty acids using microbes like acidogenic bacteria, followed by removing any solid particles and finally adding methanogenic bacteria to release a gas mixture containing methane.

Ethanol

13.32 There is a process – the Algenol system – which is being used by BioFields in Puerto Libertad, Sonora, Mexico using seawater and industrial exhaust to produce ethanol.

Green diesel

13.33 Algae can be used to produce 'green diesel' (also known as 'renewable diesel', 'hydrotreating vegetable oil' or 'hydrogen-derived renewable diesel') through a hydrotreating refinery process that breaks molecules down into shorter hydrocarbon chains used in diesel engines. It has the same chemical properties as petroleum-based diesel, which means that it does not require a new engine, pipelines or infrastructure to distribute and use.

Jet fuel

13.34 Trials of using algae as biofuel were carried out by Lufthansa, and Virgin Airlines as early as 2008, although there is little evidence that using algae is a reasonable source for jet biofuels. By 2015, cultivation of fatty acid methyl esters and alkenones from the algae, *Isochrysis*, was under research as a possible jet biofuel feedstock.

As of 2017, there was little progress in producing jet fuel from algae, with a forecast that only 3 to 5% of fuel needs could be provided from algae by 2050. Further, algae companies that were formed in the early 21st century as a base for an algae biofuel industry have either closed or changed their business development toward other commodities, such as cosmetics, animal feed or specialty oil products.

UK's first commercial jet fuel plant

13.35 The Planning Committee of North East Lincolnshire Council (NELC) approved plans for the UK's first commercial waste-to-jet-fuel plant. All the statutory consultees indicated their acceptance of plans from biofuel specialist Velocys to build a major new plant near Immingham in Lincolnshire. The proposed Altalto Immingham plant is designed to convert hundreds of thousands of tonnes a year of non-recyclable household and commercial waste, otherwise destined for landfill or incineration, into cleaner-burning sustainable aviation fuel (SAF). The project is a collaboration between Velocys, British Airways and Shell. Jet fuels made from waste materials have long been seen as a means of reducing aviation emissions, despite concerns over the cost of production and the availability of sustainable feedstocks.

HYDROGEN-POWERED CARS

13.36 There are currently only a small number of cars available that use hydrogen as their fuel. Hydrogen fuel cells are attractive, in that they emit nothing other than water vapour, have a long range (4,141 miles for the Nexo) and can be filled quickly. One of the sticking points has been that hydrogen required a lot of electricity to produce it – not such a big consideration if the hydrogen can be made using renewable energy.

Hydrogen-powered fuel cell

13.37 A fuel cell works is a similar way to an electric battery, converting chemical energy into electrical energy using the movement of charged hydrogen ions across an electrolyte membrane to generate current. There, the hydrogen ions recombine with oxygen to produce water, which is the fuel cell's only emission along with hot air.

Hydrogen-powered fuel cells are potentially an environmentally friendly alternative to fossil fuels, and they can be used to power nearly every machine needing energy. They have a number of advantages:

- hydrogen is an abundant element, but it takes time to separate the hydrogen gas from other elements that it is combined with;
- hydrogen doesn't emit harmful substances; it reacts to oxygen without burning, and the energy that it releases can be used to generate electricity that can drive an electric motor. Also, it doesn't generate carbon dioxide when burnt;
- hydrogen is a non-toxic substance;
- hydrogen-powered fuel cells are two or three times more efficient than traditional combustion engines; and
- hydrogen is renewable.

Hydrogen-powered fuel cells currently have some disadvantages:

- hydrogen is expensive;
- hydrogen is difficult to store and move around;
- petrol and diesel are still being widely used and the infrastructure that supports them cannot support hydrogen;
- hydrogen can be very flammable; and
- hydrogen energy is renewable and has minimal environmental impact; unless a renewable way of producing it can be found, its production depends on non-renewable sources such as coal, oil and natural gas.

Hydrogen production facility explosion

13.38 An explosion at a hydrogen production facility in Santa Clara, California, owned by Air Products, shut off the fuel supply to many fulling stations in the San Francisco bay area.

Exxon Mobil and Synthetic Genomics

13.39 Since 2009, Exxon Mobile and Synthetic Genomics have been working to turn algae into low-emission transport fuel.

SOLAR ENERGY

Double-sided solar panels

13.40 This type of panel works by gathering sunlight one side and reflected ambient light on the other. It also has a tracking system so that it can turn towards the sun. A team from the Solar Research Institute of Singapore has found that using panels with photovoltaic cells on both side, that also tilt and follow the sun, would produce 35% more energy and reduce the average cost of electricity by 16%. Despite both bifacial solar panels and tracking panels being currently available for commercial use, models that combine the two features are not. JP Morgan Chase[6] has completed a 2. MW rooftop bifacial solar panel installation on its Columbus, Ohio location that provides 18% of the site's electricity usage.

Organic photovoltaic (OPV)

13.41 The company Heliatek describes a solar material that is a carbon-based sheet as an 'organic photovoltaic' (OPV). The layered film can be bent into shapes or glued on to flat or curved, vertical or horizontal surfaces – where panels could not be used or fixed on without damaging the integrity of a building. Heliatek says that the film is one-tenth of the weight of traditional panels in frames (1.8kg per m^2), contains no rare earth or toxic materials, and lasts for 20 years; its efficiency in a laboratory is about 13%, but the company says that stays stable as temperatures rise in natural sunlight – a problem with traditional solar panels, although they can function at an average of 15–18% efficiency. The film collects a wider spectrum of light than other panels, while still working on grey days.

Solar skin

13.42 Designed by MIT engineers, this is an overlay that can transform the look of any solar panel. It can display branding or be camouflaged to blend in with the local environment. It uses selective light filtration to simultaneously display a vibrant image and transmit sunlight to the underlying solar panel with minimal loss of efficiency.

Solar-powered roads

13.43 Placing a solar panel on a road has a number of disadvantages. The panel is not at the optimum angle and so will produce less power and is prone to more shading. There is also the problem of dust and dirt, and so the glass needs to be much thicker than on a traditional panel so that it can withstand the weight of traffic. The panels also have no air circulation and so heat up, which causes a loss in energy efficiency.

Tourouvre-au-Perche, France

13.44 In 2016 in France, when a trial solar-powered road was unveiled, it was made of photovoltaic panels with a view to generating electricity for street lights in the town of Tourouvre. However, less than three years later, cracks started to appear in part of the road in 2018, and it had to be demolished because of the damage from wear and tear. Even when the road operated at its peak, it only produced half the expected amount of energy, as no consideration

6 'JP Morgan launches massive bifacial solar array': https://electrek.co/2019/11/11/egeb-jpmorgan-chase-worlds-largest-bifacial-rooftop-solar-fossil-fuels/.

had been given to rotting leaves. The project cost US$5.2 million for 0.6 miles (1 kilometre) of road and 30,000 square feet (3,000 square metres) of solar panels.

Decarbonising railways

13.45 Solar panels to power trains, and a system that uses hydrogen and oxygen to produce steam to power engines, are two projects awarded a share of £1.75 million of government funding for use on the rail network. One of the recipients is the Riding Sunbeams initiative, a project run by charity 10:10 Climate Action along with Community Energy South, which will see trains use PV power generated trackside. The idea of on-site solar is a cost-competitive and energy-saving option. Imperial College and 10:10 detailed how British railways could be powered by solar, connecting track-side panels and substations.

The funding comes as the rail industry addresses the challenge set by the Department for Transport of cutting emissions and removing diesel-only trains by 2040. Transport for London wants renewables installed across as many of its 10,000 pieces of land in the capital as possible.

Indian Railways – solar-powered trains

13.46 In July 2017, Indian Railways launched their first solar-powered diesel electrical multiple unit (DEMU) train from the Safdarjung railway station in Delhi. The train will run from Sarai Rohilla in Delhi to Farukh Nagar in Haryana. A total of 16 solar panels, each producing 300Wp, are fitted in six coaches. The solar panels generate about 17 units of power in a day, which powers the lighting system in the coach. Currently, Indian Railways will be installing solar panels on non-alternating current (AC) coaches only. Indian Railways have plans to generate 1,000MW of solar power in the next five years. Steps are being taken to install solar plants on railway building rooftops and level crossings across the country.

Byron Bay, Australia

13.47 The world's first 100% solar-powered train is now running in Byron Bay, Australia[7]. The Byron Bay Railroad Company refurbished a three-kilometre, or almost two-mile, stretch of track and a bridge between the town of Byron Bay and the Elements of Byron Bay resort, to provide affordable public transportation for locals and visitors. It also restored a heritage train, fitting it with a 6.5kW solar array with flexible solar panels. . 100 seated passengers and other standing passengers can ride the solar train, and there's room for luggage, bikes and surfboards.

The flexible SunMan solar panels lining the carriage roofs produce energy that is stored a 77kWh battery system, which can also charge up between trips

7 http://byronbaytrain.com.au/sustainability/.

via a 30kW solar array at the main station. The battery bank has around the same capacity as a Tesla Model S, and it can make 12 to 15 runs off one charge as it only takes the solar train around 4kWh for each leg of the trip. A regenerative braking system recovers around 25% of the spent energy each time the brakes are applied. The train's lighting, traction power, control circuits and air compressors are all battery-powered.

Wearable solar

13.48 Small electrics can be charged through a USB connection integrated into clothing. This would allow a number of devices, such as mobile phones, to be charged as people move about.

'The Starlight Catcher'

13.49 The use of wearable solar gadgets took a major step forward in October 2019 with the introduction of 'The Starlight Catcher', which the developer claims is the world's first wearable solar charger. The charger can fit into a trouser back-pocket and is sufficient to charge a smartphone: 'It is small and light, making it easy to carry, and in few hours is capable of charging the 2500mA inside battery, even on an overcast or cloudy day,' said Andrea Poma, company founder and Starlight team leader. The company has just started a 'Kickstarter' crowdfunding campaign to commercially launch the product. The Starlight Catcher uses 'Sunpower solar cells', which Andrea Poma described as 'the best photovoltaic cells available on the market'.

Super-thin organic solar cell

13.50 A group of Japanese researchers at the Riken research institute and Toray Industries Inc developed a super-thin organic solar cell that can be heat-printed onto clothes. The cells can be used to power portable devices and wearable technology. The ultra-flexible organic photovoltaics (OPVs) are said to achieve a thermal stability of up to 120°C and a high power conversion efficiency of 10%, with a total thickness of 3 microns. Thermally stable and ultra-flexible OPVs are one of the keys to expanding the possibilities of textile-compatible electronics.

FLOATING WIND TURBINES

13.51 Fixed offshore wind turbines are set on the seabed and need waters less than 50 metres deep. This often means that sites where there are very strong winds are not available for wind turbines. However, using a floating foundation means that the depth is not a constraint and, potentially, that wind turbines can be used in deeper waters. In places such as Japan and the United States, there are few shallow waters offshore which are suitable for wind turbines, and so the use of floating wind turbines is important.

Floating foundations offer environmental benefits as they are a less invasive installation.

Platform designs for offshore wind require adaptation to accommodate different dynamic characteristics and loading patterns. The first full-scale prototypes for floating wind turbines have been in operation for several years. Though it is still a small sector, floating wind power is moving towards being a commercial operation, with many farms in the planning stages.

Concepts of floating wind power

13.52 The three main types of floating foundations are spar buoy, semi-submersible and tension leg platform and some variations of these, including the mounting of multiple turbines on one floating platform.

Spar buoy

13.53 This uses a cylinder with low water plane area and ballasted to keep the centre of gravity below the centre of buoyancy. The foundation is kept in position by catenary or taut spread mooring lines with drag or suction anchors.

Advantages:

- tendency for lower critical wave-induced motions;
- simple design; and
- lower installed mooring cost.

Disadvantages:

- offshore operations require heavy-lift vessels and currently can be done only in relatively sheltered, deep water; and
- needs deeper water than other concepts (>100 metres).

Hywind, Scotland

13.54 Hywind is a 30MW wind farm off the Aberdeenshire coast. It has been in operation since October 2017 and has 5 turbines operating on a floating basis. The farm is located 15 miles from shore and in 105 metres of water. Over a stormy period in November 2018 to January 2019, the turbines managed to survive and produced 65% of their capacity as the North Atlantic hurricane produced swells of 27 feet.

Semi-submersible (or spar submersible)

13.55 This type has a number of large columns linked by connecting bracings / submerged pontoons. The columns provide the hydrostatic stability, pontoons provide additional buoyancy, and the foundation is kept in position by catenary or taut spread mooring lines and drag anchors.

Advantages:

- constructed onshore or in a dry dock;

- fully equipped platforms (including turbines) can float with drafts below 10 metres during transport;
- transport to site using conventional tugs;
- can be used in water depths to about 40 metres; and
- lower installed mooring cost.

Disadvantages:

- tendency for higher critical wave-induced motions;
- tends to use more material and larger structures in comparison to other concepts; and
- complex fabrication compared with other concepts, especially spar buoys.

Ideol, Float Gem, France and Japan

13.56 This uses a floating technology, the damping pool concept, in partnership with Atlantique Offshore Energy, Chantiers de l'Atlantique Business Unit – which specialises in offshore engineering procurement, construction and installation (EPCI) projects – and ABB. This substation will fit both bottom-fixed and floating offshore wind farms starting at depths of 40 metres. The test site at Le Croisic, France, in 33 metres of water, has been operational since 2018; and the second demonstrator at Kitakuyshu, Japan, in 55 metres of water, was installed in 2018.

Tension leg platform

13.57 This solution is buoyant, with central column and arms connected to tensioned tendons which secure the foundation to the suction / piled anchors.

Advantages:

- tendency for lower critical wave-induced motions;
- low mass;
- can be assembled onshore or in a dry dock; and
- can be used in water depths to 50–60 metres.

Disadvantages:

- harder to keep stable during transport and installation;
- depending on the design, a special purpose vessel may be required;
- some uncertainty about impact of possible high-frequency dynamic effects on turbine; and
- higher installed mooring cost.

Barge

13.58 Barge-type floating substructures balance the hydrodynamic and wind turbine loads against buoyancy of the floater, which is held in place by moorings. Electricity is exported through a flexible ('dynamic') cable that is interfaced with a static cable on the seabed or directly with the next turbine location. Barges are shallow in draft and can be made from concrete or steel.

WindFloat

13.59 Being built off the coast of Portugal in the Atlantic Ocean, the 25MW WindFloat Atlantic project (WFA) is based around a trio of semi-submersible platforms, designed by US company Principle Power, which are connected to 8.3MW MHI Vestas V164 turbines. Power was first generated on the last day of 2019 and, once all three units are connected to the grid, the array will contribute to producing power to supply 60,000 homes. This is the first floating wind industry in Europe to reach switch-on since Hywind, Scotland, but it was also built without heavy-lift construction vessels, which is a key cost-reduction issue. The floating platform technology being used on WFA was prototype-tested as a 2MW unit between 2011 and 2016, also off Portugal.

TetraSpar

13.60 The TetraSpar is designed as an antidote to the offshore oil engineering-inspired spar, semi-submersible and tension-leg platform concepts that have informed the first wave of floating wind projects. The design is a modular tetrahedral structure made up of standardised components and steel-work that can be manufactured in 'local factories' and transported to the quayside for assembly. This reduces construction time per unit delivery to 'weeks rather than months'. It features a unique triangular float-keel that is tucked up during construction in harbour and tow-out to site, and then lowered using air-filled ballast tanks to provide deep-draft stability for the unit at sea. Backed by investment from Shell and Innogy, the first TetraSpar is currently in construction in Denmark, with plans to install the prototype topped with a 3.6MW Siemens Gamesa turbine as part of a demonstrator project at the Marine Energy Test Centre off western Norway, where the first-ever industrial-scale floating wind turbine, the Hywind Demo (now an R&D unit), has been turning since 2009.

W2Power

13.61 This is the first twin-rotored floating wind power platform, and the design was brought on-line at Gran Canarias off the Spanish coast in 2019 by developer EnerOcean. The 1:6 scale unit, a triangular steel semi-submersible with angled turbines at two corners that turns into the wind, was tested in 65 metres of water in a fast-track testing programme. The 40-tonne prototype has a shallow-draft design that can be adjusted to get in and out of harbour. At full-scale, the W2Power platform is suitable for water depths ranging from 35–300 metres.

SeaTwirl

13.62 Swedish-based SeaTwirl uses a vertical-axis design. It is engineered to rotate as one unit, from blade-tip down the length of its axle, turning a direct-drive permanent-magnet generator, with seawater drawn into the structure through the shaft by centrifugal force, and then released during low-wind periods to maintain the turning momentum so that the turbine works as a flywheel.

Swing Around Twin Hull (SATH)

13.63 One of several Spanish designs, the Swing Around Twin Hull (SATH) being developed by engineering outfit Saitec is to be installed as a 'medium-scale' prototype in the Cantabrian Sea. The 1:6 demonstrator, based on a 10MW design built around conjoined cylindrical pre-stressed concrete hulls anchored to the seabed via a single-point mooring system that allows the unit to face the wind, will undergo a 12-month testing programme as part of the so-called BlueSATH project. The concept, which received €2m from the European Commission in 2019, will be tested for its dynamics in the open sea, as well as its robustness and the choice of concrete mixtures for the hull.

Chapter 14

Trends in Policies

INTRODUCTION

14.1 The United Kingdom policies are consistent with its goal to reduce greenhouse gas (GHG) emissions by at least 80% by 2050 from the 1990 levels, as defined under the Climate Change Act 2008[1]. It was in 2016 that the government adopted the fifth carbon budget (for the period 2028–32), which targets a 57% reduction in GHG emissions compared to 1990 levels. The Clean Growth Strategy of 2017 sets out policies and government funding of £2.5 billion for innovation and low-carbon investment up to 2021. Alongside Canada, the UK launched the Powering Past Coal Alliance: to date, a total of

1 www.legislation.gov.uk/ukpga/2008/27/contents.

30 countries, 22 subnational states and 28 businesses have joined the Alliance, which commits them to the rapid phase-out of coal.

The country's energy system has seen a very rapid growth in the share of low-carbon energy, which accounted for over 50% of the electricity mix in 2017: natural gas (41%), nuclear (21%), wind (15%, up from 3% in 2010), solar (3%), bioenergy and waste (11%), coal (7%, down from 29% in 2010) and hydro (2%). The UK has committed to phasing out all remaining unabated coal-fired power generation by 2025. UK energy-related CO_2 emissions have declined by 35% on 1990 levels, and total GHGs are down by 40%, reaching some of the lowest levels recorded since 1888. Power and heat, which were once the number one source of energy-related CO_2 emissions in the UK, have declined significantly (to 25% of the total) and are now far below those of transport (34%).

RENEWABLE ENERGY DIRECTIVE (RED)

14.2 The Renewable Energy Directive sets the rules for the EU to achieve its 20% renewables target. The energy sector is responsible for more than 75% of the EU's GHG emissions, and so the increasing of renewable energy across the many sectors of the economy is expected to have the effect of delivering Europe's ambition of climate neutrality.

In December 2018, the recast Renewable Energy Directive (RED II) came into force as part of the 'Clean Energy for all Europeans' package. The recast Directive moves the legal framework to 2030 and sets a new binding energy target of 32% by 2030, with a clause allowing for upward revision in 2023. There are new provisions for enabling self-consumption of renewable energy, an increased 14% target for the share of renewable fuels in transport by 2030, and strengthened criteria for ensuring bioenergy sustainability.

Under the Regulation on the Governance of the Energy Union and Climate Action[2], EU countries are required to draft National Energy and Climate Plans[3] (NECPs) for 2021–2030, outlining how they will meet the new 2030 targets for renewable energy and for energy efficiency.

National Energy and Climate Plans

Process

14.3 Under the governance Regulation, Member States had to submit their draft NECPs for the period 2021–2030 to the Commission by 31 December 2018. These were analysed by the Commission, with an overall assessment and country-specific recommendations published in June 2019. Taking these

2 Regulation (EU) No 2018/1999 on the Governance of the Energy Union and Climate Action: https://eur-lex.europa.eu/legal-content/EN/TXT/?uri=uriserv:OJ.L_.2018.328.01.0001.01.ENG&toc=OJ:L:2018:328:TOC.

3 National Energy and Climate Plans: https://ec.europa.eu/info/energy-climate-change-environment/overall-targets/national-energy-and-climate-plans-necps_en.

recommendations into account, Member States were then required to submit their final NECPs by 31 December 2019.

Each country must then submit a progress report every two years. The Commission will, as part of the state of the energy union report, monitor EU progress as a whole towards achieving these targets.

To better develop and implement the plans, the Member States were required to consult citizens, businesses and regional authorities in the drafting and finalisation process.

The governance Regulation also required Member States to submit, by the start of 2020, national long-term strategies looking forward to 2050.

The NECPs are the first-ever integrated mid-term planning tools that Member States are required to prepare in view of the implementation of the energy union objectives and, in particular, the agreed EU 2030 energy and climate targets. The NECPs describe how each Member State plans to contribute to the achievement of the common energy union objectives.

The NECPs have to follow a binding structure set by the governance Regulation to ensure comparability and policy consistency while promoting a wide European debate on energy and climate priorities. The NECPs therefore reflect the logic of the five dimensions of the energy union:

- energy efficiency first;
- a fully integrated internal energy market;
- decarbonisation of the economy;
- energy security, solidarity and trust; and
- research, innovation and competitiveness.

For each dimension, Member States are required to include targets, objectives and/or contributions as well as policies and measures to attain the national goals. The NECPs should be grounded on a sound analysis, looking at the expected impact of the proposed policies and measures. NECPs should also be discussed both with national stakeholders and with neighbouring Member States. The NECPs are essential tools to enable the clean energy transition and provide investment certainty to Europe's industry.

The Commission aims to set up the right planning instruments, support Member States and allow the Union as a whole to fulfil its energy union objectives along all five dimensions, and in particular the 2030 energy and climate targets.

The Commission can ask Member States to improve their draft plans in several ways:

- on the energy efficiency and renewable contributions, some Member States are called upon to increase efforts and better exploit their national potential, while others will need to confirm their already ambitious objectives;
- Member States are also asked to set measurable, achievable, realistic and time-related objectives across all five dimensions; and
- most Member States are also called upon to further substantiate the achievement of their national targets and contributions with more concrete additional policies and measures.

The EU and its Member States have committed under the Paris Agreement to achieve at least 40% domestic GHG emissions reductions by 2030, as compared to 1990. With the full implementation of the adopted 2030 climate, energy and clean mobility targets, GHG emissions could be reduced by around 45% in 2030, as compared to 1990. However, the initial assessment of the draft NECPs is not at this level yet.

Member States are looking at additional policies, planning to achieve their national targets for GHG emissions which are not covered by the EU Emissions Trading System (ETS). Member States' targets range from zero to 40% reductions.

The Commission has proposed that the EU become climate-neutral by 2050, and the European Parliament has endorsed this, while the Council was still discussing the matter. Under the governance Regulation[4], Member States also needed to develop their national long-term strategies by January 2020 in a complementary way to the NECPs, so as to ensure the consistency of the 2030 targets and long-term objectives.

Legislative framework

14.4 The governance Regulation came into force on 24 December 2018. It set up a common framework for energy and climate policies in the European Union and its Member States, with Member States having to show in their NECP how they will contribute to the achievement of the energy union objectives, notably the EU 2030 energy and climate objectives.

Those include EU targets of at least 32% for renewable energy and at least 32.5% for energy efficiency, as established by the revised Energy Efficiency Directive and Renewable Energy Directive that entered into force in late 2018.

RECAST RENEWABLE ENERGY DIRECTIVE (RED II)

14.5 In December 2018, the recast Renewable Energy Directive (RED II) entered into force. The overall target for energy consumption for renewable sources has been raised by 2%. Member States must require that their fuel suppliers supply a minimum of 14% of the energy in road and rail transport by 2030 as renewable energy.

Directive 2009/28/EC specifies national renewable energy targets for 2020 for each country, and takes into account both its starting point and the overall potential for renewables. These targets range from a low of 10% in Malta to a high of 49% in Sweden.

4 Governance Regulation: https://eur-lex.europa.eu/legal-content/EN/TXT/PDF/?uri=CELEX:32018R1999&from=EN.

Renewable Energy Action Plans

14.6 EU countries set out how they plan to meet these 2020 targets, and the general course of their renewable energy policy, in national Renewable Energy Action Plans[5]. The progress towards national targets is measured every two years when EU countries publish national renewable energy progress reports[6].

Sustainability criteria

14.7 The RED II defines a series of sustainability and GHG emission criteria that bioliquids used in transport must comply with to be counted towards the overall 14% target and to be eligible for financial support by public authorities. Some criteria are the same as in the original RED, while others are new or reformulated.

The RED II introduces sustainability for forestry feedstocks as well as GHG criteria for solid and gaseous biomass fuels. Default GHG emission values and calculation rules are provided in Annex V (for liquid biofuels)[7] and Annex VI (for solid and gaseous biomass for power and heat production)[8] of the RED II.

Revision and updating of the default values of GHG emissions, when technological developments make it necessary, can be carried out by the Commission. Economic operators have the option either to use default GHG intensity values provided in the RED II or to calculate actual values for their pathway.

Greenhouse gas savings thresholds in RED II

Plant operation start date	Transport biofuels	Transport of renewable fuels of non-biological origin	Electricity, heating and cooling
Before October 2015	50%	–	–
After October 2015	60%	–	–
After January 2021	65%	70%	70%
After January 2026	65%	70%	80%

As discussed in Chapter 8, although biofuels are important in helping the EU meet its GHG reduction targets, the production of biofuels often takes place on land that was previously used for other agriculture, such as growing food or feed. Agricultural production is still necessary, and this could lead to the extension of agriculture land into non-cropland, possibly including areas with high carbon stock such as forests, wetlands and peatlands. This is known as indirect land use change (ILUC) and may cause the release of carbon dioxide

5 2020 National Renewable Energy Action Plans: https://ec.europa.eu/energy/topics/renewable-energy/national-renewable-energy-action-plans-2020_en?redir=1.

6 Progress Reports: https://ec.europa.eu/energy/topics/renewable-energy/progress-reports_en?redir=1.

7 Annex V (for liquid biofuels): https://eur-lex.europa.eu/legal-content/EN/TXT/?uri=uriserv:OJ.L_.2018.328.01.0082.01.ENG&toc=OJ:L:2018:328:TOC#d1e32-147-1.

8 Annex VI (for solid and gaseous biomass for power and heat production): https://eur-lex.europa.eu/legal-content/EN/TXT/?uri=uriserv:OJ.L_.2018.328.01.0082.01.ENG&toc=OJ:L:2018:328:TOC#d1e32-172-1.

stored in trees and soil, thereby negating the GHG savings that result from increased biofuels.

The 'Clean Energy for All Europeans' package has a new approach. It sets limits on high ILUC-risk biofuels, bioliquids and biomass fuels with a significant expansion in land with high carbon stock. These limits will affect the amount of these fuels that Member States can count towards their national targets when calculating the overall national share of renewables and the share of renewables in transport. Member States will still be able to use (and import) fuels covered by these limits, but they will not be able to include these volumes when calculating the extent to which they have fulfilled their renewable targets. These limits consist of a freeze at 2019 levels for the period 2021–2023, which will gradually decrease from the end of 2023 to zero by 2030.

There is an exemption from these limits for biofuels, bioliquids and biomass fuels certified as low ILUC-risk.

The Commission adopted a Delegated Regulation (EU) 2019/807, following the two-month period of scrutiny by the European Parliament and the Council, as defined under the standard EU comitology procedure.

This delegated act sets out specific criteria both for:

- determining the high ILUC-risk feedstock for which a significant expansion of the production area into land with high carbon stock is observed; and
- certifying low ILUC-risk biofuels, bioliquids and biomass fuels.

Also adopted was an accompanying report on the status of production expansion of relevant food and feed crops worldwide, based on the best available scientific data. This report provides information that Member States can use in conjunction with the criteria set out in the delegated act in order to identify high ILUC-risk fuels and certify low ILUC-risk fuels.

Advanced biofuels

14.8 Within the 14% transport sub-target, there is a dedicated target for advanced biofuels produced from feedstocks listed in Part A of Annex IX to the RED II. The contribution of advanced biofuels and biogas produced from the feedstock listed in Part A of Annex IX, as a share of final consumption of energy in the transport sector, should be at least 0.2% in 2022, at least 1% in 2025 and at least 3.5% in 2030.

Member States may exempt fuel suppliers supplying fuel in the form of electricity or renewable liquid and gaseous transport fuels of non-biological origin from the requirement to comply with the minimum share of advanced biofuels and biogas produced from the feedstock listed in Part A of Annex IX with respect to those fuels.

Caps and multipliers

14.9 The share of biofuels and bioliquids, as well as of biomass fuels consumed in transport, where produced from food and feed crops, should be no more than one percentage point higher than the share of such fuels in the final consumption of energy in the road and rail transport sectors in 2020 in that Member State, with a maximum of 7% of final consumption of energy in the road and rail transport sectors in that Member State.

Renewable electricity will count four times its energy content towards the 14% renewable energy in transport target when used in road vehicles, and 1.5 times when used in rail transport. The Commission will also develop a framework to guarantee that the renewable electricity used in transport is in addition to the baseline of renewable electricity generation in each Member State.

Fuels used in the aviation and maritime sectors can opt in to contribute to the 14% transport target but are not subject to an obligation. The contribution of non-food renewable fuels supplied to these sectors will count 1.2 times their energy content.

THE UK'S DRAFT INTEGRATED NATIONAL ENERGY AND CLIMATE PLAN

14.10 On 31 January 2020, the UK left the EU; as part of this, the UK set out proposals as to how it would like the relationship with the EU to work. In terms of energy, the UK wants to cooperate with the EU to continue looking towards cost-efficient, clean and secure energy supplies of electricity and gas. In terms of climate, the UK recognises the need for shared interest in climate change and the mutual benefit of a broad agreement on climate change operation. The UK intends to have high standards in domestic law which will be more stretching than the current obligations under EU law. The draft plan was submitted to the Commission in December 2018 and the final plan was due in December 2019 but has not yet been submitted.

Climate Change Act 2008

14.11 The Climate Change Act 2008 set in legislation the UK's approach to tackling and responding to climate change. It introduced the UK's long-term legally binding 2050 target to reduce GHG emissions by at least 80% relative to 1990 levels.

Its main elements are as follows:

- Setting emissions reduction targets in statute and carbon budgeting. The Act establishes an economically credible emissions reduction pathway to 2050 and beyond, by putting into statute medium- and long-term targets. In addition, the Act introduces a system of carbon budgeting which constrains the total amount of emissions in a given time period. Carbon budget periods will last five years, beginning with the period 2008–2012, and must be set three periods ahead. The Secretary of State is required to give indicative ranges for the net UK carbon account in each year of a budgetary period, to set a limit on use that can be made of international carbon credits in each budgetary period, and to develop and report on his proposals and policies for meeting carbon budgets.

- A new reporting framework. The Act provides for a system of annual reporting by the Government on the UK's GHG emissions. The Committee on Climate Change will have a specific role in reporting annually on progress, with the Government required to lay before Parliament a response to this progress report.
- The creation of an independent advisory body. The Act creates a new independent body, the Committee on Climate Change, to advise the Government and devolved administrations on how to reduce emissions over time and across the economy and, on request, on any other matter relating to climate change, including adaptation to climate change. This expert body will advise on the optimum trajectory to 2050, the level of carbon budgets, and on how much effort should be made by the part of the economy covered by trading schemes and by the rest of the economy, as well as reporting on progress.
- Trading scheme powers. The Act includes powers to enable the Government and the devolved administrations to introduce new domestic trading schemes to reduce emissions through secondary legislation. This increases the policy options which the Government could use to meet the medium- and long-term targets in the Act.
- Adaptation. The Act sets out a procedure for assessing the risks of the impact of climate change for the UK, and a requirement on the Government to develop an adaptation programme on matters for which it is responsible. The programme must contribute to sustainable development. The Act also gives powers to direct other bodies to prepare risk analyses and programmes of action, and advisory and progress-reporting functions to the Committee on Climate Change.
- Policy measures which reduce emissions. The Act will be used to support emissions reductions through several specific policy measures: amendments to improve the operation of the Renewable Transport Fuel Obligations; a power to introduce charges for single use carrier bags; a power to pilot local authority incentive schemes to encourage household waste minimisation and recycling; amendments relating to the Certified Emissions Reductions Scheme; powers and duties relating to the reporting of emissions by companies and other persons; a duty to make annual reports on the efficiency and contribution to sustainability of buildings on the civil estate.

The Act also introduced 'carbon budgets' which cap emissions over successive five-year periods and must be set 12 years in advance. It also requires the UK to produce a UK Climate Change Risk Assessment (CCRA) every five years. These assess current and future risks to, and opportunities for, the UK from climate change. In addition, the Act requires the UK Government to produce a National Adaptation Programme (NAP) to respond to the risk assessment. Finally, the Act gives powers to the UK Government to require certain organisations to report on how they are adapting to climate change through the Adaptation Reporting Power.

Request for advice on UK climate targets

14.12 In order that the UK has a robust climate framework, it needs to take account of the latest scientific findings. Following the publication of the

Intergovernmental Panel on Climate Change (IPCC) special report on global warming of 1.5°C[9], the UK Government has asked the independent experts, the Committee on Climate Change (CCC)[10], for their advice on the implications of the Paris Agreement for the UK's long-term emissions reduction targets, including on setting a net zero target; this includes:

- setting a date for achieving net zero GHG emissions across the economy;
- whether the UK needs to raise its 2050 target of cutting emissions by at least 80% relative to 1990 levels to meet international climate targets set out in the Paris Agreement;
- how emissions reductions might be achieved across the economy; and
- the expected costs and benefits in comparison to current targets.

Clean Growth Strategy and Clean Growth Grand Challenge

14.13 In October 2017, the UK Government published its Clean Growth Strategy[11] (CGS) setting out policies and proposals, through to 2032 and beyond, to reduce emissions across the economy and promote clean growth; and, in November 2017, the UK published its modern Industrial Strategy[12], which includes a Clean Growth Grand Challenge[13] that aims to maximise the advantages for UK industry from the global shift to low carbon.

Second National Adaptation Programme and the third strategy for Adaptation Reporting Power

14.14 The second National Adaptation Programme (NAP)[14] was published in July 2018 and addresses the key risks highlighted in the second CCRA, published in January 2017, and was developed working with and drawing on the 25-Year Environment Plan. It presents a set of actions in areas such as natural environment, infrastructure, people and built environment, business and industry, and local government. The Adaptation Reporting Power (ARP) set out in the Climate Change Act 2008 provides for the Secretary of State to direct reporting organisations (those with functions of a public nature or statutory undertakers) to report on how they are addressing current and future climate impacts.

9 www.ipcc.ch/sr15/.
10 www.theccc.org.uk.
11 Clean Growth Strategy: https://assets.publishing.service.gov.uk/government/uploads/system/uploads/attachment_data/file/700496/clean-growth-strategy-correction-april-2018.pdf.
12 Industrial Strategy: www.gov.uk/government/speeches/the-industrial-strategy-forging-our-future.
13 Clean Growth Grand Challenge: www.gov.uk/government/publications/industrial-strategy-the-grand-challenges/industrial-strategy-the-grand-challenges#clean-growth.
14 Second NAP: https://assets.publishing.service.gov.uk/government/uploads/system/uploads/attachment_data/file/727252/national-adaptation-programme-2018.pdf.

Strategies and legislation in Northern Ireland, Scotland and Wales

14.15 Energy policy is mainly devolved to Northern Ireland and partly devolved to Wales and Scotland. Climate change policy is devolved to Wales, Scotland and Northern Ireland, although the UK Government retains control over many energy policy areas and also some other important policy areas which deliver emissions reductions.

Northern Ireland

14.16 In Northern Ireland, energy policy and the independent regulation of energy companies are devolved matters. The energy strategy is set out in the Strategic Energy Framework[15] (SEF) for the period 2010–2020. The likelihood is that the future energy strategy will concentrate on a more consumer-led decentralised energy system and decarbonisation in areas such as electricity, heat and transport. The Northern Ireland Authority for Utility Regulation (NIAUR)[16] is responsible for regulating the electricity, gas, water and sewerage industries in Northern Ireland.

The strategic aim of the Department of Enterprise, Trade and Investment (DETI) is for a more secure and sustainable energy system where:

- energy is as competitively priced as possible alongside robust security of supply;
- much more of Northern Ireland's energy is from renewable sources and the resulting economic opportunities are fully exploited; and
- energy efficiency is maximised.

Northern Ireland has operated a single wholesale electricity market, called the Single Electricity Market (SEM), with the Republic of Ireland since November 2007, which has been undergoing extensive redesign to comply with the EU Target Model for the harmonisation of arrangements for trading electricity across Member States. These arrangements are being progressed under the Integrated Single Electricity Market (I-SEM) programme[17]. These reforms are designed to introduce efficiencies of interconnector flows, encourage new investment in the market, apply downward pressure on prices, and create enhanced trading opportunities and options through the introduction of continuous trading in the intra-day, day-ahead, forwards, and balancing timeframes. The first auction took place at the end of 2017; further auctions took place in 2018 and in March 2019.

Scotland

14.17 The Climate Change (Scotland) Act 2009[18] requires Scottish Ministers to reduce emissions in Scotland by at least 80% by 2050, with an interim target of 42% by 2020 and annual targets for each year to 2050.

15 Energy – A Strategic Framework for Northern Ireland: www.economy-ni.gov.uk/sites/default/files/publications/deti/sef%202010.pdf.
16 www.uregni.gov.uk.
17 Integrated Single Electricity Market (I-SEM): www.uregni.gov.uk/i-sem.
18 www.legislation.gov.uk/asp/2009/12/contents.

The Climate Change (Emission Reduction Targets) (Scotland) Act 2019[19]:

- amended the Climate Change (Scotland) Act 2009, setting targets to reduce Scotland's greenhouse gases to net-zero by 2045 at the latest; and
- s aninterim targets for reductions of at least 56% by 2020, 75% by 2030, and 90% by 2040.

The Scottish Energy Strategy[20] (published in December 2017):

- sets out a vision for the future of energy in Scotland to 2050;
- confirms that Scotland's electricity supply is largely decarbonised. Scotland is well on the way to its target of generating 100% of our electricity demand from renewables in 2020 – provisional statistics show 54% of Scotland's electricity needs were met from renewables in 2016, with major new capacity due to connect to the system in the coming years. It is determined to tackle the challenges of decarbonising heat and transport, in order to meet its longer-term energy and climate change targets; and
- s andenthat the installed capacity of renewables in Scotland reached 9.5GW in June 2017.

Wales

14.18 The Environment (Wales) Act 2016[21] requires Welsh Ministers to reduce emissions in Wales by at least 80% by 2050. This Act also requires Welsh Ministers to set reduction targets for the years 2020, 2030 and 2040, and establish a system of carbon budgeting that together create an emissions reduction pathway to the 2050 target.

FIVE DIMENSIONS OF ENERGY SECURITY

14.19 There are five dimensions of the EU energy and climate legislation strategy which is supported by the UK.

Energy security

14.20 Energy security is the uninterrupted availability of energy sources at an affordable price, with secure supplies for consumers, regardless of the energy mix, and delivering a diverse and reliable energy mix using smarter and more flexible networks.

19 www.legislation.gov.uk/asp/2019/15/contents.
20 Scottish Energy Strategy: www.gov.scot/publications/scottish-energy-strategy-future-energy-scotland-9781788515276/.
21 www.legislation.gov.uk/anaw/2016/3/contents. There is also an overview of the Act: https://gov.wales/sites/default/files/publications/2019-05/environment-wales-act-2016-overview.pdf.

Energy efficiency

14.21 To meet the UK's 2050 climate change target (to reduce emissions by at least 80% by 2050, compared to 1990 levels), emissions from buildings will need to be near zero, along with action on industrial processes. This requires the improvement of energy efficiency and energy management, and decarbonising nearly all heating and cooling of buildings. The UK is taking a range of actions, including looking at barriers to energy efficiency and low carbon investment and supporting organisations to access finance.

Northern Ireland

14.22 Northern Ireland contributes to the UK's energy efficiency targets, with the Northern Ireland Sustainable Energy Programme[22] (NISEP) delivering up to 200GWh per year of energy savings, as required by Article 7 of the Energy Efficiency Directive. Northern Ireland is currently developing a Northern Ireland energy efficiency action plan as part of a wider energy strategy, to ensure co-ordinated and effective delivery of energy efficiency policies and programmes across Northern Ireland.

Scotland

14.23 The Energy Efficient Scotland route map[23] was launched in May 2018. This ambitious 20-year programme contains a set of actions to make Scotland's buildings near zero carbon, wherever feasible, by 2040 and to do so in a way that is socially and economically sustainable. The programme will invest around £10–12 billion of public and private sector money in energy efficiency and heat decarbonisation over the 20-year period. Energy Efficient Scotland has two main objectives:

- to remove poor energy efficiency as a driver for fuel poverty; and
- to reduce GHG emissions through more energy-efficient buildings and decarbonising Scotland's heat supply.

Wales

14.24 The Welsh Government has invested more than £240 million since 2011 to improve the energy efficiency of more than 45,000 homes of those on low incomes or living in the most disadvantaged areas of Wales. The Welsh Government is investing a further £104 million in the Warm Homes programme for the period 2017–2021, improving up to 25,000 homes and leveraging up to £24 million of EU funding.

22 Northern Ireland Sustainable Energy Programme: www.uregni.gov.uk/publications/northern-ireland-sustainable-energy-programme-nisep-list-schemes-2019-2020.

23 Energy Efficient Scotland: route map: www.gov.scot/publications/energy-efficient-scotland-route-map/pages/1/.

Appendix

Cases

CONTENTS

William Ellis McLennan v Medway Council [2019] EWHC 1738 (Admin)

Solar panels have a right to light. This High Court ruling set a new precedent for planning and climate change law. The local authority had granted planning permission for an extension, even though this would effectively block out the sunlight which fell onto a neighbour's solar panels. The judge overturned the planning permission on the basis that the electricity generated by solar PV panels helped to mitigate climate change. This means that the amount of light falling on a solar panel should be a planning consideration.

The claimant in the case, Mr McLennan, used the micro-generation solar panel to generate up to 11kW of electricity per day in direct sunlight. In December 2018, planning permission was granted to his nextdoor neighbour to construct an extension to the rear of their property to which Mr McLennan objected. He said that the extension would overshadow his solar panels and reduce their ability to generate electricity. The planning permission was challenged in a judicial review in June 2019.

Under section 38(6) of the Planning and Compulsory Purchase Act 2004 the planning application 'must be made in accordance with the development plan unless material considerations indicate otherwise'. The main issue was therefore was whether the solar panel is capable of being a material consideration to which the council should have had regard when determining the planning application. Council planning officers had concluded that the interference was not a material consideration as it involved a private interest rather than a public one.

In court, the judge referred to section 19(1A) of the Planning and Compulsory Purchase Act 2004 which requires development plan documents to include policies that contribute to the mitigation of, and adaptation to, climate change and the provision of the National Planning Policy Framework (NPPF).

The judge concluded that the council was not entitled to reject the impact of the proposed development on the claimant's renewable energy system and that to do so was irrational. As a result, the judge quashed the grant of planning permission for the extension.

This case raises important questions for the future development of taller buildings where they overshadow solar panels on neighbouring buildings. Overshadowing of solar panels will have to be taken into account in the decision-making process as a material consideration.

However, the planning authority will have to undertake the normal balancing exercise when considering any planning application and determining how much weight should be given to the impact on solar panels on a case-by-case basis.

In *Tesco Stores Ltd v Secretary of State for the Environment and others* [1995], Lord Hoffmann says:

> 'Provided that the planning authority has regard to all material considerations, it is at liberty [...] to give them whatever weight the planning authority thinks fit or no weight at all. The fact that the law regards something as a material consideration therefore involves no view about the part, if any, which it should play in the decision-making process.'

The following message from the judgment is relevant:

> 'Whether a consideration is capable of being a relevant or material consideration for planning purposes is a question of law for the court. ... It is, however, difficult, if not impossible, definitively to resolve the question of relevancy or materiality, as it were, in a vacuum without reference to the facts of the particular case. As a starting point, I accept that the exercise of planning control should be in the public interest. It is not concerned with the creation or preservation of private rights as an end in itself (see Salmon J in *Buxton v Minister of Housing and Local Government* ... and Lord Scarman in *Westminster City Council v Great Portland Estates Plc* ...).
>
> I do not, however, accept the distinction in principle that Miss Ellis sought to draw between the effect on the use of land through overlooking or overshadowing and that through deprivation of outlook or aspect. The guiding principle seems to me to be in each case whether the private interest in question requires to be protected in the public interest. In that sense detriment to the amenity of residential user through overshadowing or overlooking is far more likely to be something to be resisted in the public interest than interference with a view. Whether or not protection of a view or private amenity is, in the circumstances of the case, in the public interest would be for the decision-maker to determine. Generally, no doubt, that decision would take into account the number of properties or persons whose view or amenity would be affected and to what degree. I respectfully accept, and adopt, the guidance in the judgment of Cooke J in [*Stringer v Minister of Housing and Local Government* [1971] 1 All ER 65] that:
>
>> "The public interest ... may require that the interests of the individual occupier should be considered. The protection of the interests of individual occupiers is one aspect, and an important one, of the public interest as a whole".'

Lawsuit challenging Biomass in the EU's Renewable Energy Directive

A group of plaintiffs from Estonia, France, Ireland, Romania, Slovakia, Sweden and the USA filed a lawsuit against the EU (March 2019) to challenge the inclusion of biomass in the EU's Renewable Energy Directive. The group argues that the EU institutions have failed to take account of scientific evidence showing that the forest biomass harvesting and combustion for energy purposes exacerbates climate change by causing deforestation outside Europe. In 2018 the EU adopted an updated version of its Renewable Energy Directive which committed to source at least 32% of its energy from renewables by 2020 – a target considered to be a central element of the EU's goal to cut carbon emissions by 40% by the same date. But the plaintiffs contend that including forest biomass as a source of renewable energy runs counter to Article 191(1) of the EU Treaty, which stipulates that the bloc's environment policy should contribute to 'preserving, protecting and improving the quality of the environment ... and in particular combating climate change'.

R (Wright) v Resilient Energy Severndale Ltd and Forest of Dean District Council [2019] UKSC 53

Severndale applied for a change of use of land at Severndale Farm, from agriculture to the erection of a single community-scale 500kW wind turbine for the generation of electricity. It was proposed that the wind turbine would be erected and run by the community benefit society. The application also said that an annual donation would be made to a local community fund, based on 4% of the society's turnover, from the operation of the turbine with a project life of 25 years.

The Forest of Dean District Council granted permission. In arriving at this decision, they had expressly considered the donation to the community fund and imposed a condition that the development was to be undertaken by the community benefit society and that the community fund donation was part of the scheme.

A local resident, Mr Wright, challenged the planning permission that was granted, on the grounds that the promised community fund donation was not a material planning consideration. His application succeeded at first instance, and the Court of Appeal dismissed an appeal by Severndale and the Council.

The Supreme Court unanimously dismissed the appeal and said that the Local Planning Authority had relied on the proposed payments which do not qualify as a material consideration. It had been argued that the concept of 'material consideration' should be updated in line with changing government policy, but the judge did not agree. He concluded that what constitutes a 'material consideration' is in no doubt, and updating the established meaning to the term would be inappropriate. A central consideration had been the long-standing *Newbury* case.

The judge carefully examined the case law, demonstrating firstly that a material consideration has come to mean a consideration that serves a planning purpose and, secondly, that a planning purpose is a purpose which relates to the character of the use of the land. He reaffirmed the long-standing principle that planning permission cannot be bought or sold. The promise of a financial contribution which does not relate to the character of the use of the land will never be material in planning terms. This statement of principle is clearly established.

Breyer Group and others v Department of Energy and Climate Change [2014] EWHC 2257 (QB)

This case came about as a result of a proposal announced in a written Ministerial statement on 31 October 2011, and the publication the same day of a consultation document. This document indicated that the cut-off date by which certain Feed-in Tariffs (FIT) paid at a particular rate to generators involved in small-scale panel installation would change. The Government felt that the rate for solar PV installations was too generous and so proposed to bring forward, from 1 April 2012 to 12 December 2011, the date by which the installation had to be commissioned/registered in order to achieve the highest FIT rate. The potential impact was for installations which would have been completed by April 2012 but were abandoned when they could not complete by December 2011. Some that were affected by this change sought judicial review. In the case of *Friends of the Earth v Department of Energy and Climate Change* [2011] EWHC 3575 (Admin), judgment was given in favour of the claimants. In January 2012, the Court of Appeal also concluded that the proposal was unlawful because there was no power under the relevant statute to give retrospective effect to delegated legislation.

The Government then changed its proposals and laid before Parliament a Licence Modification to take place on 3 March 2012 which effectively reduced the FIT rate. This proposal did not pose any unlawful issues, as the claimants had claimed that the damage was done by the making of the original proposal on 31 October 2011. The claimants also claimed that, by the time the courts ruled that the proposal was unlawful, the installations had already been abandoned so they sought damages under Article 1 of the First Protocol to the European Convention on Human Rights ('A1P1').

Preliminary issues were identified, to be tried between the parties on the basis of agreed or assumed facts. There were issues about:

- whether or not the claimants have 'possessions' within the meaning of A1P1;
- whether or not the announcement by the defendant of its proposal on 31 October 2011 could amount in law or in fact to an interference;
- whether or not, if the proposal constituted an interference, it was justified; and
- whether or not proper satisfaction would lead to a financial remedy.

The judge first dealt with the FIT scheme (see Chapter 2).

FIT scheme

Under section 41 of the Energy Act 2008[1], the defendant could modify the conditions of licences granted by the Office of Gas and Electricity Markets (OFGEM) under the Electricity Act 1989 so as to provide for financial incentives for small-scale low-carbon generators of electricity. It was pursuant to this power that the FIT scheme was created.

1 The latest version is now Energy Act 2016.

In July 2009, the Government published a consultation paper on renewable electricity financial incentives. That consultation expressly recognised the need to encourage private investors to fund the necessary installations:

> 'Some organisations have seen easy access to up-front, low-cost capital as essential to the uptake of the technologies; others are of the view that tariffs themselves will be sufficient to drive the financial market to develop products in this area and provide the necessary capital, and would be discouraged by government intervention in this area.'

In the Government's response to the subsequent consultation in a document dated February 2010, the Government set out its legislative proposals:

> 'Once an installation has been allocated a generation tariff, that tariff remains fixed (though will alter with inflation as above) for the life of that installation or the life of the tariff, whichever is the shorter.'

Other parts of the paper stressed that FIT rates applicable for later installations would be lower 'both to reflect and to encourage and drive cost reductions from the relevant sectors':

> 'But any individual installation, once starting to receive a tariff at a certain level, will continue to receive the same generation tariff level throughout its entire support period under the FIT scheme.'

It also said that tariffs 'should encourage investment in small-scale low-carbon generation that will contribute towards meeting our challenging renewable and carbon targets, and do so in a way that ensures value for money for the scheme as a whole, bearing in mind that the costs of support are shared by all electricity consumers'.

Tariff levels had been set to provide an expected rate of return of approximately 5–8% (or 7–10% because the FIT rates were linked to inflation), taking into account, amongst other things, 'the likely effect those risks would have on investors' willingness to invest':

> 'Several responses to the consultation argued that early degression would provide a disincentive for new businesses setting up. We have therefore decided that for these technologies subject to degression, its introduction will be delayed until April 2012, providing generators with tariffs at initial levels for two years. We believe this delayed start to degression will provide technology supply chain industries an indication of the costs reductions that will need to be achieved so that the tariffs can still deliver sufficient return to encourage investment from potential generators.'

An objective of the FIT scheme was to provide long-term certainty for investors, so it was important that the scheme was reviewed and adapted as circumstances changed, including technology costs and supply chains and other policy developments.

Feed-In Tariffs (Specified Maximum Capacity and Functions) Order 2010

This Order (SI No 678) came into effect on 1 April 2010. It made provision for the FIT scheme as proposed in the previous year's consultation and response papers:

- The FIT payments would be made by the electricity supply companies, who were referred to in the order as 'mandatory FIT licensees'. The cost of the FIT scheme would be passed on to all electricity consumers, so the scheme was effectively a subsidy paid by those consumers for low-carbon electricity generation.
- The FIT payments would be made to FIT generators or nominated recipients. The former were defined as the owners of an eligible installation. The latter were those appointed by a FIT generator to receive FIT payments in respect of an accredited FIT installation owned by that FIT generator and recorded as such on the central FIT register. This second category was designed to embrace installers, surveyors, brokers and investors who had arranged, put in or paid for the solar PV system for, say, a school at no up-front cost, but in exchange for receipt of all or part of the FIT otherwise payable.
- the references in the 2010 Order to accreditation and registration are important. In order to trigger the FIT payments, there had to be an eligible installation (which meant plant capable of producing small-scale low-carbon generation from, in this case, solar PV) which OFGEM had determined as suitable for participation in the scheme and entered onto the central FIT register. Accreditation was dealt with in Part 3 of the 2010 Order, and the central FIT register was dealt with in Part 5 of the 2010 Order.

Relevant rates of payment

In order to qualify for these maximum rates, the installation had to be completed by the end of FIT Year 2 (that is, 31 March 2012). Completion was achieved as follows: the authority had to accredit an eligible installation if it had been commissioned and registered. Once that happened, notice of accreditation was given which included the confirmation date, 'the tariff code for the installation, and the unique identifier for the installation'.

The cut-off date of 31 March 2012 was an important element of the FIT scheme: completion by that date dictated that the highest rate would be paid for a particular installation over a 25-year period.

Subsequent modifications

On 7 February 2011, Secretary of State announced a review of the FIT scheme which would 'assess all aspects of the scheme including the tariff levels, administration and eligibility of technologies'. Tariffs would remain unchanged until the end of FIT Year 2 'unless the review reveals a need for greater urgency'. The consultation paper sent out in March 2011 stressed at paragraph 11 that 'the Government would not act retrospectively and any changes to generation tariffs implemented as a result of the fast-track review will only affect new entrants into the FIT scheme. Installations which are already accredited for FIT at the time the changes come into force will not be affected'. However, it was noted that 'the risk of rapid and unforeseen expansion of larger scale solar PV poses a threat to the ability of the FIT scheme to keep within the budget for the Spending Review period to 2014/15'.

The claimants in the proceedings were either FIT generators or nominated recipients (although some were neither) that were working towards the installation and completion of thousands of solar PV installations by the end of FIT Year 2. On that basis, the electricity supply companies were obliged to make FIT payments to them calculated as accruing from the eligibility date of an eligible installation. If the eligible installation was completed, commissioned and accredited by 31 March 2012, and the tariff code had been assigned 'in accordance with the FIT year in which the eligibility date for the accredited FIT installation falls', the claimants would be entitled to FIT payments of 43.3p per kWh for 25 years. Or so they thought.

In a debate in the House of Commons on 20 October 2011, the Secretary of State for Energy and Climate Change (Chris Huhne) was asked about a newspaper report in the Financial Times which suggested that he was about to 'completely pull the rug from underneath thousands of people up and down this country who might have taken steps to invest in solar power for their own houses and who are now finding that their investment is being completely undermined by his decisions'. The Minister said that there was no question of anybody's investment being undermined because 'this Government are very committed to not having retrospection in legislation and legislative changes'. However, he went on to say that they were keeping all their subsidies under review.

The changes took place 10 days later, on Monday 31 October 2011. The consultation paper said that the tariff for solar PV was originally intended to provide a return of around 5%, but the Government's analysis suggested that the returns available were now substantially more than that. It was said that this was not sustainable, because it would risk solar PV generators being overcompensated, and it would very rapidly result in the spending envelope for the FIT scheme being breached. The paper indicated the significant scale of the proposed reduction. Instead of 43.3p per kWh, the proposed rate was reduced to 21p per kWh.

That the bringing forward of the cut-off date for FIT Year 2 was a central feature of these proposals can be seen in two further statements made on 31 October 2011. First, the Minister said in a press announcement that 'people who are now thinking of installing solar PV need to do so with their eyes wide open and I would encourage them to call the Energy Saving Trust for the latest advice'. Anyone following that advice would have been provided with the Trust's fact sheet, also dated 31 October 2011, which said: 'we recommend customers should use the figures in the consultation if they are planning to install after 12 December 2011'. In other words, if the installation was not completed/commissioned and registered by 12 December 2011 (six weeks from then), the Government's advice was that the rate was going to be halved.

Article 1 of the First Protocol

Article 1 of the First Protocol to the European Convention on Human Rights ('A1P1') provides:

> 'Every natural or legal person is entitled to the peaceful enjoyment of his possessions.
>
> No one shall be deprived of his possessions except in the public interest and subject to the conditions provided for by law and by the general principles of international law.

> The preceding provisions shall not, however, in any way impair the right of a State to enforce such laws as it deems necessary to control the use of property in accordance with the general interest or to secure the payment of taxes or other contributions or penalties.'

The claimants' claims in some cases were small-scale solar PV generators or nominated recipients under the FIT scheme; others engaged in a variety of businesses connected in some way with solar PV generation.

There are broadly three types of business:

- FIT-payment recipients: These companies procure, install and register solar PV systems for owner-occupiers with suitable premises. The occupier will receive the benefit of cheaper electricity but the claimant or its nominated subsidiary would be entitled to receive the FIT payments as nominated recipient, either on the basis of a contract between the claimant and the owner-occupier, or on the basis of 'block' contracts for a group of properties, between the claimant and a broker company with its own direct arrangement with the owner-occupier.
- Fee recipients: These companies procure, install and register solar PV systems for owner-occupiers with suitable premises, whether on the basis of a contract between the claimant and the owner-occupier (pursuant to which a fee would be paid to the claimant), or a block contract with a third party nominated recipient, again on the basis of a fee. In addition, some claimant companies would find and prepare sites for a third party who would arrange for the installation of the solar PV system for which they would be paid a fee and would be entitled to an ongoing share of the profit from electricity sold to the grid.
- Equipment suppliers: These companies supply solar PV equipment to other installation companies.

The claimants' claims stem from what they say was the catastrophic effect of the proposal to bring forward the eligibility date, which had an immediate and serious adverse impact on the claimants' business, which impact was reasonably foreseeable. It was not economically viable for the claimants to continue their business in relation to the installation of solar PV systems, unless such systems could be installed and commissioned by the reference date of 12 December 2011, which was six weeks from the publication of the proposal; and that the majority of installations which had been planned and contracted for by the claimants could not be completed and accredited in this timeframe.

The issues were whether the Claimants and/or any of them had 'possessions' within the meaning of A1P1, consisting of:

- an enforceable legitimate expectation, as described in the respective Particulars of Claim, concerning the timing of any changes to rates payable pursuant to the FIT scheme and the manner in which the related review process would be conducted; and/or
- the marketable goodwill in the claimants' business, as described in the respective Particulars of Claim; and/or
- the signed contracts or contracts which would, but for the proposal, have been signed, agreeing that the FIT payments would be receivable by any of the claimants, or their subsidiaries and/or their assignees.

The judgment considered that the claimants had entered into contracts by 31 October 2011, which contracts became incapable of performance as a result of the proposal, then those contracts represented an element of the marketable goodwill in the claimants' businesses, and therefore represented a possession protected by A1P1. The claimants could, in principle, recover for the loss of that element of the marketable goodwill in their businesses.

Also, even if the loss of unsigned/non-concluded contracts could be said to have affected the claimants' goodwill, such losses were properly characterised as losses of future income and were therefore irrecoverable under A1P1.

Index

[*All references are to paragraph numbers*]

www.ingramcontent.com/pod-product-compliance
Ingram Content Group UK Ltd.
Pitfield, Milton Keynes, MK11 3LW, UK
UKHW051416150926
475561UK00005B/193

9 781526 515124